This book was
recommend
Social worker &
Kalman Iss.
at Jeresolem Conference
June 2012.
Ellen- nurse prof.
? - sw.

August

Sweet Tea for the Soul

Daily Nourishment For
Living Spiritually In Tune
With Your World

by

Melody "Lil Mel" McGowan

authorHOUSE®

AuthorHouse™
1663 Liberty Drive, Suite 200
Bloomington, IN 47403
www.authorhouse.com
Phone: 1-800-839-8640

First published by AuthorHouse 10/31/2007

ISBN: 978-1-4343-4868-5 (e)
ISBN: 978-1-4343-4684-1 (sc)

Printed in the United States of America
Bloomington, Indiana

This book is printed on acid-free paper.

Looking for uplifting soul support? Spiritual nourishment? Inspiration? Motivation or guidance? Look no further!

"In *Sweet Tea for the Soul*, Author Melody "Lil Mel" McGowan, has hit upon the answers for anyone who has ever wondered how to get through life. Each of the insights that are provided are chock full of wisdom and faith. Truly refreshment and nourishment for the soul, this book can guide you through the roughest times and help you celebrate the happiest times. I intend to use it everyday and give copies to all my family and friends!"

Barbara
A Wise Woman

Dedications

This book is dedicated to my children, Anthony and Nicole McGowan who lovingly encourage me as I walk my spiritual path and who now walk their own paths. They continue to teach me the joys and blessings of motherhood. They are the sweet tea for *MY* soul!

To my dear friend Barbara Eastep, truly a wise woman and my spiritual mentor, who told me to write until my fingers were numb! Without her vision, unwavering faith and loyal support this book wouldn't have been conceived, never mind written.

Tis' truly a blessed life I live!

Acknowledgments

God sends his blessings upon me in so many ways and for this I am forever grateful. Some of His blessings are sent in human form and I wish to thank each of the following for their ceaseless encouragement and support. I give special heart-felt thanks to:

Bridgette Wallis, my extraordinary sister, who overcame life's challenges. She is a significant influence in my life, always supportive, forever loving, and she never lets me take life too seriously.

Alexus, Jessica, and Blake Wallis, my nieces and nephew, for sharing part of their summers with me and keeping me young at heart. Special hugs to Blake, my muse for *Be Seven*—may he always hold onto the spirit of being seven!

Lisa Reeves, my best gal-pal, for reaching out to me again after so many years of silence between us. Her friendship and support is invaluable to me—may we never lose track of time again!

Laurel Peterson, who helped spread the word about my first book, *Ramblings from the Heart*, encouraging me to continue with this book.

Cpl Joseph L. Santel, and the rest of our servicemen and women who have answered the call of duty and dedicated their lives to protecting and ensuring my freedoms. It is due to their courage and dedication we enjoy the freedom of religion, speech, and press.

Rhei C, a talented singer and artist; her music fused the creative forces within—inspiring me to get past those difficult moments while writing this book.

My fellow Internet bloggers, friends, and chat buddies for their never ending encouragement, support, and laughter. No artificial sweeteners among them, they are the real thing!

And of course, to my clients, who taught me to remain true to my purpose and mission. Their insatiable thirst for my *random ramblings* fanned the flame that inspired this book. Each one is the best example of how God's love and the angels work on earth and in our lives.

Contents

Foreword

In her first book, *Ramblings from the Heart*, author Melody "Lil Mel" McGowan, provided readers with inspiration and encouragement with her collection of poems, prose's, inspirational writings, and spiritual messages. Now she serves up, *Sweet Tea for the Soul*, a daily devotional book that provides spiritual refreshment for nourishing the soul. This inspirational book contains 365 daily messages that suggest a specific action you can take each day to become more spiritually in tune with your world.

Answering the call to spread messages and guidance to reach people around the world, Melody's *Sweet Tea for the Soul*, provides daily messages that help heal beliefs and thoughts, transforming them into positive empowering and loving viewpoints. Offering ideas and practical ways to enrich your life, foster character, and provide nourishment for your emotional and spiritual needs, this book can guide you on your spiritual path as well as help you with troubling emotions such as depression, resentment, boredom, stress, regrets, and anger.

This book will, I believe, be of great value to any reader whether looking for daily guidance, inspiration, support, empowerment, comfort, spiritual nourishment, or simply a way to become more spiritually in tune with the world they live in.

As we travel on life's journey, everyone needs to feed their spirit daily. *Sweet Tea for the Soul* is designed to help nourish your spirit, start each day off right, and assist you along your spiritual journey. Each page offers comforting and uplifting messages that sets a positive and healing tone for the day. It has everything you need to refresh and nourish your spirit, uplift and motivate you during trials, and give you strength needed to make it through each day.

The longing for uplifting soul support, spiritual nourishment, motivation, and divine guidance is a God thing—*Sweet Tea for the Soul*, is the answer! As you pirouette through the pages of this book you will find refreshing nourishment that your soul is thirsting for—may it keep you centered, balanced, and provide peacefulness throughout your day!

Lisa M. Reeves
Event Coordinator
Let Your Heart Heal Life Coaching

Introduction

Each day we must renew our faith, find strength to meet challenges, and draw inspiration. This devotional book is spiritual refreshment for nurturing the soul. Presented to you in a practical down-to-earth manner, *Sweet Tea for the Soul* contains 365 daily messages that suggest a specific action or attitude you can take to become more spiritually in tune with your world. Like a tall cold glass of sweet tea, these daily messages serve as a refreshing reminder that we have an all-knowing loving God, offers hope, inspiration, and encouragement for anyone seeking direction along life's journey.

Universal in its appeal and non-denominational in its approach, this book is a way for you to connect with God, with each message offering inspiration and practical guidance for becoming more spiritually in tune and enriching your day. Although this lovely bedside companion is geared toward morning meditations, as a touchstone for the day's events, you can benefit from it day or night. You can read the pages in their numbered order, or quiet your mind, relax, and let your inner guidance lead you to the messages intended for you in the moment. Each daily message is accompanied by a thought, affirmation, or prayer to further nourish your soul. Say it out loud, write it down and carry with you, or just think of it throughout the day—whatever feels the most natural. Sometimes we forget or don't have time to follow the spiritual advice for the day. Don't worry, the most important part is to read and absorb the loving energy by reading the words.

As a life coach, my clients stem from diverse religious backgrounds—I respect all religious beliefs however, I focus on the spiritually of our live here on Earth. For me personally, I believe that there is but one God. God is the Creator of our universe—meaning anything within the universe is created by God and of Him. God created angels and they are his instrument to watch over, protect, and help us here on earth. Angels act as postal carriers, delivering God's messages and love to us. It is through God and His angels that these messages were dictated for this book. Some messages teach or inspire, while others suggest a way to approach the day. God wants us to lead a healthy and happy life—He is available to all of us every moment of everyday.

It is my hope that these daily messages help open your hearts and soul, find encouragement, inspiration, and nourishment for the soul so that you too can live spiritually in tune with your world—and beyond! With this in mind I invite you to partake of this refreshing taste of spiritual nourishment as you continue down life's highway!

Daily Messages

~1~
You Are Never Alone

Rest assured that you are never alone, especially during the most difficult times. Recall the poem, *Footprints in the Sand*, and how the one set of footprints represented those times the author was carried by God. You have a powerful, loving, supportive God sending you healing energy at all times. And if that is not enough, God has a host of angels ready to lend a helping hand—you can ask the angels to help you along your journey at any time.

Stop for a moment, quiet your mind, sit still, and listen. Open your heart, your mind, and your soul to the messages being revealed to you. These messages speak only of love. These messages give solutions to everyday problems—big or small. God and the angels are here to guide you through the darkest times of your life; bring you back into the light, where love, happiness, and healing energy await.

The first step to becoming spiritually in tune with your world is the realization that you are never alone…for God and the angels will remain right by your side, they are with you always.

Today's Nourishment:
I remember that I am not alone. I have God and God's angels that are ready to help me with anything, if I just ask. They surround me with loving guidance and protect me from harm. I call upon God now to guide me, and I am grateful for God's assistance.

~2~
Slow Down

Slow down for just one minute. Remember you are not responsible for doing it all. If you are walking, slow down the pace. If you are driving, ease up on the pedal. Slow down your rate of speech. Slow down your breathing. Take time out to enjoy a quiet moment, take frequent breaks, close your eyes, breathe, and calm your body and mind. Release the anxiety that makes it difficult for you to focus and concentrate.

Anxiety causes restlessness within, however, it is created by an inner search for peace without knowing how or where to find it. Since peace is God, what you are really longing for is a connection with the Divine. You need a break from the intense situations. Everything you are longing for is waiting for you in those quiet moments. Slow down, retreat to that quiet place, for this is where peace is and where God resides. Allow yourself these moments of silence, especially during the difficult situations, or whenever you feel anxious. Give yourself time to connect with God—to feel God's loving presence, to bask in the peace…you will find the answer to any question.

Today's Nourishment:
I remember to slow down throughout the day. I will take time to enjoy a quiet moment and connect with God, feeling God's peaceful and calming presence—no matter what is going on around me.

~3~
Create A Theme For The Day

Each morning as you start your day, you set the tone for the day by your attitude. It is similar to sending out a signal to the universe. This signal creates the theme for the day and determines the type of situations, people, and attitudes you will encounter. You determine the theme for the day by your attitude and type of signal you send out into the universe. By setting a more positive theme, you will attract more positive situations.

For example, you may want to focus your mind on developing more harmonious relationships, seeing the beauty in your surroundings and others, make more money, or live a healthier lifestyle. By focusing on positive thoughts each morning you cast a positive signal to the universe—attracting situations that are apart of your theme just as you asked.

Today's Nourishment:
My theme for this day is _____(fill in the blank). I call upon God and the angels to assist me this day. I notice and enjoy the situations that my positive outgoing signal attracts.

~4~
Regulate Your Energy

Just as you control the temperature in your home, you have the ability to control your energy, moods, emotions, finances, and other areas of your life. Visualize your own internal switch or controller, by turning up the switch you are increasing the intensity and sending an important signal to the universe.

The higher the dial, the more you are in charge! By regulating your own energy you are taking back control. Once you have decided what it is that you desire, focus your energy in that direction and turn up the power! Crank up the switch on harmony, abundance, health, loving relationships, and peaceful surroundings—there is no limit to what you can ask for!

Today's Nourishment:
I take control of my life today. I take control of my energy, mood, emotions, and all areas of my life. I am cranking up the intensity of goodness and positive energy. I will follow my guidance, keep my arms open to receive, and be gracious.

~5~

Indulge Yourself

Now is the time to relax and rejuvenate in a tranquil, stress free environment. Make time to treat yourself to rest, relaxation and pampering. Surround yourself with gentleness, with soft music, candlelight, soothing smells, and absorb the bounties in your life. The only cost for indulging yourself is gratitude.

To only give without taking deprives others the pleasure of giving, causes barriers to the life of abundance you deserve, and eventually you are left sitting alone with an empty cup. By indulging in pampering, blocks are lifted; you are open to receiving more gifts. Your cup is soon overflowing again—spilling out onto others, creating a joyous circle of sharing endless gifts of life!

Make this the day that you escape to your own oasis and experience a serene atmosphere that rejuvenates and refreshes your energy. Surround yourself with beautiful soft music, light soft candles, indulge in sweet smells, talk quietly, and engage in slow rhythmic movements. Don't engage in drama or conflicts this day, become more spiritually in tuned—retreat to a quiet place and indulge yourself today!

Today's Nourishment:
Today I will relax and rejuvenate myself with extra loving attention. I indulge myself with fresh flowers, a massage, a nap, a visit to a spa, or a quiet afternoon of soothing music. Today I embrace the joy of being me!

~6~
Be Kind To Others

One single act of kindness, a token of mercy, or an expression of forgiveness each day creates a powerful flow of energy, directing your energy outward. Kindnesses extended to other less fortunate, and at a time when kindness is needed, can impact a whole society. Simple choices can promote enthusiasm and inspire similar acts of kindness in others.

One who extends loving kindness to every living being can sleep happily and wake up happily like the blossoming of a lotus. Such persons will not dream of bad dreams, will become pleasant to all living beings, and will receive blessings.

Performing one thoughtful act of kindness each day is an investment in your own spiritual growth—it's a win-win situation!

Today's Nourishment:
I will perform one act of kindness today as I feel guided. I will give of myself freely, use kind words, thoughts, and gestures. I will extend myself to others today and practice forgiveness for any perceived slights or hurts done to me.

~7~
Be Truthful

To be truthful is expressing or given to expressing the truth; making a true statement, giving truthful testimony, or being truthful. Being truthful with others moves you and your life in a positive direction. While there are many key ingredients to being spiritually in tune with your life, being truthful with others may be the most important.

With that understood, it is likewise understood that being truthful is important in everything you do and say. It is at the heart of having love, being loved, and creating trust. Honesty is at the heart of spiritual growth and progress along our paths.

Being honest with yourself is every bit as important as being honest with others. In being truthful there are no contradictions or discrepancies in thoughts, words, or actions. Being truthful earns trust and inspires faith in others. Honest thoughts, words, and actions create harmony.

Today's Nourishment:
I create harmony in my life by being truthful in my words, actions, and thoughts. I gain the trust and inspire others by being truthful. By being honest with myself and others I allow for further spiritual growth which is necessary to continue on my path.

~8~
Practice Patience

You are much too hard on yourself at times. You are evolving, learning, growing everyday, even when you are not consciously aware of progress being made. Looking back on how far you have traveled you can see lessons learned; blessings received and measure spiritual growth. You must not chastise yourself and learn to have patience with yourself and the process of life.

Your goals and desires are being realized at a faster pace than you realize. However, nurturing and patience is still required. All things begin with a seed, even the intangible; it takes time for the seed to take root, push through the ground, and grow to maturity. Each part of the growth process can bring lessons, joy, and blessings.

Enjoy the process of manifesting your dreams. Slow down, have patience, feel gratitude as each step in the process brings you closer to manifestation. Experience the lessons, love, and blessings as you allow your dreams to unfold.

Today's Nourishment:
I practice patience with myself and the process of living. I no longer struggle, feel the need to control things, or attempt to force the situation. I experience each lesson, love, and blessings bestowed upon me with each step in the process.

~9~
Release The Negative

Occasionally it seems as if you are at a standstill and your dreams are not manifesting as quickly as we believe they should. If you find yourself in such a place, look within to see if something within is causing a blockage or delays. Are you trying to force the issue? Have you truly released your desire to the higher power? Are negative thoughts, fears, or past memories creating a barrier to success?

When you find something in your world that is unpleasant or negative it affects our mental, physical, emotional, and spiritual well-being. This greatly hampers our attempts at happiness, health, success and fulfillment. By releasing past disturbances, negative memories, hurts, anger, and negative emotions, you are open to a more positive flow of energy. To release the darkness of the past creates love and light for the future. Ask for help releasing the negative and be reassured that the universe is taking care of your needs and clearing the way for the manifestation of your desires—even if it is not clear to you at this time.

Today's Nourishment:
I release the anger and negative emotions I have toward others. I forgive the wrongdoings of others, and those who have wronged me. I now ask for assistance to release all negative thoughts, memories, and hurts. I now accept forgiveness for myself.

~10~
Let Go

When you are in the storms of life and you wish to hold tightly and struggle, worry, manipulate, and fight your way out of the storm it's simply a sign of fear and mistrust. This entire process makes you weary, tired, and discouraged. It is only when you can see no other solution do you let go and let God work things out His way. Have compassion and understanding when this happens to you or with others. This tendency reveals the need for reassurance that things are happening as God intends.

The remedy for this tendency is to allow God's nurturing soothing love surround you. After all, when a person tries to have control and power over everything they most often feel out of control. If you stop, sit quietly, and listen to your inner voice you will hear God's beckoning call for you to just let go so He can work it out. Then and only then, will you be free of the storm.

Even though you can not see what lies ahead, God already knows what He has planned for your future. He is holding you in the palm of His hand. You can relax your control, stop struggling, and release it to God. By letting go, you are showing your trust that things are being worked, that you are cared for, and that your life will be filled with peace, love, and strength.

Today's Nourishment:
I take a deep, full breath and then release it. By releasing that breath, I am releasing the situation to God. I give all to God for His your care and keeping. This act of letting go affirms unlimited power of God's love.

~11~
You Are A Blessing

You are surrounded by a loving all-knowing God night and day. You are surrounded by divine loving light and energy—warmth, love, color, and compassion fill your soul. God does not see flaws or imperfections. He only sees you are a true blessing.

He sees your true self, a divine being with remarkable gifts of compassion, love, and empathy for self and others. He sees that everyone around you benefits from your existence on this plane, as your gifts touch the lives of others.

You are a blessing to your parents, to your siblings, to strangers and a blessing to friends. You are a blessing in your home, on the street, in your words, your deeds, in all that you do at work and at play. You are a blessing.

Today's Nourishment:
I am a blessing to everyone and I bring everlasting happiness to all I meet. I share my gifts of compassion, love, and empathy to others. I have a life of abundance from the universe and I am blessed.

~12~
Knowing What You Want

Today is the day to decide what it is that you definitely want. You deserve to have your desires manifested. It is natural to have dreams, intentions, goals, desires, and to ask for spiritual assistance in manifesting exactly what you want. Do not be afraid to ask for financial prosperity or material gain, as God wants you to live a comfortable life. You are worthy of good things happening in your life; you are worthy of achieving great things!

It is all within your reach. You simply have to ask, know that you deserve it, give permission for spiritual assistance, follow your own guidance, and allow your desires to manifest. When you make that affirmative decision as to what you want, and follow these steps, your angels will guide you in the steps to obtaining your desires.

As with any goal, there are steps to be taken along the way. Focus on taking the first step in the direction of your desires. You will be supported and guided along the way. Pay attention to your inner voice, a strong feeling, a dream, a thought, or even a repeated song. As you begin to notice these things, you will be on the right path to manifesting your desires.

Today's Nourishment:
I know exactly what I want in my life. I deserve to have my desires manifested. I ask for spiritual assistance with the process of obtaining my desires. I take the first step toward accepting guidance, focus on noticing and following guidance, and I graciously accept that my dreams will be manifested.

~13~
Out Of The Darkness

You can agree that you need light in order to function in your daily life. There are many different types of light. During the day, you enjoy the light of the sun. During the night, the moon gives off light. When it is dark, you can flip a switch and there is light. Whether it is stoplights for safety, soft candlelight for ambience, or putting lights on a tree at Christmastime for decoration, the power of light is evident in your life. In order to function in your daily life, you need a light source.

The problem with physical lights is that they eventually go out, thrusting you into darkness. Have you ever gone from the brightness of a sunny day into a darkened movie theater? Or exited a brightly lit room to go to the darkness of a basement? Or experienced a thunderstorm that results in a sudden power outage? Naturally you have experienced a sudden loss of physical light at some point in your life, where you are thrust into darkness. Regardless of the situation or age, everyone will undergo a sense of fear, anxiety, and a sense of urgency until a light source is found. This is true for your emotional and spiritual life as well. Whenever your thoughts or moods feel darken, you need the light and warmth of God's love to bring you out of the darkness.

When you feel yourself slipping into the emotional darkness, imagine a gorgeous sunset within you. Visualize the shades of yellow, orange, pink, and purple. Experience the radiating warmth and beauty. Continue to visualize this inner sunset until it grows larger and brighter, illuminating you from the inside, bursting outward, surrounding you with warmth and color.

As you allow the glow of this inner sunset surround you, the more your mood and energy level will brighten. Visualize angels next to you in this moment, glowing with God's love, warmth, and divine light. Lean upon the light of God when you want or need God's light.

Today's Nourishment:

I am filled with a beautiful sunset right now. Divine light, warmth, color, and healing energy surrounds me; guides me safely along my path. I have God's love inside me, illuminating me with God's love.

13

~14~
Honor Your Feelings

Do you trust your feelings and take action for yourself based on your feelings? Have you grown up learning to mistrust your feelings? Feelings are information. Feelings such as anger, depression, anxiety, are letting you know that you are treating yourself in an unloving manner.

If you went outside, and it was a mere 10 degrees, and you were clad only in shorts and a light shirt, you would feel cold. What that feeling is telling you is to *change* your clothes, to take care of yourself so that you do not catch your death of cold! This physical analogy can be applied to your emotional and spiritual welfare as well.

When you honor your feelings, you come to your own aid with personal empowerment. When you are feeling unhappy in a situation, the only thing you can do is consciously choose to make a change in your life. By listening to your feelings, you are given information that helps resolve inner struggles and needs. Without knowing your feelings, you neglect a basic need that enables you to be happy and free. Burying your feelings leads to a practice of low self esteem. It sends a message that you and your feelings are not important or worthy of being known. You must honor your feelings so that you can come make the necessary changes that are for your highest good.

Today's Nourishment:
I honor my feelings and stay true to myself. It is safe for me to listen to my feelings and use the information to make positive change in my world. My feelings are important and worthy of being known.

~15~
You Are Divine

You are divine. Pause for a moment, take a deep breath, and say out loud, "I am divine." Allow yourself to feel the words, savor how they feel rolling off your tongue, and let the words really sink in deeply. Take another deep breath, feel the words in your body, open your heart and soul, and allow your mind to rest for a moment with the sense of knowing that you are a divine being.

Know that God makes no mistakes and your creation was no accident. A lot of thought, caring, and love went into your being here. Your entire creation was carefully planned and well thought out from start to finish. Everything about you is perfect! You were personally created and blessed by God—how can you not be perfect in every way. There are no flaws or imperfections for you are a holy being created by God. Remember this throughout the day and embrace your divinity. You are of God. You are divine!

Today's Nourishment:
I am divine. My creation was planned and executed by God and everything about my creation is perfect. I am personally blessed by God. I am divine.

~16~
Create Love

Love is all things. Anything is possible with love. If you do not like a situation you can view it from a different perspective. You can change your beliefs about your life and with simple visualization you can create love in your life. You can choose a different path at any moment. You have free will and you always have a choice. Choose to make it a path of love and service and watch barriers and obstacles vanish. By creating love you can open doors to new possibilities and opportunities.

If you have loving thoughts, you are more likely to create love in your life. If your head is filled with fearful and negative thoughts, your life will be filled with fear and negativity. The energy of love is so powerful that it can heal anything, including your future. You have the ability to visualize this loving energy around you, changing your current situation or path, changing your future.

This morning, take a moment to project this caring loving energy around you and out into your day. Spread this love into each of your minutes, making sure each future moment has been touched by the healing power of love. Then as you go on with your day, know that each moment has been blessed with loving energy and healing powers. You are cushioned by love every step of the way.

Today's Nourishment:
Love is all things. I create love and send it into my day. My entire day has been saturate with loving energy. Every moment is blessed with joy, happiness, love, and all barriers have been removed.

~17~
Surround Yourself With Positive Energy

Just as you can create and send love, you can create and surround yourself with positive energy affecting those around you. You are affected by your surroundings. It is natural to feel peaceful and relaxed in a clean, well-lighted room, surrounded by happy, carefree people. However, you may experience apprehension in a space that's dark, dirty or when interacting with someone with negative thoughts or attitude. Though you may not be conscious of the emotional and physiological effects that negativity evokes, you still realize when you're in place that you feel comfortable and uplifted.

By surrounding yourself with negativity and dark or gloomy surroundings that is what you will become! You will become negative energy; harboring negative thoughts leads to negative actions and negative words. Creating positive energy is simply doing what feels rights, makes you shine, and honors your feelings.

Surround yourself with positive things and vibes; create your own positive energy! Send this positive energy to others by sending out love. Smile at your surroundings, talk to strangers, open doors, give of your time, listen and share and help people feel the energy and flow.

Today look at things a little differently. See and understand the positive aspects of people and situations instead of just focusing on the negative aspects. When you talk to other people change your negative statements to positive comments. If you're in a conversation where everybody is negative try saying something positive and see what happens.

Today's Nourishment:
I surround myself with positive things, clear my head of negative thoughts, take positive actions, and speak positive words. I create and surround myself with positive energy. I will smile at others, give of myself, use positive words, and change negative statements into positive comments

---

~18~
Use Loving Words

Words are beautiful, because they describe feelings, emotions, and thoughts. God knew exactly what he was doing when he gave us the freedom to choose and create. Words can also be the difference between night and day, right and wrong, or pleasure and pain. You are responsible and accountable for the words you choose to use.

Words affect people. You use the spiritual law of sowing and reaping every time you carry on a conversation. You must choose your words carefully, as people respond to you the way you respond to them. If you are kind, they are kind. Negative words can hurt a person, leaving scars and wound that may take a long time to heal. There is enough suffering on the earth without adding to it by tossing out evil, sarcastic, ungodly words. God is not pleased with vicious gossip and lies about others.

Using loving words blesses the lives of others and motivates them to pass it on! Loving words are as beautiful bouquets of colorful flowers. Everyone wants to receive them. You can pass out these bouquets of words to others. Doing this can be as simple as telling a server at a restaurant that she did a great job as you hand her a tip.

Hand out the gift of loving graceful words today. This is a good way to bless another and to let your light shine. When you do this you will reap a bountiful harvest of loving energy in return.

> Today's Nourishment:
> *I am accountable for the words I use. I choose my words carefully and use loving words to bless the lives of others. I do not engage in gossip, use sarcastic, or speak ungodly words. I speak, hear, write, and think in loving terms; my life is blessed!*

~19~
Ask For Divine Guidance

You do not exist alone. You do not learn alone. You do not create alone. You can answer everyday life questions by acknowledging and trusting in your inner voice which is the voice of your guardian angel or God. Through mediation, lifestyle changes, and phrasing your questions correctly, you can break down any communication barriers and ask for divine guidance directly. Learn how to *crank up the volume*, and increase the intensity of the feelings and clarity of the messages you receive in response.

Guidance comes in many forms. Family or friends may give wonderful advice or guidance in dealing with a particular issue or concern. An inspiring book might provide meaningful guidance. The most powerful guidance, however, comes in the form of divine guidance. By opening up to guidance from God you are opening your mind to new knowledge and your heart to new wisdom.

When you need to make a significant decision, or just want to calm or center yourself, stop for a moment. Take time to ask for divine guidance, for assistance, and inspiration in choosing what's best. You can do this each night at bedtime, setting time aside to ask for guidance during your sleep and dream time.

Today's Nourishment:
I am not alone. I do not learn alone. I ask for divine guidance, for empowerment and enlightenment in all that I do. I quiet my mind and feelings, putting myself in a receptive, expanded state of consciousness to receive this divine guidance.

~20~
Teach Others

You're here for many reasons—one purpose is to teach others. As you take cues from the universe around you, the faster you will be capable of teaching others. Additionally you will help heal those you come in contact as well. You can help them heal by direct assistance or by example. By teaching you will help them learn what you teach, and by learning you will help them better understand the subject that they are teaching you.

In order to get, you must give; to make yourself happy, you must make others happy; and in order to become spiritually vigorous, you must seek the spiritual good of others. In teaching others, you are learning lessons. Your efforts to be useful bring out your powers for usefulness. You have latent talents and dormant faculties, which are brought to light by exercise.

Teaching is a lot simpler than you imagine. What do you teach others when you are angry or upset? What do you teach others when they see your faith waver? When others see you at peace, they're reminded of the value of tranquility. This is teaching. Other times someone will ask you for insight or help. Then it would be natural that you give what you can to help guide or assist them along their path. However, just as the angel's assistance isn't given unless asked for; neither can you teach others anything they haven't asked for.

Today's Nourishment:
I am ready and able to teach others. I teach others by my actions, attitudes, and words. By teaching others I am learning lessons.

~21~
Find Lessons In Daily Living

Today is a good day to live! Accept and participate in whatever life offers, whether it is good, bad, or neutral. By adopting this form of acceptance you are able to acknowledge whatever life offers, just as it is, in the spiritual tradition that teaches, *be in the here and now*. By *being in the here and now*, you are required to eliminate all of the drama that may intrude upon your daily life.

Let go of any apprehension about what might happen today and accept bright, new possibilities. Relax knowing that divine order is unfolding. Everything necessary for this day to be a success is coming together. Each person involved is inspired to contribute in positive and meaningful ways. Harmony, peace, and mutual respect are evident in every interaction. The activities of this day flow smoothly and bring about exceptional results. You can learn a great deal about wholeness and happiness, peace and justice from everyday ordinary type people. Be mindful of today's interactions. Within these interactions are simple, practical, and powerful lessons on the importance of attitude, responsibility, and the tools to shape your life.

Today's Nourishment:
I accept and participate in this day. I will approach each interaction, situation, and event as an opportunity to learn. I live in the here and now and eliminate all drama from my day.

~22~
Nurture Your Heart

Today is about healing! In order to live in harmony on the earth plane, it is vitally important that you heal—physically, mentally, emotionally and spiritually. You have a role to play on this stage you call earth and it is a Divine role.

You have built up significant issues in your heart as part of the life lessons you have experienced. As a result, you have likely forgotten why you are here. Your angels are here to help you remember. They are waiting to work with you, to surround you with their warmth and love. By asking for their help in clearing your issues, you will be able to reconnect with your true heart—the one God intended you to have to achieve your souls' purpose in this life time.

You can nourish your heart by practicing discipline in your thinking throughout your day. Your thoughts and emotions are inextricably linked. Next time you are feeling depressed or angry, check your thought pattern. What thoughts were going through your mind when you began to feel depressed?

Another way to nurture your heart is with creative activities and hobbies. Ask yourself, "What stirs creativity, vision and inspiration in me?" Spend time in nature to refuel your my creativity and nourishes your heart. Besides reminding you of the awesome majesty of the Creator, nature calms the spirit, renews the faith and inspires fresh vision. Listening or playing the music and writing are other activities that nurture your heart and nourish your creativity.

Today's Nourishment:
I ask my angels to help me remember my reason for being. I pay attention to my thought patterns, and correct negative patterns. I spend time nourishing my creativity with activities and hobbies.

~23~
Be Gentle With Yourself

Be very gentle with yourself today. Your angels want you to feel peaceful and centered today. Surround yourself with gentleness, gentle people, and gentle situations. Start your day by listening to gentle music. Play it all day long, wherever you go. To actually be gentle with yourself you must know that it's alright if you don't do the laundry, return every email or phone call, do the dishes, or say the right thing at the precise moment. Know that it's perfectly fine to delay making that big decision until tomorrow.

This is not the day to engage in battles. Instead withdraw from conflict, revive your spirit, and renew your strength. This is a day to speak softly, move slowly, and engage in activities that sooth and caress your spiritual side. Be as gentle with yourself as you would with someone else who is going through life just a little too fast.

Today's Nourishment:
Today I am gentle with myself. I slow down, take it easy, seek out ways to centered myself and revive my spirit. I surround myself with gentleness, people, and gentle situations. I avoid conflict, instead withdraw and renew my strength.

~24~
You Are A Powerful Being

You are a powerful being and a child of God. You are loved. You have the power to create your dreams and do so with ease and joy. Knowing that you are made in the image of your Creator, your light is bright with truth; no mistake can undo a creation of God's. Do not be afraid of your power, know that you have the power to create your higher vision, dream, or ideal and can do so with ease.

Imagine yourself in the middle of a meadow—wide open space with beautiful wildflowers. Placing one foot in front of the other, you began running, as if a wind swooped down and lifted you. Now you are flying, soaring like a red-tailed hawk, higher and higher, feeling the power of the Creator within. Throwing open your arms, like wings, spreading them wide and the wind carries you aloft. Allow yourself this moment of peace, freedom, quiet, and relish the power of being one with the Creator.

Now visualize that which you desire to create, see it clearly in detail, in your mind. See it in its finished form. Hold the image, then release it, dropping it down to the earth, detaching from it, letting it go with the knowledge that which you desire will be brought to you in its perfect form.

Today's Nourishment:
I am a powerful being and a child of God. I am much loved. I have the power to create my dream, and do so with ease and joy.

~25~
Use Daily Prayer

God desires a personal relationship with you and that requires communication. Prayer is a form of communication with God. Prayer gives you a rewarding and life enhancing conversation with God. Prayer is a door-opener. You stand on one side; on the other side is God. When you begin to open the door, you are standing with God and all His incredible and unimaginable power. By opening the door, you are allowing that power to step through and work for God's good, and in turn for your good.

Knowing that God gave you freedom of choice and free will, prayer enables Him to step into your life. Prayer gives God permission to do what he has been longing to do all the time, to help you. Prayer draws you closer to God, releases you from your ego, and draws you closer to God.

Another reason for daily prayer is to express gratitude. God has certainly blessed you, even if your present circumstances have blinded you to your blessings. Prayer allows you to see all the good things in your life. Through prayer you quiet the inner turmoil, open your heart to God allowing you to pay attention to His communication. Oh yes, God does communicate! Keep in mind that it is rude to ignore someone who is speaking to you. It is the height of rudeness to ignore God. Use prayer as part of your daily routine to foster a personal relationship with your Creator, ask for His help, open your heart and ears to Him, and to express gratitude for the blessings you have received.

Today's Nourishment:

I use prayer daily to foster a personal relationship with my Creator. I will talk to God as a child would to a father. I will tell God everything that is on my mind and in my heart.

~26~
Don't Hold Back

Sharing with yourself is important, so do not hold back your emotions. Some emotions may frighten, intimidate, or worry you, so you push them down into your subconscious. Do not be ashamed of your feelings. You do not have to act upon these feelings, but it is important for your happiness and healing to admit them to yourself. By allowing these feelings to rise to the surface, you can examine them, gaining more understanding and insight into their existence.

The foundation of self-love begins with self-honesty and self-awareness. In order to accept yourself you must first know yourself. Spend some time today listening to your inner emotions. Hold nothing back from yourself. Allow these feelings to surface, look at them through compassionate eyes, a soft heart, and a sense of humor. Take the risk of creatively expressing these feelings—write, sing, dance, or paint.

Today's Nourishment:
I am honest with myself. I allow my feelings to rise to the surface so that I may examine them and gain an understanding of their existence. I admit my feelings to myself and take the risk of expressing these feelings.

~27~
Rid Yourself Of Guilt

Only by understanding where guilt comes from, can you begin eliminating it from your life. Guilt is a feeling caused by your thoughts not being in line with what you want or your purpose. This is not about having guilt over the choices you have made in the past. Your feelings of guilt do not occur all the time, only when you are thinking certain thoughts. These thoughts are most often about the future outcomes of the choices you have made. Guilt is a feeling caused by improper thoughts. In other words, feeling guilty is a sign from your body to quit thinking those thoughts. Think about something else.

When you give into feelings of guilt you are ultimately withholding love from yourself. You are being unforgiving of yourself. Essentially you are saying you are *bad or wrong*. That is not being open to loving yourself. Eliminate this guilt by being more loving toward yourself. Everything that has happened in your life has happened for a reason. The choices you made were the ones you made and feeling guilty serves no purpose. You are meant to learn from past choices, not feel guilty.

Stop withholding love from yourself as a form of punishment for not making the right choice. Your creator does not expect or want you to suffer. Your creator simply wants you to learn to follow your inner knowing. By being loving and forgiving with yourself the feeling of guilt will disappear.

Today's Nourishment:
I love and forgive myself. I no longer have the thoughts that caused my feelings of guilt. My feelings of guilt have disappeared.

~28~
You Can Do Anything

You can do anything that you set your mind to. Your power is unlimited. Whatever you desire is within your reach. Approach each situation with a purpose, focusing on your goal as if it has already manifested. For example, instead of saying, "I wish I would lose these holiday pounds," see yourself as if you already have. See yourself motivated to walk, run, or work out more and actually enjoying yourself. Express gratitude to the universe that you have already met your goal weight.

This works for any wants or desires. See yourself as healthy, happy, enjoying life and your personal relationships, prosperous, and anything else that you long for. You are a divine being created by a loving powerful God—you can do anything!

Today's Nourishment:
I believe in myself. I can do anything that I set my mind to. My doubts are now dreams and my fears are now excitement. God's power is within me—I can do anything!

~29~
Talk To God

Talking to God is as natural as speaking with a friend sitting next to you. While it may be hard to talk to someone you can't see, faith allows you to believe in what you can't see. You know in your heart that God exists and that He desires a personal relationship with you. A relationship requires good two-way communication.

Talking with God is not always praying. Your attitude when you talk to God should be reverent. However, God is the Almighty. He can take whatever attitude or language you bring to the conversation. While some may believe it is not proper, God will listen to you even if you are angry, upset, or crying. In fact, God is happy when you are honest with Him. When you talk to God, be real, be honest, and say what is on your mind. Tell God what is going on inside you, with your life; ask Him what you should do about it. That's real and honest.

Spend time talking to God. He already knows your heart, but like any good parent, he is thrilled when you want to chat with Him. Tell him how you feel. Let him know if you are happy, remorseful, troubled, sad, fearful—everything. However, when you have had your say be sure to sit quietly and let God have his turn. Any good relationship requires two-way communication, so listen to God when it's his turn to speak.

Today's Nourishment:
I spend time talking to God. I will tell God what is going on inside. I will tell him how I feel, whether I am happy, sad, or troubled. I will listen when it's his turn to speak.

~30~

Give Your Worries To God

God says you should give all your worries to ~~him~~ _God_. Not seventy-five percent of them, but all of them. Pretend you were standing next to a friend and you gave your car keys to them. Another friend comes along and asks for the keys to your car. You would tell them you don't have your keys that you gave them to a friend.

That's what you need to do with your worries. You need to hand them over to God and not take them back. If a worried thoughts pops in your mind, give it back to God, as all your worries now belong to ~~him~~ _God_.

Once you do that, problems you've been worrying about for weeks will start to be solved. You'll no longer be tying God's hands with your worrying. Remember, though, God will not take your worries away from you. You have to give them to ~~him~~ _God_.

Today's Nourishment:
I give all my worries over to God. I hold nothing back. Everything big and small has been released to God. I am no longer worried or anxious. I allow myself to be cared for and nurtured like a child.

~31~
Speak Loving Words

Realize the power of the words you speak. The words that we speak affect other's lives. Words of comfort, love, and peace can help someone in their time of need. Pay attention to the words you speak. Do you speak words of encouragement, or words of criticism? Do the words you say give others hope, or do they cause them to doubt their abilities? Think and speak only words of love.

Look into your heart and really think about what you say to people. Make a special effort to reach out to someone in need and speak loving words. Learn to guard your words carefully; speak loving words, it promotes harmony and peace in all that you do. See everyone through the eyes of love and understanding. Speak loving words.

Today's Nourishment:
I speak loving words about myself and others. I guard my words carefully and promote harmony and peace in all that I say and do.

~32~
Create Loving Thoughts

All thoughts are creative. Your thoughts create the life that you are living right now. What are your thoughts most of the time? Do you have thoughts, which tell you that you are smart, intelligent, attractive and deserving? And do you have brilliant thoughts that with proper action could turn into something extraordinary?

You are a master creator and you become what you think about. Loving thoughts create beauty, loving experiences and relationships. Love begins with your thoughts. Ask for spiritual assistance to guide you toward creating loving thoughts. Toady be aware of your thoughts and know that with every loving thought you are creating a shining energy of love.

Today's Nourishment:
I am a master creator. Through my thoughts and emotions, I create a flow of shining energy of love creating beauty and loving experiences.

~33~
Know That God Is Right Here

God doesn't live in some faraway land called Heaven—He exists all around you. At times you may feel His presence or see evidence that He is right here. By connecting with God moment by moment, is to experience the joy of His divine presence every minute of every day. Whether driving, during deep prayer, or while washing a sink filled with dishes, God is a constant energy.

Although God would never interfere with your free will, know that He is always stands next to you ready to help you with anything you ask for—all you have to do is ask.

Today's Nourishment:
I am loved, supported, and surrounded by God's loving energy. He will never leave my side, ready to help at a moment's notice.

~34~
Transform Negative Into Positive

Negative emotions such as worry, anger, and resentment are like poison. Now is the time to change the poison into medicine. Now is the time to change your thought process, your outlook about yourself and your life. Transform negative thoughts, situations, and events into positive. Be aware of your thoughts and how you approach each day. Keep track of the negative on a piece of paper for several days. Notice how many times you put yourself down through your thoughts or actions.

Use a piece of paper folded long ways down the middle. On one side, write down each negative thought. On the right side, write down a positive thought to replace it. Be as specific as possible. Read the positive thoughts out loud to yourself each time you find yourself thinking a negative. Continue this process until positive thinking becomes a habit!

Today's Nourishment:
Negative thoughts have been transformed into positive thoughts. I feel positive about myself, my surrounds, and those around me. I am honest, upbeat, and happy. This new outlook creates positive energy that surrounds me; energizing me and keeps me healthy.

~35~
Create A Safe Haven

You are safe. Trust your inner voice, which is the voice of God, as you are guided through all situations safely. You are warned of pending dangers. ~~His~~ God's divine love surrounds you and protects you from harm. Ask that you, your loved ones, your home, office, vehicle, and community be cleansed of any lower energy and are steered away from any harmful situations.

Let go of worries as you are surrounded with a powerful loving light that protects you and attracts loving experiences. Focus on the light and love, instead of fear, creating a safe haven for yourself and loved ones.

Today's Nourishment:
I have a loving protective God who surrounds and protects me and my loved ones. I am safe and without fear. I hear and follow my own intuition as this is the voice God.

~36~
See The Beauty Around You

Look for God's beauty around you. See the handiwork of God, for he has created all that there is. There is beauty within and surrounding you at all times. You can find beauty in nature's colors of warmth, in your interactions with others, within yourself and others. You are a spiritual being, another handiwork of God, thus you are a creature of beauty. This beauty radiates to others; through your eyes, smile, and touch. Make today's focus one of beauty. Notice beauty wherever you go, in all that you do. Realize that there is great beauty within you, in those you meet, in all situations

Today's Nourishment:
I see God's beauty all around me. I notice the handiwork of God. There is great beauty everywhere; surrounding me, within me, and within everyone I meet.

~37~
Meet New People

As a spiritual creature, of a divine nature, you have a host of angels as constant companions. They see and appreciate all your wonderful qualities. Others would like to get to know you. Now is the time to leave your comfort zone. Instead of going to the same old places, shake up your routine, go to new places, develop new interests, and meet new people. Volunteering is a perfect way to meet other good-hearted people. Clubs, gyms, or social groups are great places to meet new people and they usually welcome newcomers with open arms.

No matter what approach you choose, pay attention to the image and attitude you project. Display openness and warmth to the people around you. Show that you are interested in meeting new people. Give others a chance to see and appreciate all the wonderful qualities you have. Remember to take it slowly. Meeting new people is not an overnight process—so don't expect too much too fast. Get to know your newfound friends one step at a time—ask for spiritual assistance and guidance as you meet new people.

Today's Nourishment:
I shake up my routine and venture to the unknown. I leave my comfort zone and seek out new people. I am open, friendly, and smile at everyone I meet. I display openness, warmth, and upbeat attitude to those around me.

~38~
Accept God's Blessings

God bestows an abundance of love, support, and blessings upon you daily but as with any gift, you must accept His [God's] blessings. There are times that you believe that you are not worthy to receive the blessings; that you are not as valuable as other people. Know that you deserve good things just as much as any other person. You are worthy of support, love, compassion, and caring. Know that God desires only the best for you, as any loving parent wishes for one of their own.

Open your arms to receive God's blessings, love, and support. Accepting these gifts from God allows you to help others and fulfills God's desire to give to one of His [God's] children. Know that you are worthy of such gifts. You are an innocent, precious, and sweet child of God. There is nothing wrong with you—open your arms and accept God's blessings.

Today's Nourishment:
I am a child of God and am worthy to receive His [God's] blessings. I deserve goodness in all ways. I open my arms to receive God's blessings, love, and support in my life. I treat myself with love and respect and am loved in return. I accept God's blessings…and say thank you.

~39~
Take Chances

Fear can control, limit, and influence decisions that effect the quality of your life. Now is the time to dare to take chances, throw fears out the window, and believe in your dreams! Your fear of disappointment makes you reluctant to admit your innermost desires, take action, or ask for assistance.

Know that you are being supported in all ways. God loves you and wants you to have your heart's desires. Take a chance and allow yourself to dream. Believe in your dreams, ask for assistance, and take action to make your dreams a reality.

Today's Nourishment:
I throw fear out the window. I take a chance on myself today. I take a chance on being happy, fulfilled, and know that I have the courage to follow my dreams.

Remember To Breathe

Breathe in. Breathe out. Take several deep cleansing breaths, drawing in fresh clean air, exhale slowly and release negativity. Continue this practice throughout the day. During moments of stress, tension, or crisis you have a tendency to hold your breath. Breathing is essential to living. Breathing provides oxygen to your mind, body, and spirit.

Remind yourself the importance of breathing throughout the day. Become aware of your breathing; deepen it as you read this. Delight in the cleansing effect that deep breathing has on your mind and body. Use your breath has a bridge to connect the spiritual and physical worlds.

Spend time outdoors today and breath fresh air, or place live plants in and around your home and workplace. Spend time near running water. Breathe the fresh clean air near water and let your lung fill themselves with the powerful molecules that are vital to your health and happiness.

Today's Nourishment:
I am aware of the rhythm and rate of my breathing. I breathe deeply; inhale fresh pure air and exhale with great joy; releasing tension, stress, and negativity.

~41~
Dare To Dream

Dare to dream! Dream big, let go of limitations, fears, and doubts that hold you back. Now is the time to realize that your dreams are within reach. All your needs will be met, all the answers to your problems will be given, you will have abundance on every level—you will grow spiritually!

Today is the day to take charge of your world. Envision a future filled with success, prosperity, exotic and elaborate fantasies. Specialize in the impossible. Take your seemingly impossible dreams and choose today to make them a reality. Simplify your life and live the life you have imagined. Go confidently into your day, for today is the day you dare to dream!

Today's Nourishment:
I let go of limitations, fears, and doubts—nothing holds me back. Today I take charge and envision a future of prosperity, success, and happiness.

~42~
Give Something Back

To give you must receive and when you receive you should give something back. You are being guided to learn and be willing to receive; for as you receive you can give. Like a flowing river that starts out small and narrow and as more water is added to that river it grows wider and longer. The more you receive, the more you can give, and the more you give the more you can receive.

It is through giving and receiving that you truly prosper. Prosperity arrives in many forms such as knowledge, love, friends, money, and time. In many instances what you give is what you receive and what you receive is what you give. When you give unselfishly, you are giving with a pure heart and the right intent. When you receive with gratitude and appreciation you are receiving with the right intent.

As you go throughout your day, keep in mind the flowing river. Open yourself up to receiving more so you can give more back. If you continue to give without being willing to receive you will eventually run out of all that you have to give. You will receive all that you want and desire because you are giving with the true intent.

Today's Nourishment:
I give with a pure heart and right intent, because sharing is my heart's desire. I give something back as I receive so shall I give back.

~43~
Ask Your Angels For Help

The term angels is the name used to refer to a group of heavenly beings created by God. They are all in service to God, answer to Him, follow His directions, and are messengers of God. All angels are powerful, compassionate, divine beings of loving light. God created them to provide you with protection, strength, courage, love, and spiritual guidance.

Angels are available to respond to your sincere request for help. They stand next to you ready to help. When the angels hear your cries and pleas for help, they immediately come to your aid. They lend you strength during those times when you have forgotten your own power. This deep angelic love envelops you protectively, shielding you from any harm, soothing your fears, removing your doubts. They are here to walk with you along life's journey, helping with through life's transitions and challenges.

Ask your angels to stand by your side today. Voice any fears, doubts, or insecurities you may have. Release your worries, problems, or concerns. Do not try to fix or control things yourself; ask your angels to help.

Today's Nourishment:
I ask my angels to help me today. I release my fears, doubts, problems, and insecurities. I feel safe, loved, and cared for.

~44~
Open Your Heart

When you talk to God today, ask God to assist you to open your heart to yourself and others. It brings God joy to assist you in consciously co-create space for continued spiritual awakening, transformation, healing, and growth. At your request God will work with you in opening your heart, expanding spiritual knowledge in hopes of nurturing, healing and uplifting you.

You were made out of love by your Creator. When you open your heart you encounter God's love. Allow the angels to help you open your heart in a way that feels safe and secure. Ask your angels to sweep away old pain and resentments as they guide you. As you open your heart to be fully present in your life, for yourself and others, you call forth the miracles of healing, love and tenderness. The benefits are immeasurable.

Today's Nourishment:

I ask God to assist me to open my heart. I am made out of love and when I open my heart I encounter God's love. I ask my angels help me to open my heart, sweeping away old hurts and resentments.

~45~
Thank God

When God answers our prayers in a crisis or brings forth miracles on your behalf, it is easy to give thanks. Showing your gratitude should not be limited to special events. God is honored when you thank ~~Him~~ God for ~~His~~ God's faithfulness to provide for our daily needs or when we express gratefulness that ~~He~~ God is your ~~Father~~ God. Giving thanks to God should be an integral part of your life. Thanks and gratitude should flow from your heart on a regular basis.

Thanking God is easy. Write ~~Him~~ God a thank you letter, concentrating on thanking ~~Him~~ God for specific things, events, or blessings. Or create a gratitude list containing everything you are grateful for. Make this an ongoing project, adding to the list regularly. Read the letter or list whenever you need a quick pick-me-up, and your gratitude will lift you up once again.

Today's Nourishment:
Today I say, "thank you God!" I am grateful for_____. {Create your gratitude list containing everything you are thankful for and that which is yet to be given.}

~46~
You Are Awesome

As you begin to trust and reveal your true self to others, it slowly dawns on you that you are an awesome person! Extraordinary, caring, loving, attractive, honest, intelligent, and successful in every way! This is your true self–let your true self shine through!

You are God's miracle in human form, you are awesome. You are loved, valuable, and cherished. You are here for a worthwhile purpose. You were sent to Earth because everything you do, say, and think has a healing effect on others. Know that every one of God's children is a miracle created in human form and that includes you—you are awesome!

Today's Nourishment:
I am awesome! I am a creation of God who loves, values, and cherishes me. My true self is extraordinary, caring, loving, attractive, honest, and loved. My true self shines through.

Work With Your Angels

In order to draw your angels near you must prepare to draw them to you. Angels reside in the heaven-world, the world of God, while you live on the earthy plane. Angels naturally gravitate toward home. So if you want the angels to become closer to you, you must draw them into your world. You need to make your world, your thoughts, feelings, and surroundings more in tune with theirs.

To make the angels more comfortable you must replace thoughts of irritation and aggression with those of peace and love. Thoughts of the driver who cut you off may linger in your mind throughout the day, but you can free yourself from the irritation by communicating with your angels a few minutes a day. To become more in tune with your angels you must separate yourself from distractions. Turn off the radio and TV, go into a room by yourself or to your favorite nature spot, imagine an angel in your mind and get comfortable. Begin by asking for help to hear God's messages clearly through God's loving angels. Imagine talking to your best friend, open your mind, heart, and then your ears. After you have finished your side of the conversation, be silent and listen. Listen for the thoughts that pop into your mind, as these thoughts are messages from God delivered by God's postal carriers—your angels. .

Before long, your relationship with angels will evolve and they will help you to feel more positive and upbeat. Feeling positive will bring you closer to God's angels.

Today's Nourishment:
I replace thoughts of irritation and aggression with those of peace and love. My world, my thoughts, feelings, and surroundings are in tune with those of God's angels, drawing them near.

~48~
Feel The Angels Love

After you have established a relationship with the angels, you still need to keep yourself open to feeling their love. Free will is a gift from God—angels respect all gifts from God. On rare occasions they will intervene without your speaking up. But most often, they politely wait for you to ask for their help.

Your angels want to saturate you with their divine love. They watch over you day and night, illuminating your way with their loving healing divine light. It is important to them that you know who they are and that you feel their love and hear their messages of guidance and support. Your angel's mission is love. Your mission is to feel it.

As your awareness of the angels grows the more open you are to feeling their love. Let the angels teach you how to love yourself unconditionally as they love you. Their love extends beyond any judgments you might have about your worth of lack there of. Let them guide you with their gentle and humorous ways to love and accept yourself no matter what. Open your heart and your mind, allow their gentle loving energy to fill your heart, soul, and essence. Feel the angel's love.

Today's Nourishment:
I am aware of the angels and their unconditional love for me. They guide me with their gentle ways. I accept and love myself unconditionally as they love me.

~49~
Connect With Nature

Spend some time outdoors, blow the stink off, and connect with nature! Connecting with nature renews your spirit, revives energy, relieves stress, creates new ideas, and promotes creativity.

Being in nature synchronizes rhythms to the universal heartbeat, improves timing, allows you to be in the right place at the right time.

Revamp your daily planner and schedule time for breathing fresh air; dare to use ink! Take in the beauty of nature, hear the birds, see the butterflies, and smell the flowers. Allow nature's cleansing powers remove negative energies, breath in the positive. See the beauty in everything and everyone. Once you are upon nature, take time to drink in God's beauty, know that you are a part of this beauty. Take time to connect with nature, connect with God.

> Today's Nourishment:
> *I spend time outdoors connecting with nature. I schedule outdoor time, breathe in fresh air; soak up some of God's beauty knowing that I am a part of this beauty.*

~50~
Keep It Simple

Complications, hassles, and struggles...sound like your life? Stop for a moment andask yourself, what is the one thing that can be changed in your life to make it less complicated?Write down the firstanswer that pops in your head. Now toss that idea into the universe and ask that it become a reality. You deserve to have a simpler life, and releasing this desire to the universe canbecome your new reality.

Focus on making your life simpler today. As you approach situations, see if there isn't an easier way to obtain the same desired results. Contrary to what you may believe, struggle is NOT a necessary part of life. Open your mind to the possibility that life can be simpler and that things can be accomplished without struggles orcomplications.

Today's Nourishment:
Keep it simple! Knowing that the best things in life are simple, I will eliminate complications from my life–simplify is my word for the day!

~51~
Change Your Routine

There is comfort in having a routine for your life. Routines and habitual patterns make you feel safe, secure, and in control of your life. Going through the hum drum of each uneventful day dulls your senses to anything out of the ordinary. Now is the time to change your everyday rituals and open yourself up to a journey of change!

Take a break from your routine and begin to do things you have always wanted to or become open to new experiences. Take in an afternoon movie, explore your interest in music, and begin to see your world as fun.

Take a few unexpected detours in your normal routine day. Do your best to add something new to change your routine. Order something new off the lunch menu or take a different route to work. Do your grocery shopping during peak hours. Perhaps waiting in a long line is a good thing once in a while. Add variety to your established patterns; it keeps things from getting boring. Although you will most likely return to some of your comfortable routines, you will have incorporated some fresh approaches as well. Through the process of experimentation you will have discovered some new ways to embrace your life.

Today's Nourishment:
I change my routine and seek new experiences. I add something new to my day and add variety to my normal daily habits. I look for unexpected detours and allow myself to be guided into new territory.

~52~
Sit Quietly And Listen

When did you last sit quietly and listen? When did you last listen to the small voice inside you? Think back to the last time you sat down quietly with a cup of coffee or tea and just listened to what is going on inside you. This small voice is the angels sending you messages. They want to make sure you are doing the right thing. They want you to succeed more than anything else and they want you to enjoy your success.

Begin in this moment; be still, sit quietly, and listen. Connect with that peaceful space within where you can listen to their messages. Don't force messages; let them come to you in this quiet moment. Although you have been receiving repetitive messages through your feelings, dreams, visions, inner voice, or simple knowing you haven't been listening. The universal airwaves have been cluttered with the comings and goings around you. All this clutter and noise is causing interference with the reception. Calm your mind, body, and spirit; you are in communication with God.

Follow what is being said. If you feel a strong urge to call someone, go somewhere, read something, or do something, it is important to follow these urgings.

Today's Nourishment:
I am still, calm, quiet, and ready to listen to that small voice within. I follow what is said, knowing that I am in communication with my God.

~53~
Release Challenges

True healing can not begin until you release all challenges. Only when your challenges have been released can heavenly divine light enter. Stop focusing on *what is wrong* and accept that everything is as it should be. Have faith that God is working through all your challenges and healing your heart.

Your challenges are too heavy to manage alone. Imagine a purple square box with a red lid, remove the lid, place your challenges, worries, and concerns inside the box, and replace the lid. Now hand the box over to God. Take a deep cleansing breath, embrace thoughts of love, lift your eyes upward, and watch everything move heavenward. Give thanks.

Let this be your last day of holding tightly to challenges. Release your challenges to God as soon as they appear, walk lighter, absorb the heavenly light, and feel the healing love.

Today's Nourishment:
I place all my challenges, worries, and concerns inside the purple box with the red lid. I replace the lid and release my challenges over to God. I feel balanced, peaceful, and loved.

~54~
Accept Your Success

Like a parachute jump, it is scary and exhilarating at the same time, to know that you have achieved a goal, won a prize, or landed that promotion. Everything you are or ever will be is completely up to you. Everything that has happened and is happening in your life is because of your behavior, words, and actions.

Every success imaginable in life is yours already; there is no reason for you to search any further. You are already a success and it is time to accept that which is yours. Through positive thinking, energy, and emotions you are the creator of your own successes. Imagine the exhilaration of that parachute jump, retain it, savor it, and hold on to it. That feeling combined with gratitude will manifest all your future successes.

Today's Nourishment:
I open my arms to receive every success that God brings me. I feel exhilarated and worthy of all my successes. I deserve to be successful; to achieve all my goals, to reap all my rewards.

~55~
Ignite Your Imagination

As a child, what did you dream of being? What roles did you play? What make believe worlds did you create? Imagination is not just for children! It's pure and childlike in the most positive way. It is untamed, unrestricted, a condition for truth, and a necessity for faith. The soul journey requires the constant use of imagination. Without imagination, there are no relationships, no creativity and no soul.

What you imagine is what you experience. Using your imagination deliberately gives you the power to create your own experiences. Imagination is born on the wings of the angels and could never mislead. Allow your imagination to gallop wildly and embrace the wonderful creations. Inspiration, creativity and dream-like visions fill your mind space. These creations are gifts from your Creator that are conjured in your mind and born into reality. Ignite your imagination and liberate yourself—live your life without limits and soar!

Today's Nourishment:
I ignite my imagination and am liberated. I am aware of all my creative thoughts, emotions, and dreams, unleashing them and free to soar.

~56~
Create A Meditation Spot

Meditation is an experience of the heart, not of the mind. To learn how to meditate you need to trust the messages of your heart. After a period of time, you will realize the benefits of meditation in your life, even before you fully understand what meditation is.

It is best to create a permanent meditation place. Your meditation place may be anything from a quiet room in the house, a table or a corner of your study desk, to even the shade of your favorite tree in the backyard. It doesn't matter where it is, just as long as you are able to find peace of mind there and access it regularly. Put simply, your meditation spot is an entrance to your heart; a shrine to your soul. Whatever inspires you spiritually is perfect for your meditation spot.

If possible have a small table or shelve to place inspirational objects. Objects such as flowers, beautiful crystal, photo, candles, or sacred object are placed upon the table or shelve. Ideally you have a permanent meditation spot, but if you don't just have the objects in a bundle, ready to go.

If you already have a permanent meditation place, in which case you might like to make sure it is clean, and if possible, light a candle and some incense, place some fresh flowers on the table. It is helpful to use this time to begin to focus on your spirituality. Prepare the meditation place with reverence – pay attention to your movements and feel the grace that comes with the joy of spirituality. Light the candle and incense, place the flowers, with no other thought but the now. If your meditation space is temporary then as you are setting it up the same applies.

Today's Nourishment:
I trust the messages of my heart and realize the benefits of meditation in my life. My meditation spot is clean, quiet, and inspires me spiritually. I pay attention to my movements, thoughts, and feelings while preparing my meditation spot.

~57~
Flex Your Body

Today's focus will be on flexing your body. God wants you to feel good in your body. God wants you to maintain a healthy lifestyle that includes exercise and healthy living. More importantly God wants you to accept and enjoy being in your body. Understand there is a close connection between exercising and flexing your body.

The need to stretch and flex is instinctive in the animal world. Visualize a cat waking up from a nap and engaging in a full-body, paws to toe stretch. Flexing is inspiring and is a means to open you up to information, feelings, and is one of life's simple pleasures. It is natural to flex and stretch out a bit before getting out of bed in the morning. Flexing your body opens and loosens you up, helps you breather better, move more easily and feel less tired.

This is a day to practice flexing your body at regular intervals throughout the day. If you want to have freedom of movement, creative thoughts, increase your imagination throughout your life, you need to work towards maintaining your strength and flexibility.

Today's Nourishment:
I enjoy flexing my body throughout the day. I focus on stretching my mind, flexing my body, and increasing my imagination.

~58~
Exercise Your Body

You are a divine spiritual being created by God and your body is but one of God's His gifts. Your body is important to God. God wants you to be healthy so you can fulfill your life's purpose. God He promises that when you ask God He will give you the power, self-discipline, determination, and motivation to exercise your body. When you exercise your body you will feel more alive. You will experience greater energy and vitality to do what you love and achieve what your heart desires.

When you treat your body as a gift from God that you are privileged to help build and maintain, you not only benefit physically, but experience mental calm and spiritual well-being. Exercise increases your physical strength and vitality which is imperative to your emotional well-being. When you honor your body through healthy eating and exercise you can achieve a truly remarkable level of emotional and spiritual growth.

Today's Nourishment:
I am blessed by God with the strength, vitality, self-discipline, and motivation to exercise my body. My body is a gift from God and I honor this gift through healthy eating and exercise.

~59~
Prioritize Your Life

By prioritizing your life you free up time to enjoy the people and things that are important to you. Accept that you can not squeeze any more into your day and being okay with that. Take an honest look at what you want to accomplish in your life and letting the rest go. You have relationships to nurture, dreams to follow, activities you enjoy, and work responsibilities. These are your priorities.

Understand that no matter what you do, there are still only 24 hours in a day. You are in charge of your schedule; you set your priorities and it is up to you to decide what you can deal with.
Everyday God gives you 24 hours. By breaking it down and factoring in sleep and job related time realize that you only have five hours a day.

You decide how you want to spend your five hours a day. By spending the rest of your day cooking, cleaning, paying bills, doing laundry, helping with homework, chauffeuring your kids, running errands you miss out on personal time, relationship time, and quality family time.

You can not manage what you don't have—you have to prioritize your life. Look at the big picture—spirituality, family, health, work; now list everything in order of personal importance. Keep your eye on the top priorities and do your best to stay focused. When it comes to accomplishing your goals, there is little time for being side tracked.

Today's Nourishment:
I can not manage what I do not have. I can not squeeze any more into my day—I am okay with that. I keep my eye on the big picture, prioritize, and stay focused throughout my day.

~60~
Declare A Day Of Love

Today is a day of love! This day is dedicated to the magic of love! Strip off the mask of illusion and see that love is the essence of all life. Penetrate the illusions of personality and the destructive nature of negativity; realize that we are, at our core, a fountain of love!

Find ways to celebrate love throughout the day. Let your focus beon caring, compassion, and affection. Be affectionate, express your feelings to your family and friends, and be kind to yourself and others today. Open your heart to the love within knowing that the essence of love is the basic and fundamental substance of life. Without love nothing can grow or flourish—life would cease to exist. Let yourself explode with expressions of love today!

Today's Nourishment:
I dedicate this day to the expression of love. I celebrate love throughout my day and focus on caring, compassion, and affection. I generate loving thoughts, feelings, and acts toward myself and others.

Embrace Your Inner Child

In order to grow stronger in self-esteem, you will need to embrace your inner child who lacks the experience of being freely accepted and loved in an unconditional manner. By embracing your inner child you gain inner healing and increase in the strength needed to pursue ongoing recovery when feeling lonely, forgotten, or abandoned.

Spend time reconnecting with the trusting, fun-loving and imaginative part of you that may just have disappeared under piles of hard work and life's trials. Spend time doing the things you loved doing as a kid. Such things include going to the playground, the toy aisle or a cartoon movie session. Stop obsessing over the small things. Kids are carefree! Let go of worries and see if the world around you tumbles. You'll be surprised that it doesn't. And maybe you'll regain some clarity and perspective.

Today's Nourishment:
I spend time doing the things I loved as a child. I visit the playground, swing high, build sandcastles, and make mudpies! Today I will embrace my inner child—provided nurturing, love, fun, and playtime.

~62~
Sing

When you want to nurture your body, mind and spirit, your angels invite you to sing. There is music within your heart that desires to be set free. It does not matter if you sing off-key or forget the words to a song. Music helps you relax, reduce stress, sleep better, and connect with your spiritual essence. Singing allows you to express deep emotions, is therapeutic, and great for your self-esteem.

Even if you are shy and uncertain of your abilities, sign the permission slip today and allow yourself to contribute to the musical notes in the universe. Sing to the music you play on the radio in your car, sing in the shower, sing to your animals or children, hum a tune from days gone by—it doesn't matter how you do it—just do it! Express yourself and sing!

Today's Nourishment:
I nurture my body, mind, and spirit and sing for the fun of it. I release the music within my heart. I sing throughout the day—expressing myself freely, openly, and joyfully.

~63~
Dance

Discover the secret place within your soul with music and movement. Let yourself be swept away, inspired, and uplifted with the power of dance. Experience the healing benefits of dance movements, gentle swaying, and meditative powers. Deeply relax your body and mind; soaring into a powerful magical transformational dance explosion.

Make time to dance. Turn on some music and let yourself experience the power of dance. You need not learn complicated dance steps to experience the emotionally therapeutic power of dance. Even if you are a non-dancer let exotic, primal world beat rhythms set you body, mind, and spirit free. Enjoy an aerobic workout that never feels like exercise. Dancing helps regain a connection to your physical and spiritual essence. As you sway and move you will realize that you are a graceful, attractive, and spiritual being created by a loving gentle caring God. Indulging in the movement of dance can be life-changing as old energies which weigh your down are dissolved. One dance session will leave you feeling light as a feather and deeply at ease.

Today's Nourishment:
I make time to dance. I play music or dance to the music in my head. I discover the secret place within my soul with music and movement. I allow myself to be swept away, inspired, and uplifted with the power of dance.

~64~
Play With Children

Remember what it was like to be kid, running around without a care in the world? Well, stop remembering and start revisiting your childhood! Today is a day to engage in the art of play by allowing yourself the joy of playing with a child. Fun and play is the angels' way. Add some fun to your life; sing, dance, laugh, and be silly!

If you have kids, do the stuff they like to do. Swing with them, play dress up, play in the rain, and eat ice cream; what could be more fun? See the world through a child's eyes. Build sand castles and mud highways with them. Get dirty, blow bubbles, toss balls over the neighbor's fence and fetch them back sheepishly. Jump rope and eat snack-sized puddings.

Stop obsessing over calories. Have a lollipop. Have a chocolate fudge coated something that looks so fattening it just screams *eat me*. Run around madly afterwards as a kid would do and you'll soon burn off those calories!

Return to your responsible adulthood tomorrow, but learn from the fun that childhood teaches. Learn to always cast back your memory to fun childhood times and the things that made you feel safe, fulfilled and happy. Build on those memories in a way that allows you to be the responsible adult influenced for the better by the carefree child inside.

Today's Nourishment:
I will revisit my childhood. I take time out of my day to engage in childlike play. I play with my children or other children. I see the world through a childs' eyes—tomorrow I return to adulthood but learn from the lessons of childhood.

~65~
De-Clutter Your Life

Is your car junky? Are your closets a wreck? Does your desk look like a war zone? Take the time to inspect your surroundings. Look at your car, your house, and your desk. Organizing is a way of gathering your thoughts so that you have less stress finding important papers, clothes to wear, or fixing yourself a meal. You can feel the difference in your energy flow when you are in a clean area versus a messy one.

If you don't know what you have, then clearly you are not attached to it and you can get rid of it. If you haven't used something in two years, chances are you are not going to use it. If you have had it longer than two years, it is probably out of style anyway. Secondly, if you are simply hoarding things, make no mistake you are creating stagnant energy in your space and are blocking blessings and prosperity from coming into your life. Think about it, energy flows through physical structures similar to the flow of water or air. When you have so much stuff cluttering up your environment, that flow is obstructed.

Today is a perfect day to de-clutter your life. It's time to clean out that closet, straighten your work area, donate unwanted or unused items, or hold a garage sale. De-cluttering your life, even in small ways, will make room for more energy flow and as that energy increases you will find you have more blessings and prosperity in your life.

Today's Nourishment:
I inspect my surroundings and clear away clutter from my environment, one area, and one object at a time. If I do not use, want, or need an object I sell it or give it to someone who can benefit from it.

~66~
Do Something Extraordinary

You are an extraordinary person! Being the extraordinary person you are, anything is possible. Today is a great day to seize every opportunity to make anything happen. With the spiritual fan club you have backing your every movement, thoughts, and feelings, this is the time to grasp hold of whatever strikes your fancy and go for it!

What would you like to do today? The choices are unlimited—parachuting, parasailing, white water rafting, rock climbing, ballooning, or anything outside your normal routine qualifies. What you do is not as important as seizing the moment to do something different. Embrace the unknown, flag down the unfamiliar, discover hidden talents, and let today be the catalyst for wonderful new possibilities! Doing anything out of the ordinary makes the day extraordinary—do something extraordinary!

Today's Nourishment:
I am an extraordinary person capable of doing something extraordinary with my day. I will seize every opportunity to make something different happen in my life. Today I do something extraordinary!

~67~
Relax, Let It Happen

Let go of the, *it's me against the world*, attitude, stop holding on tightly as it will only lead to failure. Stop struggling with the concept of letting go. When you struggle against life, as you do when you hold on too tightly, you are fighting against the flow of life. Everything you want is in the flow of life. Nothing is upstream, you do not have to fight or struggle for anything that you desire.

If you truly believe in the, *ask and you shall receive concept*, put some faith into it. Take some time to get into the grateful place in your mind and hear. Be grateful, totally and completely grateful for what you already have. Spend some time visualizing your goal but be at a place of gratitude in your heart. Then release it to God, let God handle it for you. Make sure to watch for inspired actions to take and follow through, but relax and let it happen. Release the resistance of trying to force it to happen, trying to make it happen, being determined it will and relax—let it happen.

Today's Nourishment:
I stop trying to force things to happen and relax. I no longer struggle against the flow of life and let it go. I create an attitude of gratitude, release it to the universe, and relax. I let it happen.

~68~
Plant A Garden, Watch It Grow

In the midst of your crowded life you forgot that gardening is as simple as it has always been. You plant a seed, take care of it, watch it grow, and smile in delight! Gardening is the basis of life. The world is a garden, with Mother Nature the ultimate landscaper. From her humankind has learned to plant, water, and harvest, both for food and pleasure. Gardening has both emotional and spiritual rewards. In other words, by creating an outside space you are nourishing your inside!

The message for you today is to plant a garden and watch it grow—literally. Purchase a package of seeds from the store. Before you put the seeds in the earth think of a project or goal you would like to see manifest. Hold the seedlings in your hands as you visualize your desire, inserting your energy within the seed. Then plant the seeds in the earth. You have planted a garden, now watch it grow.

You don't have to be a landscaper architect to reap the benefits of gardening. Simple things like potted plants, window or planter boxes, and hanging baskets are wonderful ways to nurture a garden—even if you don't have a yard.

Nurture both your garden and inner self. As you tend to your garden you build your connection with nature, enriching your appreciation of its gifts as you enrich the earth. Gardening is a sensory experience; nourishing your need to touch things, to work with your hands and to literally get into the nitty-gritty. Your labor comes to fruition with colorful, fragrant flowers, fruits, vegetables, and herbs—a feast for the senses. As you tend to your garden take daily steps to reach your goal or desire that you inserted within the seeds you planted.

Today's Nourishment:
I plant a garden along with my desires, goals, and dreams. As I tend to my garden I connect with nature and find peace and balance within the earth. I nurture both my garden and my goals.

~69~
Have An Adventure

You hold on to your routines because you are afraid of the unknown. Change is necessary for growth. What would happen if everything in your life stayed the same? You wouldn't find new ideas, your life would stagnate, and you would get stuck in a rut. To be successful, you need to take risks. To take risks you need to be open to change. Variety in life brings excitement and is a breeding ground for inspiration, innovation, and a higher level of creativity.

Become a natural at embracing change—be more adventurous. You don't have to wait to go on vacation to have an adventure. Start small but start today. Create your own adventure starting with making changes in your routine. Change the way you do things, try a new food, visit a new place, and stay open to new ideas. Today is the day to become daring, spontaneous, impulsive, and adventurous.

Get excited about the possibilities. Instead of fearing the worst expect the best and look at change as a fun adventure. Stay open to new ideas; make room for a higher level of creativity and inspiration. Schedule half hour of open time to do something different than what you normally do. It doesn't matter what it is as long as you do not write it down on your schedule ahead of time. Figure it out when the moment arrives. Do whatever comes to mind in that half hour. You can nap. Go for a walk. Ride your bike. Draw a picture. Read a book. Jump a rope. It doesn't matter, as long as it is something different than what you would normally do at that time. If you don't feel like doing anything, then don't. Doing nothing is still something!

Today's Nourishment:
I embrace change and am adventurous. I create my own adventure today. I schedule half hour of open time to have an adventure. I will not write it down on my schedule. I will figure it out when the moment arrives.

~70~
Nourish Yourself

You are a participant in the everyday marathon of life like a human pinball zipping through time. Many things happen throughout your day, but you take in but a handful. You have been pushing yourself too hard—now's the time to relax and nourish yourself. Clear your mind, rest your body, and focus on nourishing yourself with spiritual and emotional food. While in this resting state, focus on being true to yourself; what you want and how you truly feel.

Find a place where the world doesn't penetrate and visit for five minutes or five hours and let your spirit find its strength. Create your own cocoon; whether it's the bubbly warmth of an aromatherapy-scented bath, your favorite recliner, a spot in the backyard swing, or a view from the deck, you need to create your own personal island of calm and serenity. It doesn't matter what the activity you engage in, as long as you spend some time nourishing yourself.

Today's Nourishment:
I relax and nourish myself. I notice my surroundings and the blessing of my day. I spend time in my cocoon and retreat to my personal island of calm and serenity—I emerge refreshed, vitalized, and nourished!

~71~
Be Creative

Be creative with your life; express yourself in everything you do; acknowledge your creative gifts which come from your Creator. You are constantly presented with opportunities to expand your personal horizons. You are encouraged to make the world a more beautiful and joyful place.

Stimulate your senses and soak in beautiful colors, hear stimulating music, and read a variety of good books. Your creativity can be expressed in many forms in the way you dress, the food you cook, the way you decorate your surroundings, or the manner in which you plant your garden. You can be creative through painting, dance, music, or writing—you choose!

Today's Nourishment:
I express myself in everything I do. I stimulate my sense and soak in beautiful colors, hear stimulating music, and express my creativity.

~72~
Surprise A Loved One

Everyone expects something special for their birthday and wedding anniversary day, but just imagine how amazed a loved one would be when they get an unexpected surprise out of the blue! Just as you like pleasant surprises, so do others in your life. When you give to another person you are in fact giving to yourself. You are putting forth energy into the universe that you like happy surprises yourself.

Giving gifts or personal acknowledges on birthdays, anniversaries, or holidays are nice ways to show your love. But you need not wait for a holiday or birthday to surprise a loved one. Moving, final exams, or any life transitions can be stressful. Creating happy surprises *just because*, are the most fun. Let your loved one know that you are thinking of them with a surprise.

Created with a personal touch from the heart, surprises always bring a smile and are a great way to show your love and support. Surprising a loved one doesn't have to be in the form of a material gift. There are several inexpensive non-materialistic ways to surprise your loved one. Cook dinner for them or have someone cook dinner for you both. Show up unexpected, make something, or compile photos of the two you, showing how much creating memories mean to you. Doing something nice and unexpected for a loved one such as clean the house, draw a bath, light candles, or a personal serenade session is a perfect way to show your appreciation.

Today's Nourishment:
I experience great joy today creating a happy surprise for a loved one. Giving to another person is truly giving to myself; putting forth energy to the universe that I like surprises for myself!

Listen To Your Body

Your relationship with your body is the key to personal, emotional, and spiritual growth—it is a primary relationship. This relationship is the foundation for all of your creations and your relationships with other people. When you do not treat your body well, when you don't listen to what it needs, when you abuse or neglect it, you cannot create a full and balanced life because your primary relationship isn't working. The only way to take good care of your body is by listening to what it needs. A good foundation combined with communication between body and spirit creates a more balanced, happy and loving life.

Even though you are aware of the importance of this relationship, you do not take the time to listen to your body. You don't get enough sleep, eat healthy, exercise, and most of all, you do not listen when our bodies start to complain. This creates a tremendous amount of stress and it makes life much more difficult because it means you are not *in sync* with your body. Your life, relationships, career, and spiritual growth suffer tremendously because spirit and body are not creating together.

God wants you to pay attention and listen to your body. Listen to what your body is telling you. Develop new healthier habits; get more sleep, eat healthy, eliminate toxins, exercise, and lose your cravings for unhealthy substances. You have unlimited spiritual assistance at your disposal to help motivate and find the time to develop a new healthier lifestyle; simply ask for assistance and it will be given. As you listen to you body and follow its guidance, you will experience increased energy, happiness, and a sense of true freedom.

Today's Nourishment:
My relationship with my body is a primary relationship. I listen to my body and take good care of it by listening to what it needs. I get more sleep, eat healthy foods, eliminate toxins, exercise and avoid unhealthy substances.

~74~
Feel Your Desires Manifesting

You hold the power within yourself to create the life you desire! You have the power to create a more abundant life, decrease stress, achieve a healthier lifestyle, ignite passion in your relationships and yourself, and increase your intuition. You can fulfill your life purpose and create the life you truly love by simply applying the principles of manifestation. Awaken your true power within and claim the joyous abundant life you deserve. You will bring your desires to life!

Fear not, beloved child of God, your desires are manifesting as you read this. You no longer need to struggle with pushing the elephant through the keyhole. God has everything under control. Don't worry about how things will manifest or come to be—simply know that it is already happened. When you ask for something it is always given. It may not appear like it in the moment or manifest as quickly or in the manner you believe it should. But rest assured everything is as it should be. Continue to nurture your desires today by thinking about them and surrounding those thoughts with positive energy. Create an attitude of gratitude and say 'thank you' to the universe for manifesting your desires.

Today's Nourishment:
I feel all my desires manifesting at this moment! I am grateful that everything I wanted is now a reality. I feel a deep sense of knowing, warmth of gratitude, and tingle of excitement knowing that my desires are now a reality.

You are a unique, radiant, exquisite child of God. You are made in the likeness and image of God—perfect in every way. You are a rare and incredibly beautiful jewel that captures lights full spectrum of rainbow colors. When you walk into a room you capture the attention of everyone there. You are the symbolism of the intricacies of spirit, individuality, and achievements. Your true beauty comes from the reflecting your uniqueness.

You are a mirror of God's love; you are loved and supported. Because you exist as part of God's creation, not separate from it, you are entitled to love, respect, and prosperity. Accept yourself as you are-a radiant jewel in a physical body.

Today's Nourishment:
I am a unique, radiant exquisite child of God created in God's likeness and image. I exist as part of God's creation and am entitle to love, respect, and prosperity. I am a radiant jewel.

Express Yourself

Within you lies a creative spirit longing to break free. True self expression is when you are able to articulate what is originally within. It is about being able to say what you mean or want to say. It's about expressing yourself in words, music, painting, or any activity that allows your inner expression to come forth.

Release that which is in your heart through creativity. The manner of expression is not important as long as it brings you a sense of happiness. Let the means of your creativity be emotionally driven and sensory in nature. You can express yourself through jewelry making, web design, writing, sewing, painting, interior design, circle dance, singing, gardening, wall murals, scrap booking, collages, or anything else that you can dream up—the possibilities are endless!

Today's Nourishment:
I release my creative spirit and express myself. I allow myself to release what is in my heart through creativity. I relax and allow my creative nature to gallop wildly, leaving me feeling recharged, revitalized, and rejuvenated.

Acknowledge Your Thoughts

Your thoughts create your reality allowing you the power to heal, love, and transform. Transformation begins when you embrace your purpose in life, trust your hearts intuition, and learn the habit of positive thinking. God loves you and wants you to experience peace and love. He wants you to help you create a life of abundance and balance.

Pay attention to your thoughts today. When your mind begins to wander, noticing where your thoughts lead you, both the happy and fearful places. You can easily recognize signals of distressing thoughts. When you are afraid or anxious your body will tense, your heartbeat and breathing increases, or your stomach may tighten. This is the time to ask God for assistance. The instant you think of the Divine power for your asking; whether it is God himself, or you ask your angels, you will begin to feel a sense of calm and love wash over you.

Acknowledge your thoughts today. If you have negative thoughts that cause you to feel anxious or afraid, simply ask that they be removed and replaced with positive thoughts. God will instantly infuse you with a sense of divine love and calmness throughout your mind, body, and soul. Allow God to assist you with inner freedom and peace by removing your negative thoughts.

Today's Nourishment:
I pay attention to my thoughts today. I recognize the signs of negative thinking and immediately call for spiritual help. I engage in conversations with God throughout the day, allowing Him to fill me with a sense of love and peace.

~78~
Let Go Of Your Fears

Fears create limitation by building temporary barriers that block the view of your true potential. These fears might be fear of failure or success, fear of being alone, fear of disappointing yourself or others, or a number of things. All fears come from a place where you feel alone, overwhelmed, and isolated. You have been a slave to your fears far too long; leaving you an angry and scared individual.

Today you will focus on letting go of your fears and begin the path to freedom. Begin by naming your fear. Then ask for help to let go of this fear. Focus on letting go of your fears; one fear at a time. Lighten your load, tear down the barriers, remove the limitations, draw a new map, and take a different path. If you become stuck ask your angels to assist you in releasing your fears and moving toward a more enduring vision of life.

Let the angels help you discover your true potential. If you ask, they will help you let go of your fears and realize that you are loved and cherished. Constant rays of loving healing light will sooth and comfort you during your moments of fear. Purge your mind of thoughts of suffering aloneness and isolation on this earth. Tell yourself, "I am not alone, now or ever" as you visualize handing over all your fears to the angels waiting with outstretched hands.

Today's Nourishment:
I let go of my fears and begin the path to freedom. I give all my fears to the angels, my load is lighter, my barriers removed, and I feel joyous and carefree. I am not alone, now or ever. I am loved and cherished.

Smell The Coffee

The phrase stop and smell the coffee is a way to convey that you need to slow down, take a break, rest, and enjoy the moment. God continually sends you this message. Today you are being asked to take this advice literally.

When starting your day, while having that first cup of coffee, instead of turning on the news or reading the paper, take time to look out a window, or to sit on the deck—a mug of steaming coffee with a side order of nature. Literally smell the coffee, take a deep quieting breath and savor the aroma of fresh brewed coffee. Be in the stillness of now and see what thoughts rise to the surface. Be happy to be sharing your coffee with nature instead of crawling through morning traffic.

Today make a point to inhale this refreshing delicate aroma. Give your nerves and your spirit a rest this morning. The aroma of coffee awakens the senses and refreshes your mind, rejuvenates, and jump starts your spirit! Expand your horizons and try different blends of gourmet or flavored coffees. Indulge yourself in the various Jamaican Blue Mountain coffees with their gently bittersweet character.

Carry this energy with you throughout the day. Stop by your local coffee shop, indulging yourself for a few moments and rejuvenate your soul. Know that you are being guided to stop and smell the coffee today.

Today's Nourishment:
I stop and smell the coffee, take in deep quieting breaths and savor the aroma of freshly brewed coffee. I revel in the stillness of now and pay attention to my thoughts. I allow myself the luxury of taking the time to smell the coffee as I know I am being guided to do so.

Smell the Coffee (Photo by Nicole McGowan)

~80~
Watch The Birds

At its simplest, watching birds is fascinating, relieves stress, and is peaceful. Birds are symbols of innocence and freedom, and bird watchers gain a measure of relief from the day to day stresses of modern daily life simply by looking at these little winged wonders of nature. Similar to angels, birds are God's winged creatures soaring above; all seeing, free of problems and limitations.

Bird watching gives a sense of something new every time you see a new breed. They are a joy to behold due to their colorful nature—they are usually colorful, flashy, and really fun to watch. While some species of birds squawk or shriek, there are songbirds with melodic voices. These song birds show the importance of a sense of harmony in your life.

Spend some time today watching these winged creatures. Watch as they fly through the air creating their own sanctuary of peace and tranquility. Notice their behavioral patterns—they are more whimsical and playful than most other types of wild animals. Place bird feeders and bird baths around your yard or toss bird seed on the lawn to attract the birds. As you watch the birds, know that these feathered wonders of the sky work closely with your angels and bring you messages of love.

Today's Nourishment:
I spend time watching the birds today. I take note of their flashy colors, the songs the sing, and the message of love that they bring. I feel peace and tranquility today knowing that God is sending me messages of love on the wings of a tiny feathered creature.

~81~
Extract Lessons From Life

This is your life and you determine the outcome. Every choice you make contributes to your happiness, success, failures, and pain. God talks to you through your intuition and guides you to make the best choices for your life. If you listen to that wisdom and take heed, your life would be forever changed for the better.

Focus on what you have learned from your life experiences up to this point. Imagine that you were writing a letter to a young loved one filled with what you had learned up until this point in your life. What advice would you give? What lessons would you share?

Everyday life experiences, situations, relationships, and people that you meet teach patience, compassion, empathy, and other important life lessons. Find some time today to reflect on what you have learned from the past; from yesterday or even today. God gave you the ability to create the best life possible and to learn something everyday that improves you as a person, therefore improving your life.

Today's Nourishment:
I review what I have learned from life—seeing the lessons in every experience and relationship.

I look for lessons in everyday life experiences, situations, and relationships. I value what I have learned.

~82~
Sign The Permission Slip

Do you remember as a child needing a permission slip for things like leaving class to go on a field trip or to the bathroom? As an adult you already have your permission slip. You are in charge of your life. You just need to sign the permission slip and give yourself permission to use it!

It is time to sign the permission slip and give permission to please yourself. At first this may feel a bit strange and wickedly selfish, but God wants you to go ahead and do it anyway. Give yourself permission to take a day off, no fair checking messages or calling into the office. But if you have trouble with that, give permission to check your messages!

Give yourself permission to act out of character, play outdoors even if it's raining, to be fearless, and permission to not know all the answers. Grant yourself permission to stay up late or go to bed early, and permission to say no. Permission to say yes or no has unlimited usage and does not have an expiration date. The possibilities are endless! Go ahead; sign that permission slip to change your hair color, skydive, and throw a spontaneous *come as you are* party. Play more, take a trip, or buy a puppy or a new car! Remember it's your life—give yourself permission to enjoy it!

Today's Nourishment:
I sign the permission slip to enjoy life, to please myself, and to take control of my life! I am the boss of my life and I have the right to follow my own Divine path and to enjoy myself along the way.

Take Walks

Walking benefits your mind, spirit, and body. It improves your mood, relieves stress, and allows you to connect more deeply with your spiritual side and with your loved ones. Your Creator wants you to be happy, enjoy a stress*free* life, experience harmonious relationships, and foster a deeper connection with your spiritual nature.

The simple act of walking can be meditative and allows you to get into your head, hear yourself think, and work through issues. Sharing a walk with a loved one or a friend is therapeutic as well. A leisurely walk will leave you feeling refreshed, renewed, and relieved that you took time out of your day to do something for yourself.

Find time for a walk today. Not simply for exercise but walk at a more leisurely pace. Take time to stop and chat with people, soak up the sights, sounds, and smells of nature, or simply enjoy connecting with your spiritual nature. While leisurely walking isn't a cardio workout, it does work wonders on the heart's capacity to absorb love.

Today's Nourishment:
I take walks. I walk at a relaxed leisurely pace, stopping to chat with people, soak up the sights, sounds, and smells of nature. I connect with my spiritual nature and enjoy a stressful walk anytime I want.

~84~
Honor Your Promises

Honor your promises. This is a very simple statement, yet not so easy to do. Trust is a touchstone of success. You must have self-trust. You must believe in yourself. If you are not confident in yourself, no one else will be. Just as important as self-trust, you must have trust of others. You must be a person of your word. You must honor your promises or people won't trust you.

When you honor your promises your inner self feels good and your confidence increases. When others know that they can always count on you to honor your promises, the relationship will be mutually beneficial, will last, and strengthen over time. By honoring your promises you gain the respect of others and in turn respect yourself. When you treat others with respect and honor, you are rewarded by being treated the same. In other words, what you put out into the universe comes back to you tenfold.

Today honor your promises and deal with others with integrity. Be aware of your choice of words, if you tell a person you are going to do something, make sure you're a person of your word and follow through. If something changes and it is not possible to honor your promise, make sure you explain the situation to that person and make amends.

Today's Nourishment:
I honor my promises and foster trust with others. I treat others with respect and honor and am treated with respect and honor. I reap the benefits of living my life with integrity.

~85~
Bless Your Food

Saying grace before a meal is one of the most common and universal forms of spoken prayer, the one sacrament many of us hold onto after others have faded from use. Blessing your food and drink with a prayer before consumption infuses it with healing energy nourishing your body as well as your soul. Invite your Creator to join you at mealtime. Admit and honor the giver of life—God or the divine principle—through acknowledging the gift of food. By admitting God to your table you are fostering a personal relationship.

Develop a healthy habit of blessing your food and drink at each meal. Say a pray or affirmation that your meal be infused with healing loving energy that nourishes your body, mind, and spirit.

Admit God to your table and experience the love and beauty of your personal relationship.

Today's Nourishment:
I bless my food before consumption, infusing it with the healing properties of divine love and energy. I invite God to join me at mealtimes fostering a personal relationship. I bless my food, my food blesses my body and soul—God blesses me!

~86~
Practice Forgiveness

Eventually all the feelings, resentments, guilt, or humiliation you hold within creates a harmful energy that affects you and those around you. By holding onto such feelings, nurturing them, and refusing to let them go breeds anger, contempt, and feeling of worthlessness. This negativity seeps into your life blinding you to the everyday blessings that await you.

Child of God, you are much too hard on yourself. Your belief that you must be perfect in order to be valued promotes feelings of self-loathing and guilt. You need to keep in mind that you are lovable even when you are not perfect or when you stumble. Actually, you are even more lovable during the times you stumble. By taking the risk of trying you learned, grew, and then moved on. God is on the sidelines cheering you on—God is your biggest fan club!

Focus on forgiving yourself, others, and release the resentments that blind you to the many blessings that wait. As you practice forgiveness and lovingly embrace yourself, you project a loving healing light that touches those around you.

Today's Nourishment:
I am a child of God, worthy of love, compassion, forgiveness, and a life of abundance. I forgive myself, those who have caused me pain, and release feelings of guilt and resentment.

~87~
Surrender Yourself To God

The path to a state of blissfulness and spiritual healing starts by surrendering yourself to God. By surrendering yourself to God you are making a commitment to living a life more spiritually in tuned with your physical world. Making this commitment is an ongoing process throughout your life, involves having a personal relationship with God, and really listening when He speaks to you. Sometimes keeping busy helps avoid the still, quiet place where God can really speak to you. It is in this solitude that creates an awareness of the closed doors, the true motives behind certain actions, and the areas of your life that haven't been surrendered.

When you were a child you took pride in doing things on your own. As a child of the Creator, you do not have to do things on your own. You have the ability to infuse a power life force into every situation. Let God be the foundation in your life—your stability. There is infinite love, wisdom, and abundance available to you upon request. Your free will prevents God from imposing his help upon you without being asked.

Surrender yourself to God and remember this commitment in all that you do. Surrender each decision, task, and question over to Him. Let Him guide you in all ways. Find a still quiet place, a moment of solitude, where God can really speak to you.

Today's Nourishment:
I remember to surrender myself to God. I make a commitment to live more spiritually in tune with the world around me. God is the foundation of my life—my stability. I allow Him to guide me in each decision, task, and query.

~88~
Take It Easy

Today's message is; relax, don't worry, and slow down. It is time to take it easy, relax and do a whole lot of nothing! With all that you accomplish in your daily routine; work, family, cooking, cleaning, and catering to others, it is time to step back for a moment and take it easy for just a few hours out of this day. You deserve a few hours of doing absolutely nothing, to relax, let go of the normal day-to-day activities, and sit on the porch sipping a tall glass of sweet tea.

Focus on forcing yourself to sit a spell for a few hours today. As you sit on the porch sipping your sweet tea, reflect on how wonderful it feels to take it easy and relax. Contrary to what you may believe, taking it easy on occasion is not selfish or neglectful. Find time today to sit a spell, sip some sweet tea, and open your mind to the notion that sometimes you can accomplish more by sitting a few hours than you can in an entire day!

Today's Nourishment:
I take it easy! I find time to sit on the porch sipping sweet tea, doing a whole lot of nothing! I am not selfish, neglectful, or lazy—I accomplish more sitting on the porch for a few hours than I do in a day of rushing!

~89~
Let Go Of Resentments

Many times it is another person's behavior that causes us hurt, anger, or humiliation; generating feelings of resentment toward the person. When you hold these feelings of resentment within, you are only hurting yourself.

Life is full of choices; therefore it is your choice whether to hold onto resentments or to release them. You only hurt yourself by letting resentments reside within; lowers your own energy level, creates lack of enthusiasm, and reduces your effectiveness.

When people act inappropriate or unkindly toward you, you must strive to not take it personally. For their behavior is but a reflection of where they are in their life; not a true picture of who you are. Others bad behavior or unkind acts diminishes love and light from their own lives, creating their own unhappiness and discontent.

Naturally, you should not spend time with a person who behaves inappropriately or is unkind toward you. God does not want you to be in an abusive situation. A good rule to follow is use of the key phase; *forgive the person, not the behavior*. In other words, it's acceptable to send this person loving caring thoughts from a safe distance. When you send out loving thoughts toward the person you harbor resentments toward, you are healing yourself. You free yourself from the pain and anger.

Since you attract that which you think about, releasing negative thoughts allows for a more positive attitude. By letting go of the resentment and forgiving the person, you are breaking patterns, changing thought processes, and creating a more loving attitude; benefiting yourself and the other person.

Today's Nourishment:
Today I will let go of resentments and forgive those who have acted unkindly toward me. I will turn old anger into a healing energy of loving caring thoughts.

~90~
Know That You Are Loved

To God you are the most lovable person around. He sees within your heart and through the outer shell you present to the world. He sees past the illusions you create to keep others from see the real *you*. He see the goodness, the compassion, the gentle loving nature you—He sees you!

Know that you are worthy of love. Each breath you exhale sends out beautiful loving energy to everyone around you. Every part of you is loved. Your personality, thoughts, feelings, your eyes, smile, and your body are completely adorable. You are perfect in all ways—you are loved!

Today's Nourishment:
I am loved. God sees the true me; from the inside to the outside. He loves me for whom and what I am. This love makes it safe to share my true self with others.

~91~
Write In A Journal Daily

Writing is a meditation. It settles the mind. It is a de-stressor and it releases tension. Writing in a journal is like having your own private confessor who keeps your secrets safe. It is also a mood-changer, with the capability of making you happy. It is an outlet, for it helps you let go of your negative thoughts. It is creative, cathartic, and curative. When pen and paper connect, thoughts are released and your mind becomes more focused as you are instinctively drawn to that quiet place within.

Writing in a journal daily gives new insights into yourself and your relationships with others. It is a way to connect with your spiritual side. Writing in a journal is completely honest—for what do you gain by lying to yourself? Writing is therapeutic for everyone not just for the disturbed, distressed or dying. A journal, like books, is a voyage into one's inner self, where body, mind, and soul shift course and become the center of existence.

Make writing a part of your daily life starting today. Create your own a journal and write in it daily as part of your spiritual quest—let your soul search for the truth through writing. Writing is magical; it can heal a heart, transform relationships, and create new beginnings.

Today's Nourishment:
The urge to write, to put my thoughts on paper, is strong within me. I write in a journal, letting my emotions flow from my heart through my pen. My writing is part of my spiritual quest and blessed by God. My writing heals my heart, transforms my relationships, and is part of my daily routine.

~92~
Stroll Down Memory Lane

Take a stroll today! Not a run, nor a walk, but a leisurely stroll. This is not a stroll in the physical sense mind you. Although you could start with physically taking a stroll; allowing your mind travel down memory lane. Let your mind take you back to visit some pleasant memories you have placed in storage. Take some time today to reminisce, recall, and re-visit happy moments from your past.

As you stroll down memory lane take notice of special occasions; birthdays, holidays, your first kiss, your first love, or the birth of a child. Recall the emotions associated with these happy events. Allow yourself to relive the excitement of that first kiss, the exhilaration of that first love, and the happiness and joy of celebrating moments with others. As your mind wanders down memory lane, only stop and visit those pleasant memories. It's alright to acknowledge those not-so-pleasant memories, but simply nod a brief acknowledgment, and continue on your way.

Take this moment to take a stroll down memory lane. Recall a cute, funny, or momentous thing that happened to you. Pull it from your memory bank, hold it in front of you, review it, examine it, feel the pleasant emotions associated with the moment—smile! Wrap those positive loving emotions in your heart so you will be infused with positive emotions throughout the day.

Today's Nourishment:
I let my 'mind travels' take me on a journey down memory lane. I recall special moments in my past that evoke feelings of happiness, joy, love, and excitement. I place these positive emotions within my heart to carry with me throughout the day.

~93~
Tell Yourself, I Love You

So often you hear about the importance of self-love and surrounding yourself with self-love. The simplest way to begin loving yourself is to start by saying it! In order to surround yourself with self-love and create a bubble of love, you need to learn how to say, "I love you" to yourself. You can do this silently, but it is more powerful when you actually speak the words, "I love you" out loud to yourself.

Make saying, "I love you" to yourself part of your morning ritual—look into the mirror and say out loud to yourself the words, "I love you". This may sound awkward or strange in the beginning, but over time, these three powerful words will make all the difference in how you feel about yourself. Everyone needs to hear that they are loved and cherished. Stating, "I love you" to yourself is affirming that you are a lovable child of God worthy of love.

Today's Nourishment:
Today I look in the mirror and tell myself I love you. I embrace myself and allow myself to feel love and warmth. I surround myself with a bubble of love—starting with telling myself I love you!

~94~
Visualize Your Dreams

In a seated position extend your arms with your hands open, facing upward. Close your eyes take a deep breath and exhale. Take another deep breath and exhale again. Do this several times until your body is thoroughly in a state of blissful tranquility. With your eyes still closed visualize what it is that you desire. If it's a new car, visualize the car that you want. See the make, color and year that you desire. Really, see it! Clearly in your mind, be there. See yourself driving this car to the beach, to the mountains or around town - whatever strikes your fancy. See your family and friends admiring your car. Visualize them riding with you, enjoying the ride and the good company.

Make this visualization as real as you can. Feel the security and safety you enjoy in your new car. Feel the joy of knowing this is your car and most importantly. Know that this is your car, bring this visualization inside you and recognize the emotional and physical change that has taken place in your mind and body.

Keep your eyes shut and your hands open. Draw this image into your body through your left hand. Fill your heart with your visualization. See exactly what you saw only moments earlier, only now, that image is thoroughly branded into your heart, can you feel it? See you're new car, job, soul mate or whatever you want in as much detail as possible. See it. Feel it. Smell it. Touch it. Taste it. Hear it. Love it. Vividly experience your *hearts* desire.

Enjoy this vision that you have created for prolonged periods of time. A minute, an hour, whatever you want. This is your dream take the time to enjoy it. The stronger this vision is, the greater the possibility that you will call it into being. Lastly, here's the secret that will totally empower your dream, your vision. After you have visualized what you want and have drawn that visualization into your heart and into your being, execute one more vital component. Transmit your dream to the world. Using your right hand as a communication disc, project the energy of your visualization out into your physical reality. This broadcast, this literal proclamation of your desire allows the Universe to go to work on it immediately.

Today's Nourishment:
I visualize my heart's desire—making it as real as possible. I draw the image of my desire through my body into my heart and project it out into the Universe.

Give Yourself Approval

When you make others responsible for your sense of worth, you have to constantly try to figure out what someone else wants of you to get approval. Your good and bad feelings are dependent upon how you look and how you perform, so you have to be constantly on your toes. This is a very hard way to live.

Instead of working so hard to win the approval of your parents, teachers, siblings, and peers, give yourself approval. Let go of the need to be liked or valued by everyone else. It only matters that you value yourself. Other's opinions have no bearing on who you are or your value.

Give yourself approval to like yourself. You no longer need the approval of others to be valued.

Take on the responsibility of defining your own worth. See yourself through the see of love, not the eyes of judgment. Start by accepting the fact that God created you perfectly. He wants you to see yourself as He sees you. See your innocence, your lovingness, your sense of wonder, your creativity, your aliveness, and your spirituality. You need not strive for more greatness, as you are flawless in every way right now.

Think of the amount of time you have put into worrying about gaining the approval of others. Wouldn't it be wonderful to only worry about gaining your own approval? Today is the perfect day to adopt this new healthy attitude of giving yourself approval.

Today's Nourishment:
I no longer need the approval of others. I let go of the need to be liked or valued by everyone. God created me perfectly. I see myself through the eyes of love. I see myself as God sees me; flawless in every way.

~96~
Send Love To Yourself

Love lives at the center of every living cell in your body, and in the heart of all living things. Open your heart to the love within you and find that the essence of love is the basic and fundamental substance of life. Without love, nothing could grow or flourish, and life would cease to exist.

Give extra love to yourself today—send love to yourself. Nourish yourself with the energy of love. Infuse your body with the essence of love, letting it become grafted on to your soul. Reassure yourself that you are a loving child of God; that you are safe and protected. Show yourself love by maintaining a healthy lifestyle. Eat a healthy diet and get adequate exercise. Maintain a healthy emotional balance by participating in loving relationships and situations that are good for you—as you are guided. Avoid those that are not good for you.

See yourself as the beautiful living creature that you are, worthy of love. Send yourself loving tender thoughts throughout the day, knowing that you are creating an abundance of love within yourself.

Today's Nourishment:
I am a beautiful loving creation of God—God's child, worthy of love. I send love to myself, nourishing my body, soul, and mind with loving energy. I grow and flourish by nourishing myself with love.

~97~
Smile

The benefits of a positive attitude, happiness, and smiling are endless! People who are optimistic, those who are out there smiling, are healthier physically and are actually able to fight off illness better than pessimists. Science has shown a direct link between optimistic attitude and good physical health. The same applies to your spiritual health. Having an optimistic outlook on life, a positive attitude, and go through the day smiling creates a positive loving energy that affects those around you.

A smile makes you look happy, confident, and self-assured. It makes other people's day brighter. Most people can not help but mirror what they see; they see a smile on your face, they in turn will smile too. Not only does a smiling face put others at ease, it shows friendships and is a great way to attract new friends. A simple smile could be the start of a lifetime relationship!

Make a point to smile at everyone you cross paths with today. Send out smiles and watch them come back to you tenfold! Enjoy the exchange of smiles today knowing that you are sending out positive loving energy to those you meet. In turn you will benefit physically, emotionally, and spiritually!

> Today's Nourishment:
> *I smile because I have a life of abundance and much to smile about!*
> *I smile at everyone I meet today and watch as they smile back at me,*
> *knowing that I am exchanging loving energy that benefits everyone!*

~98~
Laugh Out Loud

Laughter is truly the best medicine. According to the researchers, regular laughter in your life could help decrease your chances of becoming ill—especially stress related illness. . They recommend 15 minutes of laughter a day as well as regular exercise to reduce your risk of cardiovascular disease. A positive outlook on life and having a good laugh is much more than keeping your heart healthy.

The sound of laughing out loud not only reduces stress and makes you feel better, it benefits those around you. Laughter is contagious. If you had occasion to be sitting with someone who has the *giggles* in church you know how contagious laughing can be. Whether is a stifled giggle or a powerful laugh—those around you will absorb its energy. The act of laughing out loud immediately lifts your mood, projects positive energy outward, elevating the energy of the space around you.

Seek out ways to laugh out loud today. Try watching a funny video, read a funny story, or swap jokes with friends. Become a carrier of laughter—infect those around you. Find the humor in everyday situations and share the sound of laughter throughout your day. Notice the shift in your mood when laughing out loud or hearing the sound of others laughing out loud.

Today's Nourishment:
I find the humor in everyday life situation. I become a carrier of laughter, infecting those around me, elevating the energy of the space around me. I watch a funny video, read a funny story, or swap jokes—I laugh out loud throughout my day.

~99~
Be Happy

Everyone wants to be happy. That's why people go on diets, spend too much money for clothes, or spend time with the precieve *right people* - because they think it will make them happy! Happiness can be a "comfortable-good" or an "excited-good" or a "chilled-out-good" because it has many flavours and faces, depending on whom you are with, or what you are doing. However, if you get to know all different people, you will see what makes the happiest people happy.

Happiness is a state of being, an attitude, and a choice that is yours to make. You have the power within you to choose to be happy regardless of the way you look, dress, or whom you spend time with. Happiness is the one emotion that can heal hearts, mend disagreements, and restore faith. Today, make the choice to be happy. Allow yourself to accept all the blessings that God has brought to you and just be happy. By choosing to be happy you are expressing your faith that your prayers have been heard and answered.

Make the choice to be happy today. Be a beacon, lighting the pathway for others to make the same choice as well. The best way to teach is to lead by example—choose to be happy.

> Today's Nourishment:
> *I choose to be happy. I embrace all of God's blessings and know that my prayers have been heard and answered. I spread my happiness to those around me-inspiring them to make this same choice.*

~100~
Forgive And Forget

Child of God, has anyone ever offended you? Has your spouse been unfaithful? Have your children disappointed you? Has someone cheated you in business? Your response to the difficult experiences of life directly affects your spiritual well-being. How deeply have you been hurt, little one? Have you become bitter or unforgiving in your attitude?

Forgiveness is an important step in maintaining your spiritual well-being. When you forgive yourself or other person, you are freed from hate, bitterness, and anger. Many lives are spoiled by bitterness and a lack of forgiveness. People go through physical and emotional breakdowns because they refuse to forgive others. The longer you carry a grudge, the heavier it becomes. You cannot afford to harbor bitterness in your soul. When you withhold forgiveness, you allow anger to eat away at your heart. The word 'disease' as it relates to heart disease means 'ill at ease'. In other words, your heart is ill at ease. This cannot only affect your spiritual health, but it can also be detrimental to you physical and emotional well-being.

Forgiving someone who has caused you harm, not only frees you of the burden, but you actually gain power over the situation. Anger or revenge only escalates the problem within your spirit. Forgiveness, however, does not mean you must continue to interact with the person.

As you begin your day, lay aside the bitterness and anger you have toward those that have wronged you. Forgive and then forget it. This is the secret of spiritual health. Don't harbor bitterness and guilt within the closet of your soul. Ask for assistance from your angels, let their love be the divine spotlight in your heart. Ask that they clean out every closet in you soul. The loss of your anger and bitterness creates a spiritual gain with unlimited benefits!

Today's Nourishment:
I forgive and forget the harm that was caused by _____. I release the anger, bitterness, and feelings of revenge. I am freed from the guilt, negative feelings, and bitterness; my spiritual gain has unlimited benefits!

~101~
Love Your Body

Do you love what you see when you look in the mirror? The fashion, cosmetics and diet industries work hard to make people believe that their bodies are unacceptable and need constant improvement. Print ads and television commercials reduce people to body parts — lips, legs, breasts — airbrushed and touched up to meet impossible standards.

You are being urged by your angels to love your body—as is. You are being asked to take care of your body, eat healthy foods, exercise regularly, and to avoid toxins. More importantly though you are being asked to accept and love your body as it is right this minute. Exactly the way it is! Not when you get fit or wear a smaller size, but right now at this moment, "as is". Your body is beautiful just as it is—believe it!

Make a pact with yourself to treat your body with respect, and do things to promote positive body image. Start by taking a break from glamour or fitness magazines and the mass media. Try a new physical activity just for fun, not to lose weight. Stop weighing yourself, and change your goal from weight loss to improving your health. Don't worry about losing weight, focus on gaining spiritual health. Take action—throw away the following items: bathroom scales, diet books, tapes or videos, calorie counters, and tape measurers,

By following these suggestions you will feel terrific. Let your increased energy and happiness is your reward. Today is the perfect day to love your body—as is!

Today's Nourishment:
I watch what I put into my body, eat healthy, exercise, avoid toxins, and treat it with respect. I accept and love my body as it is at this moment. I am consumed with my spiritual health; my energy level is high and I am happy with my appearance.

~102~
Realize That God Understands You

At first thought, God seems so omnipresent it's frightening. In reality, no one understands you like your Creator. God knows all about your present weakness and trials. He knows what you are going through. He understands your hurts and your fears. He has never forsaken you or forgotten about you. He is the one whom has your best interest at heart. God is the creator of all things; sunsets, sight and sound, touch and taste, life and beauty, and love.

God not only knows your heart; He understands you better than you understand yourself. He knows each prayer before it's even uttered whether mentally or orally. He understands you and your specific needs intimately; physically, emotionally, spiritually, and even your material needs. God understands, when it's seems literally impossible that anyone could comprehend He understands the most hideous things, unimaginable and unbelievable.

Focus on the realization that God understands you; inside and out, upwards and downward, and in all ways. When you really think about it, what could be more exciting, fulfilling and rewarding than God's understanding of you? When you accept that God understands you in a way that no one else can, you will have the ability to travel to the most amazing destinations!

Today's Nourishment:
God knows and understands all my weakness, strengths, hurts, and fears—He has my best interests at heart. I feel safe and secure knowing that He understands me like no other.

~103~
Create Your Own Magic Wand

Have you ever wished you had a magic wand that you could wave over yourself or others to change things? Have you wished that a few magic words would transform your life? Wouldn't it be wonderful to wave a magic wand say "abracadabra" and presto—your wishes are granted! Believe it or not you have that power within you. Like Dorothy's ruby slippers in Wizard of Oz, the magical gift to transform lives and make wishes come true has been in your possession all along—the magical power of love.

The emotion love has its own magical healing properties. By surrounding yourself and others with the magic of love and all its forms—compassion, empathy, understanding, patience, and kindness—you create your own magic wand. Let your magic wand heal hearts, mend wounds, soothe tensions, and bring balance to the imbalance. If you feel you need a *booster* or *jump start* for your magic wand, ask God for help. He would be more than happy to jump start your magic wand with the power of His divine healing love!

Today's Nourishment:
I create my own magic wand with the power of love. I infuse myself and others with this powerful emotion, transforming lives and making wishes come true. My warm thoughts, loving energy, and well wishes are my best magic!

~104~
Be Spontaneous

The ability to be spontaneous is a natural part of being human. If your mind is cluttered by memories of the past that you can't release or fears about what the future might hold, then you'll find it difficult to let your natural spontaneity shine through. Being spontaneous will help you release those regrets and alleviate your fears, allowing you to clear your mind of these inhibiting factors and live for the moment. By being spontaneous, you will begin to feel more positive and focus aware that the past is gone and the future is yet to be determined. Living in the moment will release those negative thoughts lingering in your head and give you back your zest for life.

Today you are guided to be spontaneous! Enjoy living in the moment and rediscover your power to live life to your full potential. Do something last-minute that you would not normally do. Make those spur-of-the-moment decisions; invite friends over for a last minute barbeque, cut your hair, sign up for a dance class, sing along with the elevator music, or book that weekend getaway!

It may take practice to come up with new ideas and adventures. Being a last minute traveler makes some of the greatest memories. Look for others who are spontaneous and be around them. Great minds think alike and remember the important word, *serendipity*. Look for something, find something else, and realize that what you've found is more suited to your needs than what you thought you were looking for.

Today's Nourishment:
I drop any resistance I may have to living in the moment. It is safe for me to be spontaneous, try new things, live in the moment, and live my life to my full potential.

~105~
Pat Yourself On The Back

Everyone likes a pat on the back every once in a while. And there's no better time to get one than when you're out of your comfort zone, challenging yourself to improve, nervous about whether you can succeed. Your angels are always bestowing positive words upon you, telling you what a good job you are doing, even though you may not hear them or believe it. Still you long to hear encouraging words or receive a pat on the back from a human counterpart.

When others praise you it may feel good, but you may not completely believe or accept it. You scurry away from their praise, afraid of the power and energy in the words. The recognition that you crave most comes from yourself. While hearing praise from others feels good, it is more important to pat yourself on the back.

Today, give yourself a pat on the back—tell yourself what a good job has been done! The size of the accomplishment does not matter; finishing a major report, taking out the trash without being asked, or stopping to chat with a lonely elderly neighbor. If you praise yourself for even the smallest of achievements you will be encouraged about tackling the next one!

Today's Nourishment:
I deserve praise and recognition for all that I have accomplished. I pat myself on the back and tell myself, 'good job!' It is important to acknowledge my achievements, no matter the size, for I have come a long way, overcoming difficult times. I thank myself and God for being able to overcome so many challenges along my journey.

Stop Rushing

Are you rushing yourself to an unhappy life and an early death? You should stop rushing, put the emphasis on quality, not quantity, and most of all, be happy now, not later. When you are rushing the body literally is in panic mode. Your physical body feels as if it is constantly being stressed to meet imaginary deadlines. An occasional shot of adrenaline might be good for you but a steady stream wears down your body leading to illness, fatique, enervated, and listlessness.

When you are rushing mentally, your mind is always 'on'; thoughts of things to be done and yet to do steadily stream through your mind making you feel out of sorts. You may even feel panicked and have trouble sleeping and relazing. Instead of turning to chemical sleep aides, your angels are here to help you change your habit of rushing.

Today, become aware of your habit and thoughts. Most of the time you are not even aware that you are rushing because it is such an automatic response. Identify how you can slow down. For example, if you walk fast naturally, simply practice strolling or walking slower. If you have trouble shutting off your mind at bedtime, change your routine an hour before bedtime. Turn off the television and refuse to think of thoughts of the day or tomorrow. Try to relax. Sit outside and watch the stars.

Avoid conversations which requie a lot of active thinking. Have gentle relaxing conversations about simple relaxing things—like the sound of crickets, moonlight, or feel of the breeze. Invest in a recording of the sounds of nature— a gentle waterfall, night sounds, or play some relazing music. It is never easy to break a habit, but it is well worth it to your mental, physical, and spritual well-being to spend the time and energy to break the habit of rushing.

Today's Nourishment:
I stop rushing. I am aware of my rushing habits and find ways to slow down. My movements are slower, my pace is slow, my mind no longer feels panicked. I am relaxed, calm, and spend time listening to relazing sounds, doing relaxing things, and feel my body relax.

~107~
Retreat To Peacefulness

There is a place within that you can retreat and surround yourself with peacefulness. An escape from conflicts, paradoxes, fears, noise and chaos, where you can be at peace with yourself; a place of calm, contentment, and tranquility.

By closing your eyes and breathing deeply, you can find this retreat with ease. Appeal to your angels for peace of mind, heart, and soul as you become internally peaceful and less reactive to external conflicts. Ask to be guided toward healthy situations and to people who will allow you to live in peace.

Retreat to this inner place of peacefulness throughout the day. This peacefulness is lasting and sustaining—draw upon its strength whenever you need it.

Today's Nourishment:
I have perfect peace within me and befefit from these feelings of calm and contentment. I am interanally peaceful and no longer feel the effects of external conflict. I am at peace with myself.

~108~
Light Candles

Lighting a candle is a spiritual tradition that dates back to the discovery of fire. Candles are used as a prelude to meditation, as an expression of prayer, and as a method of illuminating and stimulating senses. A candle is a symbol of service; it gives of itself, during down in an offering of light and warm.

burning

Lighting candles can bring a deeper insight into your own spiritual experience. When you light candles you are not simply putting flame to a wick, you are awakening something deep inside. Call it what you may, some ancestral memory, or universal consciousness that connects you to the energy of fellow humans seeking the spiritual experience. As with life, a tiny glowing ember can burst into light, while a full burning wick can be extinguished with a single breath. Like love, one candle can light many without diminishing it.

You are being guided to light candles to express your intentions and to reflect your hope and desires. Light candles as part of your prayer ritual, as a light in the window awaiting a loved one's return, as ambience, or aromatherapy. Light candles of your choice, traditional votive candles, taper candles, or glass cylinder jar candles. As you put a flame to the wick think of the meaning behind the action—channeling positive energy, connecting to history, an act of devotion, prayers, and evidence of your love and creation of light.

Today's Nourishment:
I touch a flame to the wick, draw back the match and watch as one flame splits into two; the candles become a dance floor for a waltzing flame. I express my intentions and reflect my hope and desires by lighting candles. A symbol of service, giving of itself, offering light and warmth—lighting candles illuminates my spiritual awakening.

Spiritual Illumination (photo by Nicole McGowan)

~109~
Have A Happy Heart

You often hear people talk about beingoverjoyed, however, since everyone carries unlimited amounts of happiness how can such a thing exist? Having a happy heart is healthy; both physically and emotionally!Some people distrust happiness or feelings of pleasure—almost as if they believe they don't deserve itand theystand aroundholding their breath waiting for the proverbial other shoe to drop! Today's focus is on beingcontent,being lighthearted, and having a happy heart!

Being content or creating happiness in ones' heartis the safest, most natural, state of being. When a person is joyful or feeling happy, they are truly being *themselves*. The act of being lighthearted means bringing light into your heart. Begin byvisualizing breathing in healing light and energy, by sending love to another person (even those who have passed over to the other side), or by thinking carefree thoughts. Savor your happy and healthy heart—for you are a messenger of love and light.

Today's Nourishment:
I am lighthearted and have God's light and love within my heart. I embrace the radiance of my happy heart and allow it to feed and nourish my very core. I will share this gift with others, through my eyes, my breath, and the words I speak. Every word I speak with is filled with healing loving energy.

~110~
Let Go Of Anxieties And Worries

When you feel that life is meaningless, when you are bored with life, when you feel dead in your spirit, with your emotional hurts and pains, with your mental confusion; when you are anxious and worried about the future you are forgetting the love that God has for you. For when you know and accept the unconditional love God has for you, then you are able to let go of anxieties and worries. Total acceptance of the fact that you are blessed with a love more powerful than anything here on earth causes any mental confusion to disperses like fog on a summer's morning. The anxieties and worries of your life are released by His presence. Boredom is a word that can never be used of a person who walks in the love of God. This is the answer. It is the final key to all of your spiritual, mental, emotional health and, indeed, and your physical health, too.

Your task for today is accepting the love, which God has for you, and letting go of anxieties and worries. As a true believer of God's love, accept that anxiety, worry and fear have no place in your life. Believe that with all your heart. Your mind should not be troubled by anxiety and worry if you live in the consciousness of the love of God has for you. God wants you to let go of anxieties and worries.

Today's Nourishment:
I let go of anxieties and worries. I accept that I am blessed with the unconditional love of God. My life is anxiety and worry free—I am happy, content, and open my heart to receive all of God's blessings.

~111~
Release Nervous Tension

Nervous tension is usually the result of emotional and physical stresses encountered in daily life, such as relationship problems, financial difficulties, job demands, traffic jams, and crowded or noisy environments. Even seemingly happy occurrences such as a marriage, a promotion, or a move to a new home create a state of emotional and physiological arousal that can easily turn into nervous tension. When you are feeling this emotion it is similar to a wild animal who is on the lookout for predators—you feel like the prey and fearful for your safety.

You need not fear, as you are not prey for predators; you are protected by a spiritual team that surrounds you with divine loving protective light. They ask that you release nervous tension by using a physical and emotional approach to soothe yourself. Start with relaxing your body, for as your body relaxes it's easier to quiet your mind. You are being asked to take steps to unwind today. You will be guided individually for the method that fits with your schedule and preferences. When you feel a strong inclinations to exercise, flex your muscles, take a walk, drink more fluids, take a bubble bath, or sit on the front porch as sip on some cold sweet tea, know that these messages are coming from your spiritual team; guiding you to relax.

As you relax your body, begin breathing deeply, sending your breath to your muscles. Exhale any nervous tension, fears, or anxiety and inhale a sense of calm and peacefulness.

Today's Nourishment:
I relax my body and let my spiritual team watch over and protect me. I breathe deep throughout the day, exhaling nervous tension and inhale a sense of calm.

~112~
Believe In Yourself

There are times when you believe in everything and everybody but yourself. There is a constant search for mentors and role models when they exist within you. The most brutal beating that you take is the one that you inflict upon yourself. You make one mistake and you count yourself out before the referee can blow the whistle.

Believe in yourself and all you want your life to be, because the challenges and changes will only help you to find the goals that you know are meant to come true for you. Imagine yourself as a confident person free from self-doubt. Hold this image everyday until it sinks into your spirit. Whenever negative thoughts about yourself enter your mind, erase them immediately.

When you wake up in the mornings get a clear picture of a self-image in your mind. What do you want to accomplish today? Write it on a piece of paper and post it on the refrigerator, mirror or someplace readily visible. Engrave it on your heart. Follow these suggestions and believing in yourself will become a way of life for you!

Today's Nourishment:
I remember that my angels believe in me. I ask that they help me to believe in myself. I am optimistic about myself and see myself as a confident person free of self-doubt.

~113~
Keep Working Toward Your Dreams

Most of your dreams and goals require a lot of your time and energy, and it's easy to become distracted or procrastinate. Your journey will take longer if start on your goals and then you stop. Then, you start again and then you stop. Goals are reached when you are working towards them on a regular basis. They take longer if you are standing still wishing things were different. This does not mean that you cannot take a break, but recognize that long term breaks lead to long term delays in your realizing your dreams.

Your focus this week is to keep working towards your dreams. If you've ever had something great happen to you (a new job, a promotion, a raise, etc.), it happened not out of pure luck, but because you were in action. You can ask your angels for assistance to keep you motivated, clear your calendar, and overcome procrastination. Keep moving with smaller steps taken over time will lead you to the finish line. You can wonder if things will really work out or you can use that energy to make sure that they do.

Today's Nourishment:
I ask for assistance in motivating me to keep working toward my dreams.
I allow myself to enjoy the sense of accomplishment with each small step
I take toward my dream. I realize this use of my time and energy is an
investment in me!

~114~
Keep Life In Perspective

One of the most difficult things to do is to keep life in perspective. Everyone has those days where everything you touch seems to turn to garbage. You oversleep and jump out of the bed running ninety miles an hour, bang your shin, and cut yourself shaving. From that moment the day continues to go steadily downhill. Dressed and out the door, you realize your tank is on empty, and rushing to fill the tank you spill gasoline on your pants and shoes. You finally get on the freeway only to run into a massive traffic jam caused by construction two miles down the road. Desperate to get to work, you follow all the other cars and make your own exit ramp just in time to be greeted by your second policeman of the day. Ticket in hand, you manage to arrive at work, one hour late, only to be greeted by a glaring supervisor. Somehow, you manage to make it through the day, arrive home to discover that your new puppy missed the puppy pad fives times and chewed up your favorite pair of shoes!

It's hard to keep life in perspective when a day turns into a disaster. The only way you can keep life in perspective is to continually remember that you are not alone. Remember you have a loving all knowing God that is in control of every step you take, every move you make, and every breath you breathe.

You are being asked to remember when your life resembles a junk heap, or experience a disastrous day, remembering that you are not alone only God will help you keep things in perspective. Of course, having the ability to tackle life with a good sense of humor, positive thinking, and perspective helps as well!

Today's Nourishment:
I keep life in perspective by remembering that I am not alone. I have a loving all knowing God that is in control of my life. I use humor, positive thinking, and perspective to maneuver myself along life's journey.

Listen To Your Inner Voice

You are being guided to listen to your inner voice; notice the loving guidance you hear inside your mind or that sense of simply knowing something without knowing exactly how you know it. Connect back to a time that you had a *gut feeling* about something—the job that you knew you shouldn't take, even though it looked good on the surface or the relationship that just felt right for you. That's your Divine guidance talking to you. It comes in the form of repetitious messages, urging you to take a specific action or attitude for yourself or others.

Listening to your inner voice, or gut feelings, provides a wealth of information. Remember, your inner voice is never wrong, although your interpretation of it may be incorrect. When your inner voice speaks to you, trust it. Practice makes perfect when it comes to using and interpreting your inner voice effectively.

The next time you need to make a decision, check in with your inner voice or intuition. Experiment with trusting it. When you follow your inner voice, what happens? When you hear it and disregard it, what's the outcome? Ask for help from your angels if you need clarification on anything your inner voice tells you.

> Today's Nourishment:
> *I listen to my inner voice and follow the loving divine guidance given.*
> *I practice listening and following the advice given. I ask my angels for clarification of my messages.*

~116~
Let God Work Out The Details

You are being asked to turn everything over to God and let God work out the details. That's it, in a nutshell—at least for this moment. Just keep turning it over to God and asking to do God's will. That's the one simple solution. Whenever you have a problem, turn it over to God—whatever you believe God or a Higher Power or the creative force of the universe to be.

Just keep asking to do God's will, let God work out the details, and your problems will dissolve. You will be shown, step by step, intuitively, what to do. You never need to worry about your life once you really turn it over to God; for you aren't in charge of your life any more—God is in charge. Continue to ask what God's will is, and you'll be guided in your life to do exactly the right thing for you. You might take your life in completely unexpected directions! It doesn't matter—God is showing you where and how to go. God is directing the show.

Today's Nourishment:
I turn my problems, situations, and life over to God as I know God. I ask to be shown God's will and let God work out the details. My problems are being dissolved one by one. God has shown me, step by step, exactly what to do. I am no longer in charge of my life—God is and God will work out the details.

Embrace The Innocence

Within everyone is an innocent child of God who is doing the best that he or she can. Sometimes children make choices that hurt themselves or others as a way to cope with their own fears, anger, and insecurities. Through thoughtless behavior these people are attempting to cope with their fears. If you look past the behaviors, you will see a child of fear lies beneath the surface; God's child of innocence. The more you focus on the pure innocence of the child, the less you see the thoughtless actions.

You are being guided to see the innocence within yourself and others. Instead of turning away from those people who display thoughtless behaviors and lack of concern, embrace the innocence and create healing energy. It is your life purpose to teach love and you can start by noticing the love. Your love can be a catalyst to breaking the cycle of fear-based thoughtless behavior.

See past the behavior, through the illusions, and embrace the wide-eyed child of innocence with others and yourself.

Today's Nourishment:
I am an innocent child of God. I forgive myself and others for thoughtless behaviors, wrong doings, and past hurts. I embrace the innocence within me and others.

Light The Flame

If you want more happiness and direction in your life, you must light the flame of passion in your heart! Playing it safe no longer works; it leads to depression and aloneness. There is a light within you that can never be extinguished—it's pure in nature and stoked by love. The warm feelings that you feel within your heart are fueled by this flame.

Take a moment to feel the flame within, focus on the inner glow, and pay attention to how your body feels. Take a risk and follow this flame—let it consume your heart. Let the passion in your heart lead and guide you.

Today's Nourishment:
I focus on the flame within me, feeling its steady warmth. This flame fuels my passion for life—creating a passion for life! No longer content with playing it safe, I embrace life and eagerly await the next challenge. The passion in my heart leads me to where I must go!

Live Up To Your Potential

Begin today by making more of your talents and live up to your full potential. You have the power to change your habits—to acquire new skills and fully use the skills you now have. You can improve your performance, your productivity, and the quality of your whole life.

Your success at business, friendship, love, sports is largely determined by your own self-image. Your unhappiness is something you choose. So, you're thinking no one chooses to be unhappy. Well, maybe not but you have to consciously choose to be happy, self-confident, and successful. Happiness is elusive when we go after it directly. So is self-confidence. Both seem to be more side-products than something you can achieve in and for it. So how, then, can consciously choosing to be these things be of any value? Well, the secret is to focus on other things.

Today, focus on living up to your potential. Begin by making a complete and accurate assessment of your potential. To do this you must take an inventory of yourself - you will make a few lists. Sit down and make a list of all the things you can do well. Be honest with yourself. When that list is done, make a list of all the things you like to do, even if you think you can't do them well. Then, make a list of all the things you would like to do, if you could.

Look over your lists. Focus on what you can do then make the choice to live up to that potential. Make it a habit to focus on your strengths. Don't forget to include your undeveloped potential, as well. Train yourself to focus on living up to your potential instead of your limitations.

Today's Nourishment:
I make the most of my talents. I live up to my potential and allow myself to feel complete happiness. I have the power within me to change my habits, attitude, and life!

~120~
Speak With Love

The words you speak are powerful, contain charge, and emotionally driven. Some words present more impact than others. Harsh words can build walls and create misunderstandings. Tender words can bridge gaps and unlock hearts. Even a person who has closed their heart from love will respond positively to loving words.

Seek out opportunities to speak with love in all its forms; compassion, kindness, gentleness, understanding, and patience. Use words of love in your conversations today—words that are gentle, sincere, warm, and thoughtful. Convey your kindness in a loving manner with loving words—knowing that every word spoken today is a gift from the Creator.

Today's Nourishment:
I speak words of love today as I am a loving person. I speak words filled with kindness, caring, and compassion.

~121~
Finish Projects

It feels great to bring a project to completion! Today you are being guided to finish a project. What is the first unfinished project that comes to mind while you are reading this? That is the project you are to finish. Make time today to complete this project—you will feel a wonderful sense of accomplishment when you are able to admire the results.

As your insides smile with a sense of accomplishment, you will reward yourself for completing this project and know that you have the power to do anything that you put your mind to!

Today's Nourishment:
I invest time in completing an unfinished project; I feel good about myself as I stand back and admire my finished project.

~122~
Visualize Financial Security

This is a day to take charge of your financial world and envision a life of prosperity and abundance. You are not being greedy or selfish to ask for material things and prosperity. You have a Creator that loves to bestow blessings upon you—simply ask and let Him bless you! You are loved very much and He is happy to help you in this way.

Your material needs are provided for as you follow your inner guidance, visualize financial security, and manifest your dreams into reality. You are provided with the necessary tools to prosper; some may come in the form of ideas and some will come as opportunities. Ask for spiritual assistance and work together to realize your highest dreams and become financial secure. As you open your arms to receive these blessings, give thanks, and pass along the blessings to others as well.

Today's Nourishment:
My material needs are provided for and I am financial secure. I let go of fears and doubts and accept the financial blessings bestowed upon me. I am grateful for such blessings and pass them along to others.

~123~
Set Boundaries

Learning how to set boundaries is a necessary step in becoming a friend to yourself. You are a loving, compassionate, caring, sensitive, and honest person who cares for others. You would never do anything to hurt another person's feelings. Unfortunately, not everyone views the world through your eyes and possesses the capacity to treat others with the same respect and honesty. You have been blessed with the ability to set boundaries for yourself in how you are treated by others.

Focus today on reviewing and setting healthy boundaries. The purpose of having boundaries is to protect and take care of oneself. You need to be able to tell other people when they are acting in ways that are not acceptable. A first step is starting to know that you have a right to protect and defend yourself. You have not only the right, but the duty to take responsibility for how you allow others to treat you. Accept no less than what you deserve and treat others as you would like to be treated. Speak kind words, be respectful, honest, caring, and compassionate toward others and expect the same.

Today's Nourishment:
I state my feelings out loud, affirming that I have a right to feel. I speak up for myself, take care and protect myself when necessary. I have healthy boundaries and treat others as I would like to be treated and expect the same in return.

~124~
Speak Kind Words

The spoken word is extremely powerful! It can make us, break us, hurt others or heal others. Think before you speak. Literally bite your tongue if necessary. Once blurted out, you cannot take your words back. They sting, they can destroy. Destroy a person's self esteem and self worth. Unkind words can create hate and malice. Cynicism is destructive. Today, focus on the energy of kindness with each word that you speak.

Your words are your thoughts broadcasted from your soul. Use words of compassion to create an energy that is uplifting and nurturing. When you speak kind words you are connecting two hearts; yours and the receiver. Be aware of not only what you say but how you say it; be a source of encouragement to others. If you speak kind words of praise about others, they will speak kind words of you.

Today's Nourishment:
I speak kindly to myself and others, using words of compassion to create a loving energy. I am a compassionate, caring person and I surround myself with like persons—life is kind to me!

~125~
Accept Compliments Graciously

Notice what you tend to say when given a compliment. Do you minimize, argue, or find yourself so uncomfortable that you are at a loss for words? If you are uncomfortable with praise and compliments you may be so busy judging yourself harshly that you don't quite know what to do with positive feedback. Learn to accept compliments more graciously. Don't reflect kind words—accept them graciously. A warm and heartfelt, "thank you", coupled with a smile, is always appropriate and is usually enough. Reject the feeling of needing to explain, justify, or return a compliment automatically.

When someone pays you a compliment, stop before you respond. Take a deep breath and remember your wish to accept compliments more graciously. Focus on being kind and courteous to that person. If you make them feel good by accepting their compliment with genuine appreciation, they'll remember that and speak up the next time they have something positive to share with you.

Another way to get better at accepting compliments is to give more compliments. Notice how other people receive them. This can improve your relationships greatly, because now you'll be focused more on the other person. As you're looking for positive things to compliment them on, you'll also be keeping your thoughts more positive overall, and you'll have less time for worrying and negative thinking.

Today's Nourishment:
I accept praise and appreciation graciously and gratefully. I reject the need to explain, justify, or return a compliment automatically. I return compliments with a sincere, "thank you", and a smile. It feels good to accept compliments!

~126~
Take Naps

Naps aren't just for the very young, old, and slothful. As a small child you typically enjoyed an afternoon nap, however, as an adult you have fallen out of the habit of napping. Your mid-afternoon slump in mood and alertness is not caused by eating a heavy lunch or a poor night's sleep—this occurs because you are meant to have an afternoon nap!

Nature intended that you take a nap in the middle of the day. There is scientific research that shows the mid-afternoon slump occurs regardless of whether we eat lunch or slept poorly the night before. It is present even in good sleepers who are well rested. Curling up in a sunny patch on the floor or even lying your head down on your desk for a quick snooze brings relaxation and increases mental alertness. Starting today find a quiet, comfortable spot and take a nap. Even a short power nap can leave you feeling refreshed, renewed, and more focused. Sleep well!

Today's Nourishment:
I empower myself and take time out for a nap! I am not being lazy; napping will make me more productive and more alert. I routinely take a midday power nap—I awake feeling refreshed, alert, and rested!

~127~
Keep Promises To Yourself

Many times it's easier to keep promises that you make to others than to keep promises that you make to yourself. In fact, many of the promises that you make to yourself are not known to anybody else. Something like "I will read this book daily" is known only to you. Days pass by and you haven't read any further in the book. Nobody knows that you made a promise to yourself and you feel a bit guilty for not keeping the promise but you are smart enough to justify why you were not able to keep your promise. Most often, the justifications for not keeping the promises are more compelling than the promises themselves.

When was the last time you made a compelling promise to yourself and worked hard to keep it? You can fix this—start out with small promises to yourself and try to keep them. Keep doing this until it becomes a habit. It should become your second nature to keep the promises you make for yourself. If this not working, ask for help from your spiritual team to keep promises to yourself. What if you practiced this for the next thirty days? Would that make a difference—you bet it would!

Today's Nourishment:
I make a promise to myself and keep it! I start out small and work hard to hold myself to my word. I ask for spiritual help to keep my promises and honor my word.

~128~
Be One With Nature

When you think of nature, what do you picture? Do you have visions of majestic, scenic vistas from mountain tops, crystal blue glaciers, or rain forests? These things *are* all part of Nature, but what about the little woods at the end of your street? What about the river winding through your city? What about the little creek a couple blocks over? These are all part of nature—and they are right in your own little corner of the world!

Nature is all around you—even if you live in a city, there are patches of nature here and there. There may be parks with natural areas or small undeveloped areas with woods where you can find wildflowers in springtime. You may find a small creek where turtles, frogs, and small fish live. Look around. Explore. Take walks. You need to spend time in nature—hear the sounds, breathe the smells of nature, and be one with nature!

Look in your own back yard. If it isn't a natural area, make it friendly to wildlife! Garden it so you can provide the things wildlife need; food, water, shelter, and places to raise their young. Of course, it won't be a true natural area, but you can transform it into an area more naturalistic. Spend time with your hands in the dirt and reconnect with the Earth! Nourish your soul, and you will start to see how things are connected, and be one with nature. You will enjoy being outdoors and won't want to come inside. Embrace the changing seasons and notice how everything is related to one another.

Start spending time outside, even if you don't plant a garden, just spend time outside. Go for walks. Ride your bike to work. Sit and stare at the river for 20 minutes every day. Just get out there and be one with nature. Feel the wind on your face. Look at the moon in the sky. Catch snowflakes on your tongue. There's a *world* out there! You need to feel a connection to it for your own mental health and spiritual health.

Today's Nourishment:
I connect with nature. I enjoy spending time outdoors with plants, animals, and the elements of nature. I notice how being one with nature makes me feel in my heart and body—I truly connect with nature and give thanks for being spiritually in tuned with my world!

~129~
Always Say, Thank You!

At times a single phase can express a lot; 'thank you' is one of them! People just don't say, *"Thank you"* like they used to. Today is about raising your awareness and suggest that you work to create a kinder and more grateful society. If you don't currently do so, make today the day you begin to show appreciation by saying, *"Thank you!"*, when someone does something kind or helpful for you.

It only takes a moment and it will make you and the other person feel acknowledged and appreciated! When you're driving and someone is kind enough to let you merge into the traffic in front of them, wave to them. Or if someone holds the door open for you as you approach with your hands full, thank him or her. It's only a small step for creating a kinder world, but a step in the right direction nonetheless!

With that said, I'd like to say, *"Thank you"*, for reading this book today!

Today's Nourishment:
I show my appreciation by saying, "Thank you." to others today. When someone does something kind or thoughtful for me, I look them straight in the eyes, smile, and say, "thank you!" I express my heartfelt gratitude to friends, family, co-workers, and strangers by always saying, "Thank you."

~130~
Connect With Your Inner Child

The child within is a symbolic representation of the part of self that represents the emotional body. The emotional body is the part of self that enables us to feel love: the love of our own spiritual body, the love of other souls as well as the love of our Creator. An emotional body that presents itself to us as a small child obviously does not have the resources, maturity or strength to feel love. Small wonder most of us are incapable of experiencing, trusting or holding onto our self-love, others' love for us or the love of God. Our immature emotional bodies simply don't have the wherewithal.

Most people are aware of their inner child. You are invited to be open to recognizing your inner child. There are dozens of ways you can connect with your child and help them to heal, feel loved and be happy. There are ways to talk to your inner child. For instance, many people begin talking to their inner child through writing. Others engage in childlike activities as a means of connecting and nurturing the inner child. Whichever method works for you, continue talking to your inner child; soon you will start to hear the child.

As your inner child is small and fearful, you must listen softly so you can hear what is being said. Once you start talking and spending time with your inner child, you'll be much happier than you are now. You'll find yourself singing and maybe even taking silly little dance steps in the street. The people around you will start smiling for no apparent reason because their own inner child will recognize yours and will also pop up to the surface.

Allow your inner child to come out and play—you can have a great time together!

Today's Nourishment:
I get in touch with my inner child and build a loving relationship. I connect with the part of me that needs to heal—allowing it to feel loved, nurtured, and happiness. I engage in childlike activities as a means of nurturing my 'inner child'.

~131~
Acknowledge Accomplishments

You have a tendency to forget the things that are accomplished during your life. You have accomplished much in your life and you are appreciated. You have traveled a long way and learned many life lessons along your journey. You have developed a strong empathy for others; find time to listen, and your heart overflows with compassion and understanding. You are giving, kind, and live a gracious life!

Today, you are to appreciate yourself and acknowledge your accomplishments. Start by giving yourself a pat on the back for a job well done. You are to praise yourself for being the person you are and acknowledge how far you have come and what you have learned along the way.

Today's Nourishment:
I acknowledge what I have accomplished, the lessons I have learned, and how much I have grown. I give myself praise for the person I am and I appreciate myself!

~132~
Speak Three Wishes

Today, state out loud three wishes! Three wishes for yourself, a friend, or a family member it doesn't matter as long as you say them out loud. What is the first thing that comes to mind? Now say it out loud—do not whisper it, say it out loud! Speak in a clear firm voice, with conviction, as if the wish has already been granted.

Let yourself feel the energy and excitement at the wish materializing right in front of your eyes—then release it to the Universe with gratitude to affirm that the wish has already been granted. Now do this two more times with your second and third wish.

Throughout the day recall the moment you spoke your wishes. Envision your wishes materializing right before your eyes. See them happening. Feel the excitement and express your gratitude.

Today's Nourishment:
I say three wishes out loud. I speak in a clear firm voice, with conviction, affirming that my wish has been granted. I express gratitude to affirm my belief that they will come true.

~133~
Make Healthy Life Choices

Although living a healthy lifestyle is a choice, you must start by focusing on taking care of yourself; physically, emotionally, and spiritually. Everyone is faced with making choices everyday. Everything you do in life is based on choices.

The results of your choices made today will determine your outcome tomorrow, next month, and in the coming years.

- Do you believe that you can do something in the next few days that will make your life worse?
- Do you believe that you can do something in the next few weeks that will make your life better?
- Do you believe that the choice is yours?
- Do you believe that every choice you make has an end result?

If you answered yes to all of these questions, you have just agreed that no matter how good or bad your past was, how good or bad your present situation is, there is something that you can do at this moment that will either make your future situation better or worse—and it's your choice.

Making healthy life choices sometimes means entering the abyss of the unknown. Yet if the intent is to improve your situation or for the betterment of yourself, know that you are supported completely.

Today, take the step in the direction of making healthy life choices—set into motion the actions that improve your quality of life, health, and emotional and spiritual well-being.

Today's Nourishment:
I love myself. I take a step in the direction of a healthy life style; I make healthy life choices and treat myself with love.

~134
Eliminate Drama

Your purpose is to become more spiritually in tune with the world around you; to feel and teach love. That which pulls you from your path is but a tool for learning—if you recognize it. Engaging in conflict or drama creates turmoil and threatens your peace of mind. You have the power to choose to engage in drama or eliminate it from your life.

You are a powerful caring and supportive person who cares for others—you do not need to take part in negative situations, thinking, or behavior. Eliminate drama from your life by asking for spiritual assistance to stay balanced and focused on your life's purpose. Hold fast to your path and respectfully eliminate drama from your life today.

Today's Nourishment:
I am drawn into harmonious situations today. I am peacefully balanced and centered—I share this peacefulness with others. I stay calm, compassionate, drama free, and focus on my life path.

~135~
Practice Unconditional Love

God loves you unconditional, meaning…*no conditions.* It must be made clear in this example, that unconditional, means that there are no conditions, to God's love. Do you understand and agree, that unconditional means no conditions apply? You are the child of God, created by ~~Him~~ God, and are of a divine form—as with all life on this planet.

You are loved and cared for unconditionally. God is patient and has complete faith in you as ~~His~~ God's child. ~~His~~ God's faith in your choices and decisions never waver as ~~He~~ God knows all paths eventually lead you back to ~~Him~~ God. This is the power of unconditional love.

Do your best today to love others and yourself with no conditions or reservations. Look past faults, flaws, and errors in judgment—see only the pure divine nature of the person. Your unconditional love helps form a support system and will raise you to the next level in becoming spiritually in tuned with your world…and beyond.

> Today's Nourishment:
> *I practice unconditional love—unconditional love for others and myself. God loves me unconditionally and has faith in me. I honor ~~Him~~ God by practicing unconditional love.*

Feel Love

Today is a day to feel love! We are surrounded by reminders of love—pay attention, sit quietly and absorb this wonderfully joyfully emotion. Make a point of noticing evidence of love throughout your day—caring gestures, signs of affection, a child's laughter, or a couple holding hands.

As you witness these acts of love, drink in the powerful magical potion of love and let it refresh your body, mind, and soul. Let these feelings of love spill outward by showing affection, express feelings of love to your family and friends, and be kind to yourself and others today. Let yourself be nourished with love today!

Today's Nourishment:
I feel love everywhere and witness it on the faces of those around me. I drink in the powerful energy of love and let it nourish me—I am grateful to feel love!

~137~
Retreat

Escape from noise, chaos, and anxiety—retreat to that place inside of you where you feel perfect stillness. Pause for a moment, within this quiet spot, refresh yourself, drinking in the silence of peacefulness.

Close your eyes breathe deeply and find that quiet place within. Retreat to the calmness and tranquility of your inner self—your own heaven within.

Borrow moments throughout the day to retreat to your quiet place. Visit this place often knowing that you are becoming spiritually in tuned with your world.

Today's Nourishment:
I am calm, centered, and at peace. I travel to my 'quiet spot' within often so that I can rest my mind and refresh my soul. I breathe deeply throughout the day—drinking the silence of tranquility.

~138~
Connect With God

What does it take to begin a relationship with God? Wait for lightning to strike? Devote yourself to unselfish religious deeds? Become a better person so that God will accept you? *None* of these things are necessary to connect with God. God created you. Not only that, he [God] loves you so much that he [God] wants you to know him [God] now and spend eternity with him [God]. God is not only your Creator; he [God] wants to know you personally!

You are eternally connected with God—the infinite love, wisdom, and life of abundance are waiting for you upon request. Much like logging onto the Internet, when you ask for spiritual assistance, you are immediately connected with an abundance of gifts, unconditional love, and blessings.

Become more spiritually in tune with your world by connecting with God in everything you do.

Remember to connect with God throughout your day, ask for Divine support with every decision, question, and action. With your spiritual team at your beckon call, they will help you to remember to do so and clear the way for communication—all you have to do is ask.

Today's Nourishment:
God is watching from a distance. He [God] is my higher power, the man [God] upstairs and divine imminence. I connect with him [God] throughout my day; asking for assistance in all things. I thank him [God] for his [God's] constant help and am grateful.

~139~
Welcome Divine Love

Open your arms to welcome Divine love that is yours for the asking. You have been loved since your soul's inception. You are God's perfect creation and His love for you as never wavered. God is forever by your side. Welcome God!

You are deeply cherished, child of God. It is your birthright, as God's child, to be loved. You do not need to do, say, or prove anything to earn this Divine love—it is yours forever.

Today's Nourishment:
I am cherished and loved at this moment. I welcome this Divine love—it is my birthright as a child of God to be loved. I am deserving of this love. My heart is open to receive Divine love.

~140~
Quiet Your Mind

Avoid conflict and chaos today, choose peacefulness instead. You need a quiet reprieve from the stormy seas of your day. Quiet your mind and focus on peace instead of conflict and power struggles. By focusing the mind and using positive thinking you can have lasting peace, a deeper spiritual practice, and lasting true happiness.

Make use of the consistently occurring daily "rest" moments—waiting in line, or brushing teeth to quiet your mind. Stand still, close your eyes, breathe deeply, be mindful and serene, and feel your body and emotions. When you are upset or need to calm down or refocus – at any time, in any place – breathe – in and out – slowly, deeply, consciously – to bring peace and tranquility and consciousness to your body and spirit. Throughout the day, gaze out the window and just 'be' and observe beauty. Be still, breathe, relax, and quiet your mind. Breathe again – and again. Let a little time pass doing nothing, and repeat. Revisit this a few times each day.

Today's Nourishment:
I quiet my mind throughout the day and bring peace and tranquility to my body and spirit. . I dance with serenity and inspire others. I have a calming effect on those around me—being of quiet mind and serene nature.

~141~
Visualize Success

You have to not only want success, but create it. And one of the ways of creating success is to act with the self-confidence of a successful person. Visualize success to achieve success. Whatever your specific goal is, picture the scenario and see yourself acting successfully.

Imagine yourself enjoying success in your life today. See yourself smiling, feeling upbeat and elate as every door is automatically opened for you—you triumph in every thing you do! Make this vision a gift to yourself. Reward yourself today by seeing everything in life working out in your favor, be uplifted—visualize success!

Today's Nourishment:
I am successful in every way and I am deserving of this success. People like and respect me because I value myself and my achievements. I deserve the blessings bestowed upon me—as do all God's children.

~142~
Honor Your Physical Health

While it is important to nourish your spiritual side, being spiritually in tuned requires that you honor your physical health with respect to your body. To create a sense of harmony and balance in your life you need to take excellent care of your body.

Ask for spiritual assistance to help you honor your physical health. Whether you need to exercise more, change your diet, give up smoking, or other addictive habits detrimental to your physical health, your angelic teammates stand ready to help! Whatever is necessary—coaching, trainer, cheerleaders, support team, or healing, simply ask for help and it is readily given.

Today, take one step toward honoring your physical health. It is not necessary to give up all your bad habits in one day. Even a slight change is a step in the right direction—eliminate unhealthy food from your diet, take a brisk walk after a meal, drink more water, or cut back on a an unhealthy habit such as smoking. These baby steps can eventually lead you to a healthy lifestyle allowing for better care of your body.

> Today's Nourishment:
> *I honor my physical body and work toward a healthy lifestyle. I take at least one step toward changing the way I treat my body. My inner radiates as I have more energy, mental alertness, and become more spiritually in tune with my environment!*

~143~
Give God Your Worries Over Loved Ones

It's scary to think that someone you care about could be harmed. It's natural to worry about your friend or relative—at least some of the time. God has assigned everyone a guardian angel to watch over them at all times, this includes your loved one as well. When worries become too intense or start to threaten your emotional well-being, ask for additional angels to surround your loved one. The moment you ask for help—it is given immediately!

Each angel illuminates a loving protective shield around the person they are asked to help; the more angels the more powerful the shield. So call upon a choir of angels to surround your loved one to keep them safe. Call upon your angels to help you give them your worries, to calm you, and to ease your concerns. Ask the angels to help you find activities that help you feel calm. For some it might mean listening to music, playing an instrument, reading a book, enjoying nature, relaxing quietly, or spending time with a pet —whatever soothes you best.

Relax in knowing that at this very moment, as you are reading this page, your angels are watching over you and your loved ones. Let God have your worries about them, and know that because of your prayers, your loved ones are protected.

Today's Nourishment:
My loved ones and I are watched over by God and the angels all the time. I release my cares and worries over to God—knowing that we are protected, loved, and cherished. I thank God for watching over those that mean the most to me—my loved ones.

~144~
Take Action

You have been asking for guidance, direction, and wondering if you are on the right path in fulfilling your life's purpose. The universe has responded to your inquiry and wants to reassure you that you are on the right path. Every action or attention you have given to your life's purpose is meaningful and yields positive results.

Today you are being guided to take action toward your life's purpose as you are guided. Do not worry whether it is the wrong or best action—give that worry over to God. Trust that you are being guided on the right path for your life's purpose.

Today's Nourishment:
I acknowledge that I have a much-needed life purpose, which I eagerly look forward to fulfilling. I focus only on the now and trust that my actions of today lead my tomorrows to work out well. I take action toward my life's purpose as I feel guided.

~145~
Talk To Your Angels Daily

The topic of angels has been covered previously and you know that angels surround you all the time. They are standing next to you as you read this, they will never leave you, and you can talk to them anytime you want. You don't need any special powers; anyone can talk to angels.

You can begin talking to your loving guardian angel right now. Just close your eyes imagine your angel in front of you and have a mental conversation with him or her. At first this will feel like you are making it up. But it's real. Thousands of people have been talking to angels for many years and have helped many people learn how to talk to their angels too.

You can talk to your angels about anything—talk to them about everything! They love to hear from you. Ask them anything you want; ask for their help with anything, nothing is too big, too small, or too personal to discuss with your angels. Keep an angel journal. Try to set aside 15 minutes every day just to talk to your angels. You will be amazed later when you look over your notes how accurate they are. Ask the angels questions then right down the first answer that pops into your head, no matter how absurd it seems. Trust in this process—it works!

Today's Nourishment:
I talk to my angels about everything—big, small, personal, or just have a casual conversation. I ask them for help when I need it, guidance or direction, or simply their name! It doesn't matter to them, they are happy to hear from me!

Receive Heaven's Gifts

Instead of searching for what you want, focus on visualizing your heart's desire. Your heart's desire is already found the moment you think of it. Similar to placing an order over the Internet, once you click that *order now* button you sit back, relax, and know that your desire will be manifested. That is heaven's gift to you—the ability to order anything you desire and wait for delivery!

After you placed your order, surround it with faith, trust, gratitude, and a sense of security—trust that your hearts desire is on its way! Do not worry about how your desire will manifest, simply trust that it will arrive when it is suppose to, right on time. Do you concern yourself with the details of how your Internet order item will be handled and delivered? No, you do not. Your job is to sit back, wait, and open your door to receive heaven's gifts.

Today's Nourishment:
I no longer search for what I want for my desire is manifesting at this moment. I open my arms to receive heaven's gifts; trusting that it will arrive promptly on time—I deserve heaven's gifts.

Accept God's Love

You are reminded today, the number one reason you were born is because God loves you. That's right; you were created by God to love and to be loved. God's love for you is probably the greatest thing in the entire universe. The very essence of God's being, His personality, and His very nature - is love. God's love for God's children is so profound that it surpasses all boundaries.

One of the greatest mistakes that you can make is measuring God's love for you by present circumstances. You think that if things are going bad for you, then God must really be upset with you. But if the birds are singing and the sun is shining, and you are happy, then God must really love you. You also assume that God works only through your successes and not through your weaknesses. The truth is that even though your circumstances are constantly changing God's love is always with you. God's love for you does not ride the waves of your feelings.

God's love is not based on what you have, what you do, or your achievements. God's love is not determined by your behavior or conduct. It is not dependent on your background, birth, or status in society. God's love is not influenced by anything that you do. When you are good God loves you and when you are bad God loves you. This unconditional love is given to because you are God's creation—accept God's love.

Today's Nourishment:
I was born because God loves me—God loves and cherishes me very much. God's love is unconditional, constant, and is always with me.

~148~
Trust In Divine Timing

Everything operates in accordance with the universal laws of divine timing, meaning that similar to a puzzle, some pieces must be in place before the other pieces fit. Have you worked a puzzle with several pieces been lost or misplaced? Or have one piece that looked like it should fit, tried to force it to fit, but in the end it just did not fit? It's frustrating to see partial results after working so long on the puzzle. The same holds true for your prayers—rest assured, all prayers are answered at the precise moment; when all the pieces are in place.

Answering prayers is a process often involving a series of actions—some prayers require a multitude of actions, especially if it involves other people. You must practice patience and nurture your desires with trust, love, positive energy, and guided actions. Your prayer is being answered, even in this exact moment. The divine timing ensures that your prayer is answered completely, at the right moment, not a moment too soon, and without missing puzzle pieces!

Today's Nourishment:
All my prayers have been heard and answered. I will see results when the timing is right and all the pieces are in place. I trust in Divine timing and have patience.

~149~
Taste The Sweetness Of Life

Like a cold tall glass of sweet tea, your life's intent is to bring you sweet enjoyment, even as you fulfill your destiny and follow your designed path. Happiness doesn't just happen by taking time off or enjoying a holiday—most of life's joys come from helping or caring for others.

Never underestimate the power of your touch, a smile, a kind word, a listening ear, an honest compliment, or the act of caring; all which add to the sweetness of life. You can enjoy the sweetness of life more simply by noticing it. Babies are sweet. Intimacy is sweet. Love is sweet. Your innermost self, is sweet. Think of the names you call babies and lovers, the people we know most intimately: honey, sugar, and sweetie. True sweetness is found within. The experience of coming inward, coming back home, connecting with the divine, is one of ineffable sweetness. The term "sweet Jesus" is no accident!

Pay attention to every situation today; look for the sweetness within each interaction, encounter, and experience that you have. Like a glass of iced sweet tea, drink in the sweetness of each moment that today brings you—and every day!

Today's Nourishment:
I notice and embrace the sweetness in my life. I am grateful for everything and everyone in my life. I look for the sweetness within each interaction and experience I have.

~150~
Lay Your Burdens Down

Imagine walking through a crowded airport. You're late for your flight, and the wheels just broke on your over-packed suitcase. With no other option, you're forced to carry the luggage and slowly maneuver through the congested lobby toward the ticketing area. You cannot move without bumping into someone. Almost immediately, someone offers to carry your bags, but your pride won't allow you to accept help. When you realize the ticket counter is two levels up, you make your way to the stairs. You realize it would be easier to take the elevator, but you are determined to carry your bags on your own.

As you finally make it to the top of the steps, your arms feel numb from the pressure of your bags. Your legs are starting to buckle from the weight. Your back is aching from supporting the heavy load. Then, you spot a collection of unused baggage carts. But you ignore them, hurried and self-assured that you can handle the bags yourself. Sounds rather silly and foolish for you to continue struggling doesn't it?

Why would you prefer to carry such a heavy burden, ignoring every opportunity to lay it down? God has beckoned you to lay your cares at God's feet. But when you fail to come to God in prayer, you appear just as foolish as if you were staggering with your bags through the airport.

Are you trying to carry a greater burden than you can bear? Don't ignore God's offer to help—lay your burdens down, let God carry them. The truth is, you really can't do it *yourself*, and God never wanted you to try.

Today's Nourishment:
I lay my burdens down at God's feet, breathing a deep sigh of relief that I no longer have to carry the load by myself. I no longer have to struggle with a greater burden than I can bear; I have a loving all knowing compassionate God who loves me. I readily accept God's help!

153

Bless Everyone You Meet

As you become more spiritually focused your interactions with others will change. While you should not try to convince or convert anyone to your new way of thinking, you are a walking advertisement for the benefits of living more spiritually in tuned with your world. The best way to handle yourself is by being peaceful and happy; others will soon take notice and ask about the secret to your happiness.

Today, make it a point to bless everyone you meet, be it a loved one, stranger you pass on the street, a co-worker, or a casual friend. A simple blessing works fine, such as, "I wish you peace, joy and happiness." Blessing everyone you meet creates a sharing of energy and they receive your peacefulness. As you continue this practice you will notice that you are blessed in unexpected ways.

Today's Nourishment:
God, please help me to remember to bless everyone I meet today. Please send healing energy through me to those I interact with so that they may feel my peacefulness.

~152~
Daydream

Sometimes the best activity is *no* activity! Sometimes the best thing to do is *nothing!* Your imagination is the place where you envision your future—the place where daydreams reside. Daydreaming is the spontaneously recalling or imagining of personal or vicarious experiences in the past or future. You are like the artist who chooses and controls colors splashed upon the canvas. What would you like to create today?

This is the time to allow yourself to expand your world and improve your creativity through daydreams. Allow your mind to take a break, a mini-vacation in which to release tension and anxiety and *return* refreshed. Silently think about a pleasant place, memory, friend, and let your mind wander. You can reminisce, plan, or create a fantasy. Envision whatever elaborate and exotic future you desire. That is the beauty of daydreaming – there are no rules.

Today's Nourishment:
I spend time doing nothing! I allow my imagination to create visions of places, situations, events, memories, and people—letting my mind wander to fantasy land. I release my fears, doubts, and insecurities and spend creating my future in my mind.

~153~
Set Healthy Boundaries

The purpose of having boundaries is to protect and take care of you. You need to be able to tell other people when they are acting in ways that are not acceptable to you. Take the first step and know that you have a right to protect and defend yourself. You have not only the right, but are responsibility for how you allow others to treat you. Call upon your spiritual teammates to help you set healthy boundaries.

Today, it is important to state your feelings out loud, and to precede the feeling with "I feel." When you say "I am angry, I'm hurt, etc." you are stating that the feeling is who you are. Emotions do not define who you are, they are simply an inner form of communication that help you to understand. To verbalize, "I feel…" is accepting ownership of the feeling. By stating the feeling out loud you are affirming that you have a right to feelings.

Learning how to set boundaries is a necessary step in learning to love yourself and become more spiritually in tune with your world. You have the protection of heavenly beings at your beckon call, but it is still necessary to stand up for yourself- to protect yourself when it is necessary.

> Today's Nourishment:
> *I call upon my spiritual allies to help me set healthy boundaries. I let others know when they are acting in ways that are not acceptable to me. As a child of God, I have a right and responsibility for how others treat me.*

~154~
Release Regrets

Regrets dilute your present. Regret is like a blind spot in your life. When you are driving, you know there is a blind spot in your mirror, so you compensate for it. Similarly, when you navigate life, regret will be lurking there. Take the appropriate measures to maneuver around it. You are guided to release feelings of guilt, shame, and regret.

You are reminded that as a child of God, you were perfectly created and it's impossible for you to interfere with that perfection. You are loved and cherished unconditionally and always—nothing you can do or say can change or lessen that love. As long as you carry feelings of regret in your mind or heart, you are inflicting pain upon yourself and those around you.

Today, release those feelings of regret, shed the dark shadows of guilt and shame—forgive yourself and remember that you are loved and cherished. Release regrets and feel your energy lift, your mood and outlook improve, and your spirit soar!

Today's Nourishment:
I no longer have feelings of pain, guilt, shame, or regrets—I forgive myself. I am a child of a God who loves me unconditionally. Nothing I do or say will damage that love. I am at peace with myself.

~155~
Embrace Your Uniqueness

No two persons are exact—no two are the same, even twins, neither are ~~the~~ like the other. God created you to be your own person, with unique qualities, talents, and skills. You are unique! There are times you doubt your self-worth or feel out of sync with the rest of the world. Rest assured God does not make mistakes—you are perfect just as you are!

God does not want you to change who you are to fit in or belong. God wants you to recognize your unique qualities and embrace these differences. Look in the mirror and see the lovable person you are. The more you embrace your own extraordinary qualities, the more at ease you feel with yourself. Enjoy the fact that you are different. Today, get comfortable with who you are—embrace your uniqueness.

Today's Nourishment:
I am loved and cherished just as I am. My unique qualities set me apart from others, making me an interesting and unique person who is admired by others. I embrace my uniqueness and am comfortable in my own skin!

~156~
Invite Love Into Your Life

In this day and age, your lifestyle determines much of your ability to have a loving relationship with a partner in your life. There is only so much energy available; how can you parcel it out among work, activities, families, and lover without reaching a burnout? Whether you have a current love relationship in your life or desire one, rest assured that by inviting love into your life, you will be blessed with an abundance of love.

You are offered the possibility of knowing God's love in a meaningful and intimate way. As a unique individual you are offered the gift of God's love in unique ways that are perfect for you. It is your choice to open your heart so that you may be receptive to love. When you choose to invite love into your life you are embraced by the angels of love who fill your heart with Divine love. This miracle of love is best expressed through human interactions; for holy love offers its most beautiful reflection in your relationship with another.

Your angels stand next to you in this moment, awaiting your request for help with attracting an emotionally healthy partner. Whether you need help removing obstacles, hidden agendas, fears, doubts, and insecurities, they stand ready and able to assist you with this endeavor. Make a pact with yourself and your angles to invite love into your life today. Whether you need a complete attitude adjustment or minor adjustments to be more love based, they are anxiously awaiting your request…just call upon them!

Today's Nourishment:
I offer up prayers to bless me with the most precious gift and invite love into my life. I am a loving, kind, caring, and compassionate person ready to be paired with an emotionally healthy partner.

~157~
It's All Good

Look around, God is everywhere, in everything and within everyone—see that it's impossible for anything to be anything but Divine and heavenly. Hold fast to that knowledge today, and realize that regardless of the situation it's all good, because it's all God.

If you find yourself feeling stressed, anxious, worried, or confronted with conflict, breathe in deeply and remind yourself, "It's all good, because it's all God." Everything is how it should be in the moment. Sometimes what appears to be a problem is an answered prayer in disguise. Know that any changes you face today are for the betterment of yourself and your highest good.

Today, God is within you, guiding you, from the moment you awake and throughout your day He is leading you. Pay attention to your inner voice, gut feelings, the knowingness, or your visions for that is Divine guidance reminding you that everything is as it should be—it's all good.

Today's Nourishment:
God is everywhere, in everything, and within everyone. I remind myself that everything is how it should be in this moment. It's all good, because it's all God.

~158~
Celebrate Life

Life should be a celebration, plain and simple. You need to embrace your life and thank God for the opportunity to love, work, and play. Dive in and plunge into its depths. Everyone dies, but not everyone lives, and you should refuse to join those who merely exist. To be or not to be is not the question. To live or not to live; that is the question.

Celebrate life by living courageously. Savor your existence and live your life like there is no tomorrow. The only thing you need to fear is living too cautiously. Ironically, life is most exciting when we love someone or a cause more than our life.

Today, attack your life with boldness. Pay attention to the sights, sounds, and smell of life—the aroma of the soft grass you lie on while absorbing the warm rays of a summer day. Savor the taste of blackberries just plucked from a bush. Listen for the sound of a frog splashing into a pond. Watch a blinding flash of lightning sparkle in the eyes of an animal. Feel the spring mist that silently hides pastel blossoms. Life is all these and a great deal more. Life is a boundless tapestry that we observe, weave, and experience. Life is a feature film, projected one frame at a time, and we are the director, main actor, and audience member.

> Today's Nourishment:
> *I choose to celebrate life and thank God for the blessings God has given me. I live my life courageously, boldly, and savor each day—drinking it all in, refreshing and nourishing my soul!*

~159~
Transition Through Life

Life is jam-packed full of milestones!Life *IS* transition. From childhood to teen years, to adulthood, to middle age—from school to work, from kids to no kids, from empty nest to grandchildren, from job to job, location to location, making new friends, losing old friends, losing loved ones—health issues, financial issues, to name a few; and some aren't easy. For each milestone comes a transitional period; each transitional period brings new stressors into our lives. However, to not transition, is to stagnate!

As with any life transition; retirement, starting a home based business,divorce, separation, kids moving away,health, or financial issues the process takes time. Part of this transition involves establishing new roles, new responsibilities, new relationships, and a new perspective. The trick to adjusting to all this *newness* is in the attitude or perspective; overcome the challenge by looking at it as an opportunity!

Today, see challenges as opportunities for growth and learning. Acknowledge to yourself that a successful transition does not *just happen*, it takes time. Allow yourself a fair amount of time to adjust to the new arrangement before throwing in the towel, pulling your hair out, or resorting to anti-depressants! The key to a successful transition is to develop a new routine, re-define roles, consider all your possibilities, express creativity, and find some new hobbies or interests. Focus on what works for you; see what options are available; volunteer or community work, clubs, or church groups.

Today's Nourishment:
I look at new challenges as opportunity for growth and learning. I allow myself the time to adjust to new situations. I look for new ways of doing things, change my routine, and adapt to new roles.

~160~
Create Self-Love

Have you ever found yourself holding onto resentments, guilt, or humiliation? Holding these feelings inside, feeding them, and refusing to release them often breeds anger, depression, and a feeling of worthlessness. These negative thoughts and attitudes seep into your daily life, blinding you to the everyday blessings.

As a human, you are much too hard on yourself. Many humans believe that being perfect is a requirement for being valued. Having worked at something only to fall short of set goals can cause feelings of self-loathing and guilt of having failed yet again.

What you need to keep in mind is that you are lovable even as you stumble; even more so when you fall. For by taking the risk of trying, you may stumble, but you learn, you grow, and then you move on. Trust that you can experience more learning and growth during the times you stumbled and fell; even if it does take a while to get back up.

By releasing and ridding yourself of the harmful buildup of resentments, you start to forgive yourself. This process can bring you everything we seek; ability to concentrate, renewed energies, clarity, love, and a sense of playfulness…you name it. The rewards are endless!

Today, it is important to learn to practice forgiveness starting within yourself. For as you begin to forgive yourself, release the resentments, and lovingly embrace yourself, we project a loving healing light that touches those around you.

Today's Nourishment:
Today I make a pact to work on releasing any feelings of resentments, guilt, and self-anger I may have within. I start by letting go of the negative thoughts, attitudes, and self-image. I surround myself with self-love; creating a warm bubble of pink, capturing allowing only Divine love to penetrate this bubble. Today I forgive myself and accept that I am an awesome human being.

Forgive Past Loves

As you begin to seek inner faith and develop your spiritual awareness, your must learn how to open yourself up to love. Before you can begin to trust yourself and open your heart up to love, you must first cross a small bridge—the bridge of forgiveness. At this point in your journey you make the emotional decision to forgive past loves. Now you must step upon this bridge of forgiveness so as not to carry the pain, hurt, and sadness from the past into your future relationships.

Put your hand on your heart, take a deep breath and relax. See yourself standing at the foot of a bridge. Stand there quietly. Take a brief moment to look back. See the past loves you leave behind. See the old disappointments, sorrows, and hurt as vague shadows far in the distance. You do this so you may release them. The way to let them go is to forgive.

Take another deep breath. Calm yourself. Even though this is a small bridge it can be a difficult one to cross. As you start across the bridge you will begin to call forth all those past loves and who have hurt you. Allow into your awareness the faces of those who have caused you pain. Some people will appear suddenly before you, people you have almost forgotten, and people you remember all too well. With each face, each name and each memory of pain, begin to forgive. Just let them go, retaining the love and lessons from each relationship. Feel your heart opening and all the old anger, resentment, tensions, worry, guilt, and shame seeping out—swept away by your angels.

On the other side of the bridge is a clear path leading to new love, new relationships, and new beginnings. You are disentangled from your past, ready to open your heart to new love.

Today's Nourishment:
I now forgive _____. I let go of old pain, anger, resentments to make room for a new relationship. I embrace pure Divine love; suffering is no longer an option. It is now safe for me to experience new love with a new partner. My angels protect and guide me along this new path.

~162~
Keep A Positive Attitude

Thoughts are very powerful. They affect your general attitude. The attitude you carry reflects on your appearance, too—unless of course, you are a great actor. Listen to your thoughts. Now think about what thoughts fill your head? Would you label them as positive, or negative?

Your attitude can also affect people around you. The type of attitude you carry depends on you. It can be either positive or negative. Positive thoughts have a filling effect. They are invigorating. Plus, the people around the person carrying positive thoughts are usually energized by this type of attitude. A positive attitude begins with a healthy self-image. If you choose to love the way you are and are satisfied, confident, and self-assured, you also make others around you feel the same way.

A positive attitude promotes relaxation, clear thinking, and reduces stress. Vow to keep a positive attitude today no matter what. To promote a positive attitude you could see a funny movie, play with children, or spend some time telling jokes with friends. All these activities fill you with positive stimuli, which in turn promotes positive attitude. Although it is impossible to block the negative things around us, you can still carry a positive attitude by focusing on the good things, the positive things in life.

> Today's Nourishment:
> *I feel positive about myself. I feel positive toward all those around me. I am honest, upbeat, and happy. This type of outlook creates positive energy that surrounds me; energizing me and keeps me healthy!*

~163~
You Are Powerful

You are powerful! You are a child of God and He supports you in all that you do. Use the power He has given you to manifest all that you desire. You are a star, wise, strong, talented, and filled with unshakable faith. You have the courage and strength to do anything that you set your mind to.

Now is the time to summon all your spiritual strength and realize that you are a powerful instrument of God—say prayers for guidance and state your intentions. Use your faith in God, listen for guidance and manifest your desires.

Today's Nourishment:
God is within in me, supporting me, making me strong. I am powerful and attract and manifest all that is desirable. I do not abuse this power--it is safe for me to be powerful.

~164~
Find Daily Balance

Today is devoted to finding balance in your life. The key to finding balance in the most effective way possible is awareness. You know very quickly when you're hungry or tired, but how long does it take you to realize that you need to spend a little time in prayer or meditation or just reading a good book?

Write up record goals or descriptions of what you hope to be and do regarding your physical, mental, emotional and spiritual balance. Revise these at any time as you want something easier or more challenging. The more you surround yourself with balanced people, the easier time you will have keeping yourself balanced. The happier you will be. The more fun and success you will have. You can be inspired by their lives and vice versa. Keep a positive attitude, use prayer to fill your heart and mind with love, and call for spiritual assistance when you need it!

Today's Nourishment:
I make time for myself today; time to relax, be playful, carefree--for this is as important as working. I chose to have a balanced life--balancing work, responsibilities, and play. I allow myself to give and receive equally.

~165~
Overcome Challenges

The challenges you have faced in the past have made you stronger, taught you lessons, and brought you to where you are today. Your new level of spiritual understanding has filled your heart with compassion and love. No longer bitter, you have released all resentments, anger, blame, and any feelings of being a victim. You are not a victim of past challenges or difficult situations— you have overcome challenges and have a positive attitude and outlook on your life.

Focus today on maintaining your positive outlook so that you can attract loving solutions to any current challenges and new situations. Ask for guidance for you and everyone involved to act in loving ways. Keep a merciful outlook; treat each other with respect, a sense of caring, and love.

Today's Nourishment:
The worst is behind me now. I have overcome previous challenges. I am stronger because of the challenges I have endured. These challenges have taught me new lessons. Instead of feeling bitterness or like a victim, I feel compassion toward others in similar situations. My outlook is positive and loving!

~166~
Invest In Faith

Think back to all the energy spent worrying over a particular issue—in most cases these fears never materialized. There never will be anything that merits being anxious, because the time, energy, and emotions spent on worrying far exceed any actual issue that might arise.

Investing time in faith is a far more valuable way to spend ones' energy. Positive belief creates positive energy and allows you the freedom to be happy and enjoy yourself. Improved physical and emotional health is another benefit to investing in faith. Also, you are more attractive in every way when you are relaxed and carefree.

Naturally you will worry occasionally and by no means should you ignore these worries. Today you are being reminded that since you have the universe within your reach, it's just a matter of handing *it* over!

Today's Nourishment:
I give my worries to God. I am completely safe. All my needs are provided for today and in the future, and I am filled with faith--creating positive energy, thoughts, and a feeling of well being!

Know Your Right Path

When you are given complex choices which require making difficult decisions honor your inner voice and listen to your heart. You are being guided toward what will serve your growth and help you develop your strengths and gifts. As you develop your spiritual understanding and awareness you will recognize the voice within, a sense of knowing, that helps you know your right path. Listen to what is being said, choose what is really good for you and know what will serve your highest good and greatest joy.

When you focus on the light you are able to rise above the clouds of confusion and see what is for your highest good. Ask the angels to help you know what is ultimately for your greatest good. It is not necessarily the easiest or most popular path. Rest assured, however, it is the path best suited for your own good. The angels are here to help guide your way in making the wisest choices—to help you know your right path. Pray to the angels to help you develop your ability to listen to your inner voice; this will help you hear the angels whispering to you and know the right path.

Today's Nourishment:
I ask for help in knowing my right path and choose what is really good for me. I pray to the angels to help develop my listening skills, so that I may hear their whispers and make the right choices for my growth and highest good.

On Track (Photo by Nicole McGowan)

~168~
Surrender It To The Universe

Do you ever wonder why a particular expressed desire or wish has not yet manifested? And as time goes on lose faith?

Sometimes struggling with a situation so much unwittingly blocks what is suppose to happen. This is especially true when you want something so badly that you try over and over to *force* it to happen—in your time and your way!

This struggle creates fear and anxiety that maybe what you desire won't manifest—bouncing back in the form of limitations, delays, and loss of faith. Surrendering your desires to the universe brings about results. Once your wish is delivered to the universe, the fears & doubts that surround you need to be delivered as well. By letting go and surrendering your desires to the universe, you are making a statement, "I know my desire is being manifested in the best possible way, even if I am not certain exactly how it will happen."

By doing so you are demonstrating faith and allowing the universe to do the work of creating your dreams. Once you have expressed your desire, your job is done—so turn it over to the universe and enjoy the creative ways in which that desire is manifested!

Today's Nourishment:
I surrender my desires to the Universe today. I know that my desire is being manifested in the best possible way and for my highest good. I continue to have faith that all things are being worked in accordance with a Divine plan.

Acknowledge the Time is Now

The time to start living a more spiritual life is now. Not tomorrow, next week, next month or next year, but today. Focus on dedicating more time to spiritual pursuits such as meditation, talking to God, and developing the ability to listen and trust your inner guidance. Your intentions are good and you want to be more spiritual. You want to devote more time to spiritual pursuits—want to spend less, need less, and serve more. You want to have a personal relationship with an all-knowing loving God who offers hope, inspiration, and encouragement for anyone seeking direction along life's journey.

The only way to break the habit of procrastination is to make a vow of how you are going to live a more spiritual live and be a better person. Rather than saying "I will find time to meditate and talk to my Creator" you must say "I will not leave for work without sitting in meditation and I will not go to sleep at night without having at least one conversation with my Creator." You can ask for assistance with living a more spiritually in tuned life—the time is now!

Today's Nourishment:
Today I acknowledge that the timing is perfect! I want to live a more spiritual life. I want to focus on being loving, teaching love, and being spiritual in tuned with the world around me. I focus on myself, my highest priorities; get organized and motivated! I release old hurts, negative thoughts, and allow my heart to heal.

~170~
Stay Focused

Expect the best from your mind today! Your mind is powerful and you have the ability to stay focused and concentrate on whatever it is you desire. You have the ability to learn new information and retain this information.

Today you shall say and think only positive thoughts—you shall believe in your power to stay focused! Let your mind become one with the Divine intellect of the universe—it is natural and feels good to allow your minds to do what it does best: think, learn, analyze, and stay focused!

Today's Nourishment:
I remained focused on whatever I desire--learning and retaining new information. My mind is quick, powerful, and brilliant! I am one with God's magnificent universe!

~171~
See What's Right

Have you ever found yourself upset, angry, or disappointed when a situation didn't turn out the way you expected or hoped? There is usually another way to view your situation beyond how you initially see it. Being more spiritually in tuned, gives you the opportunity to look within the situation and ask to be shown a new perspective. Because you are more spiritually in tune, blessings are bestowed upon you in every moment and each situation. Of course, you may have to look harder for the blessings—rest assured they exist!

Being spiritually in tune allows us to walk in the light and sometimes we can be blind to that light. You don't always see the *whole* picture and sometimes see everything but what is right with the picture! Today, when a situation seems to go wrong or doesn't turn out the way you want it to; look at it with a new perspective. Look at the situation and ask, "What's *right* with this picture?"

Ask to be shown the positive in what initially appears to be a negative situation. If need be, stretch your imagination to find every positive aspect as you examine the flip side of a situation. See the humor in the situation—see what's right!

Today's Nourishment:
I look for a new perspective with situations that disappoint or upset me. I ask for help in seeing what is right with a situation, instead of looking for the negative. I use humor and imagination to see the best in all my situations, interactions, and events.

~172~
Embrace The Moment

Naturally, you want everything in your life to run smoothly. No one likes pain, uncertainty, strife, or frustrations. But life doesn't always present itself wrapped up in a box with a pretty bow on top—face it, sometimes life gets messy, disorganized, challenging, and can become down-right miserable! But these *messy* times are not without their aspect of good; things can happen in the worst of times that end up being as precious as a gemstone. For it is during life's messiness you have the chance to experience spiritual understanding and growth in a much deeper way. If you embrace the moment you will see God within it!

Living a more spiritual life requires embracing each moment for all it's worth. For those times you are tempted to give into fears, frustrations, uncertainty, or anxieties over what is going on in your life, stop and see God. God is within every situation, interactions, and each moment. Having God in your life, you have everything you need for the moment. Open your eyes to the big picture—see a new perspective—embrace the moment!

Today's Nourishment:
I acknowledge that sometimes life is messy and I embrace the messiness of life! I know that walking in the light of my chosen spiritual path gives me everything I need. I see the big picture with a new perspective and embrace each moment!

Be Seven

Think back to when you were a child. Embrace the sweetness of these sentimental memories of being seven. Recall that time when life had just begun. Fondly remember the wonderment of being seven, the sights and sounds of play, and the simplicity of being a child.

Now is the time to be seven again. To have fun, draw on the sidewalk with chalk, build a sandcastle, chase fireflies, star gazing, sip on a cold glass of sweet tea, or spend time watching clouds.

Become that free spirit you were at seven, that pixie, that wild child of days gone by. You are seven. Spend a summer night playing freeze tag, kickball, hide and seek, and let your playful side emerge. Build a fire, bring on the marshmallows, the hidden chocolate, and graham crackers—make smores and tell scary stories. Today you are seven!

Today's Nourishment:
Today I am seven. I am a free spirited pixie child that embraces the joys of being seven. I spend time having fun, playing, engaging in childlike activities, or play with children. For today I am seven.

Portrait of Seven (Blake Wallis, age 7)

~174~
Cheer Up Someone

Whenever you feel down or discouraged, it helps to know that a friend or family member is just a phone call or email away. A good friend knows just the thing that can cheer you up and get you going again, whether it's a corny joke or delicious batch of brownies.

If you know someone who needs occasional encouragement, this is a reminder to help make them feel special or get their mind off their troubles. Pay attention today to those you encounter, make a point to use uplifting and encouraging words. Send encouraging notes, thoughtful cards, or even a personally written poem. Some people appreciate a tangible memento—if you live at a distance send a cookie basket or bouquet of flowers. If you live close enough, drop off a book, gift certificate, or a home cooked meal. It doesn't really matter the action, the evidence of the friendship and caring will be enough to hold you in their thoughts for days and weeks to come.

Sometimes, a simple smile and hug conveys more than words or a gift. Look your friend in the eyes and smile deeply—hug him or her. Sit by their side and merely listen to their story. Sometimes spending time with someone who does not feel up to completing tasks is evidence of your friendship. Offer your services; pitch in where needed, mop a floor, do the laundry, cook a meal, or bathe a child. Give the gift of yourself in whatever manner you are guided. The theme for today is, *cheer up someone*—the method is your choice!

Today's Nourishment:
I take time to brighten someone's day, make them feel special, and get their mind off any troubles. I look around and take notice of others moods, situations, and look for ways I can cheer up someone. My life has been blessed with love, caring, and happiness—I look for ways to share this. I feel good about giving to others

~175~
Make Amends

Learning to live a more spiritual life means you must earnestly seek the right way to go about living the kind of life that God has meant for you all along. You have been guided to release resentments, practice forgiveness, and rid yourself of guilt. In order to truly let go of those negative feelings and embrace a more spiritual life, you need to make amends to those you have hurt in the past.

Making amends is a powerful transaction which can deliver peace of mind and healing for all parties involved. If you have done harm to another in some way, whether emotionally, physically, or monetarily you need to make amends. Making amends is more than just telling that person, "I'm sorry." Making amends consist of righting a wrong, offering restitution, and work to heal the damage that was done.

Knowing that apologizing and making amends is never an easy task, because it makes you feel vulnerable, it is important to ask for help in making amends to those you have wronged. Today, seek out ways to make amends to those you have harmed. Find time to do and say what is necessary to heal any damage you have done—apologize, write letters, pay back debts. Ask God for the insight, courage, and dedication to make amends and bring goodness to others.

Today's Nourishment:
I seek out ways to make amend to those I harmed; emotionally, physically, or monetarily. I ask God for guidance, insight, and courage in this process. I follow the guidance given and find time to make amends.

~176~
See Others Through The Eyes Of Love

When you go out into the world, what do you see? More often than not, you see the faults of those you encounter. Although you try so hard not to judge, the human ego often gets in the way. You will always be troubled if you pay attention to the human ego because you will only notice the faults, imperfections, and bad behaviors of others.

When looking at the faults of others, you are in no way seeing others through the eyes of love as your Creator would. How can you? Your eyes are focused elsewhere, noticing faults and imperfections. Focusing on others faults soon leads to fears that goodness is a myth and that you are alone and unloved. The only way to break this pattern is to view yourself and others through the eyes of love.

If you want to experience a greater sense of love and feel more secure, stop judging others and seeing imperfections and faults—that's the human ego at work. Look past the faults and imperfections to that place where love and light reside. If you truly see others through the eyes of love, you will uncover a peacefulness that you'd long forgotten.

Today's Nourishment:
I look past faults, imperfections, bad behavior and focus on the love and light within others. I set aside my human ego and focus on viewing others through the eyes of love. The more I see it within others, the more I feel it within me!

Expect A Miracle

Miracles are regarded as *works of God*, related to life, intrigue and inspire, create hope, and point toward God's love. Your spiritual awareness requires faith, faith in the miraculous; for if you do not believe in miracles, you can not believe in the omnipresent God. There is no room for any middle ground, you must believe or doubt—accept or reject the concept of miracles.

How often do you expect miracles to occur? When was the last time you asked for a miracle in your own life? Your angels have come to you to say it is time to begin asking now! Miracles are composed of love, making it easy for the Universe to give. Miracles come from a God whose love for you knows no bounds or limitation. You are being reminded that you are never alone, help is always available and miracles can flow in abundance if you are open to receiving them. Do not be afraid to ask for a miracle—you are worthy of receiving as many miracles as you can think to ask for. Your prayers and requests for miracles are always heard and answered.

Is there something in your life right now that you want to see impacted by the energy of miracles? Write it down, what ever it might be and at the top put the words "I expect a miracle now". Carry this with you as you go about your day to day activities or place it where you can see it often. You may want to visualize the angels sending love and light to your request or see it being gathered up in angelic hands. The important thing is to remind yourself frequently ~~that this~~ that the loving angels are drawing to you all the elements of your requested miracle and all you need do is open your heart to receive it!

Today's Nourishment:
I become more aware of the small daily miracles around me—I feel joy and gratitude for these miracles, attracting even greater miracles to me. I feel a strong uplifting presence surrounding me as my miracle is being worked—I feel that anything is possible. I am grateful and say thank you as the miracles begin to unfold in my life.

~178~
Renew A Passion

Are you living in the land of lost dreams with no idea of what you want, or how to get what you want? Has your life become so busy that you have forgotten you ever had dreams, goals, or passions? Many times goals, dreams, and visions get lost in the daily activities of life and you feel as if you have lost your passion for life.

You have a great deal of passion within, but you have lost touch with it. It is there within you, waiting to be renewed. A good way to renew a passion is to notice how something makes you feel. When you do something, pay attention to how you feel—does it light you up or shut you down? Ask for help in identifying the things that light you up and for the courage to engage in those activities. This process requires you to be completely honest with yourself in what makes you feel good. Once you begin to engage in activities that make you feel warm and fulfilled, let go of the activities that leave you cold or empty. This can as simple as selecting a restaurant you want to go to for dinner or which movie you want to see. Over time, as you build your skill at staying in touch with your true desires, you will start to feel more alive and passionate about life.

When you are honest and real about the little day-to-day decisions you become connected to your overall sense of passion about life and your purpose here.

Today's Nourishment:
I reclaim my passion for life! I notice how each activity makes me feel and recognize that which makes me feel alive and passionate. I eliminate activities that leave me feeling cold and empty. I ask for help in identifying that which lights me up and the courage to engage in those activities.

~179~

Walk In Humility

Humility is the attitude of a person who knows they can not do it alone. A humble person will pray a lot and follow spiritual guidance, instead of leaving things to their own understanding. Being self-sufficient and having pride in yourself is important, being humble means being realistic about your own fallibility.

Today, walk in humility, embrace divine love, and follow the spiritual advice given to maneuver through life events. Think about certain situations you are dealing with right now. What can you learn from them? Have you asked for spiritual assistance in handling your circumstances today? If you will ask, follow the spiritual guidance and walk spiritually in tuned with your world, you will be transformed, strengthened, and energized.

Today's Nourishment:
I accept that, as a human, I can not do everything by myself, and have spiritual assistance readily available. I walk in humility and realize that I can not maneuver myself through life; I ask and follow spiritual advice given. I am transformed, strengthened, and energized!

Write Your Thoughts

There are benefits to writing your thoughts down on paper. You don't have to be witty and scandalous like *Bridget Jones*. In fact, you don't even have to write in full sentences, as long as you honestly write down your experiences, feelings and thoughts. Yes, you have a busy life—running to and from work, making dinner, taking care of others, or finishing up a term paper leaving you with no time for personal reflection. As the benefits to writing your thoughts outweigh the benefits of running non-stop, it is being suggested that you begin writing your thoughts, starting with this moment.

Writing your thoughts keeps you honest with yourself. Getting thoughts and experiences down on paper while they are still fresh in your mind helps avoid fabricating emotions after you had time to reconsider them. Part of being more spiritual aware is to learn and grow from your experiences. Developing a healthy self-awareness about your actions and reactions in specific situations is key point to learning. Writing down your thoughts in an uncensored manner will help you learn more about yourself; you will learn which *triggers* provoke anger, what makes you happy, what saddens you, and what motivates or challenges you. You can go back at any time and review your previous journal entries in order to recall specific events or to learn how to handle situations in a different, more effective way going forward.

Not only does writing your thoughts lead to growth and learning, writing your thoughts relieves stress. Writing provides a way for you to get any negative thoughts out of your system, therefore releasing any stress and frustration you may feel. Today, reap the benefits of writing your thoughts, grab a notebook and enjoy some much-needed *you* time!

Today's Nourishment:
As part of my spiritual growth and learning, I write my thoughts, feelings, and experiences. I review what I have written and develop a healthy self-awareness about myself, feelings, emotions, and experiences. I am happy and stress free as I write my thoughts.

Heal Your Heart

The emotional pain inflicted on us by others can be far worse than the physical wounds we experience. What is the right ointment for wounded hearts? Do you have a broken heart now, or have had your heart broken in the past? Do you have this huge gaping hole in your heart that was left by someone or circumstances? Have you felt that this hole can never be filled and that you will be left with the hollow in your heart forever?

There can be many reasons for a broken heart; the death of a loved one, divorce, loss of a job, loss of status, loss of health, betrayal by a friend, loss of a child and, yes, loss of your childhood.

Along with enormous blessings, everyone also experiences great sorrow in their life. Even though you have a pain in your heart, there is healing available. You have a host of spiritual teammates who are of the greatest healers of them all. God wants to heal all of your wounds—all you need to do is ask.

Seek God as your healer! Just like you tell a doctor your symptoms, tell God how much you were wounded and need God's healing touch. God hears the cries of the broken. God wants to reach down, take your hand, and walk you through your pain. It may take weeks, years, perhaps even a lifetime to close the wounds of your hearts completely. God will spend as much time and as many years as necessary to help you through it.

It takes time to heal. Every time you feel God's presence, every time you see God's intervention in your life, every time you reach out to someone else, every time God grants you blessings, the hole in your heart will get smaller and is being replaced with God's love.

Today's Nourishment:
I ask God to heal my broken heart and believe that God will. The hole in my heart is getting smaller over time with God's help—the hole in my heart is being replaced with God's love.

~182~
Go Easy On Yourself

Naturally you want to be happy, healthy, and prosperous but you must go easy on yourself in the pursuit of these things. By going too fast or judging yourself too harshly you cause unnecessary delays. When traveling your spiritual journey, speed and pain do not bring about progress—peace and tranquility does.

You are being asked to go easy on yourself today. When meeting your responsibilities and goals, treat yourself with gentleness and tender loving care. You respond to loving care and wise counsel and deserve to take your time today.

Your spiritual path is more enjoyable if you take time to enjoy all things along the way; people, situations, nature, events, and life in general. Enjoy this day!

Today's Nourishment:
I slow down and take time to notice all the details on my path. I treat myself with gentleness and tender loving care—I respect myself. I go easy on myself.

~183~
All Is Well

Everything is exactly as it should be at this exact moment, with blessings yet to be revealed. So many times a situation, interaction, or person appears in your life that at first is viewed as a challenge or problem. Many times this *problem* is actually an answer to one of your prayers that you have yet to realize.

As part of the human race, you do not see the big picture. When a situation appears to strike you with a lightening bolt and leave your world shattered this is the Universe's way of clearing out the old to make room for the new. During this time of change, relax in the knowing that all is well—as it should be in this moment. Ask for the patience and understanding to get you through the turbulent period and know that this change is for the better!

Today's Nourishment:
Everything's happening exactly as it's supposed to and for the better. I practice relaxation and deep breathing to release my anxiety and worry. I have a sense of knowing that all is well.

~184~
Invite Peace Into Your Day

To want peace or wish for peace sends a powerful prayer to the universe. Peace is more than just a kind notion—it is a powerful action. The word itself invokes a sense of security and calm. Therefore, to merely think of peace or speak the word aloud or to yourself silently begins to create the sense of peace you are looking for.

When you invite peace into your life, you deliver peace to yourself, your immediate circle, and the world as well. You will find that life flows more smoothly, situations will be easier, and people will be kinder. Through peace you will find yourself closer to the Divine One and closer to your higher self. Peace elevates all emotions to a higher realm.Peace transforms judgment and criticism into love, light—which brings about acceptance.

Today, invite peace. If you encounter a situation that is harsh, sharp, or explosive, visualize a soft light surrounding the situation and those involved. Visualize your home or office filled with the soft light. If your main mode of communication is the phone, imagine your phone has a soft glow of light around it and *peace filter* on the receiver—transforming all callers into representatives of peace. Embrace your own peaceful side. Anytime you feel angry, judgmental or critical, take a deep cleansing breath, invite peace and let peace wash over you.

Replace negative thoughts, actions or words with the proverbial olive branch. Display items of peace in your home, office, and car. Imagine a white dove perched on your shoulder or the shoulder of someone who is exhibiting anger, criticism and judgment. Use peace to help you through your day and you will be helping the world become a better place along the way.

Today's Nourishment:
I invite peace into my day, embracing my peaceful side, replacing negative thoughts with those of peace. I surround myself with peaceful items, people, and situations. I visualize a soft glowing light around all situations, people, and items; inviting peace into my day.

~185~
Eat A Healthy Diet

You are the co-creator of your health by following your inner guidance about your lifestyle habits. Health is everyone's natural state; it's how God created all men and women. The way you eat affects your health and well-being. When you eat a healthy diet, you bestow the gift of health onto your physical body. There is a connection between our spiritual health and our physical health. Get adequate rest and resolve spiritual and emotional stress. Reach out for support—eat a healthy diet and give yourself the gift of health!

You are being given inner nudges to pay attention to the way you eat, focus on eating healthier diet, drinking more water, and eliminating toxins from your body. Begin to reprogram your mind with knowledge of what is a healthy diet for you and how your body really works.

Today's Nourishment:
I bestow the gift of health on my physical body! I pay attention to what I eat, focusing on eating healthier foods, drinking more water, and purifying my body of toxins.

~186~
Get Adequate Sleep

Your prayers for more energy, increased well-being, and happier mood have been answered. Those inner prodding's you have been getting are not intended to nag or annoy, but to prompt you into taking action in developing a healthier life style. Not only should you eat a healthier diet, you are being urged to get adequate sleep.

Sleep is necessary for growth, healing, and avoiding anxiety. Are you happy and cheerful when you get too little sleep? Adequate sleep prevents and minimizes pain; it is essential for healthy living. Things that need doing during sleep have had a chance. You need dreams. If you don't dream, you go crazy. Not to sleep is a form of torture. You should avoid torturing yourself with sleep deprivation. A regular sleep-wake cycle is the way to go. Catching an hour here and four hours there of sleep is not the same as sleeping overnight. When darkness falls, the rest of the animal world gets off their feet and go to sleep, and that's what you need too!

Today's Nourishment:
As part of my commitment to a healthy lifestyle, I get adequate sleep. I allow myself to sleep at least eight hours during the night. I awake feeling fresh, recharged, and ready to tackle my day!

Routine Medical Checkups

When you take excellent care of your body, your outlook and self-esteem naturally blossom. Heaven has a host of healers that practice preventive and curative medicine in the form of Divine intervention and guidance. When you are sick or in pain, you have angels waiting to swoop down and surround you with loving healing light and you instantly are healed.

Sometimes your angles will give you inner guidance showing how you can help with your own healing with preventive care. Open your heart to healing and let yourself be guided to the healers who do their best to help you. As you take more responsibility for your own healing, seek routine medical checkups. Routine medical checkups can find treatable problems early. For many medical problems, early treatment can help prevent more serious complications. You are being urged today, to take care of your physical body and seek routine medical check-ups.

Today's Nourishment:
I open my heart to be guided to the healers and schedule a routine medical checkup. I accept more responsibility for my own healing, and listen to my inner guidance and do what is best for my health and vitality.

~188~
Go Outside

You've probably felt the sense of spirituality that comes from the outdoors—the awe and wonder at the enormity, intricacy, and beauty of the natural world. Many find their first personal sense of spirituality in the outdoors. A sense of place in the universe and of being a part of something greater than oneself is a gift everyone should have the opportunity to experience.

You are being gently prodded to go outside, breathe in some clean fresh air, and soak up some of nature's sights, smells, and sounds. Spending time outside relieves stress, renews your spirit, and allows you to gain new creative ideas. Go outside today, even if it takes an effort or rescheduling of your day—go outside, smell nature, breathe fresh air, and renew your spirit!

Today's Nourishment:
I spend time outside today, breathe fresh air, bask in the sunlight, and drink in nature. I release all my stresses, worries, and concerns to the wind as I savor the sweet beauty surrounding me in my world.

Breathe Fresh Air

Right now in this moment, take a deep cleansing breath, hold it, and slowly exhale releasing all the tensions, worries, and anxieties. Do this several times until you feel relaxed and calm. When you face stressful situations, become upset or angry, or experience fear you tend to hold your breath. Breathing is a necessary component to life and you are being reminder that you need to invigorate yourself with deep cleansing breaths of fresh air. Write a note to yourself to breathe fresh air—to open your airways and allow fresh pure air to flow through your system.

Plan your outings to places that have lots of fresh air—near water, such as beaches, lakes, ocean, or river front. When taking your evening walk, practice deep breathing exercises until breathing deeply feels natural. Remember you are the co-creator of your health, breathing is essential to living, breathing fresh air is important to your health.

Today's Nourishment:
Throughout the day I step outside and take deep cleansing breaths; breathing in fresh air, holding it in my lungs, and slowly exhale—ridding myself of anxieties, stress, and worries. I take outings to place where fresh air is plentiful; any place near water. I remind myself to breathe fresh air today—everyday!

~190~
Relieve Stress

Your spiritual strength can help you get through even the most stressful times in life. Relieve stress by handing your worries over to a higher power. Your faith and trust in God and His angels can help you cope with events that cause grief and loss, even the death of a loved one.

Let your faith and spiritual commitment be apart of your stress management plan. Remember that you are never alone; you do not have to shoulder burdens alone. You have a host of angels that work for the omnipresent God—relieve your stress by releasing them to God. Lighten your load and lay your burdens down, give all your stresses, worries, concerns, and anxieties over to a power greater than yours.

Today, step outside, take a deep cleansing breathe, gather all your stresses and worries; exhale slowly, releasing all your stresses and worries into the universe. Imagine your stresses surrounded in a pink bubble floating upward toward Heaven. Smile and wave, *goodbye*—they are in God's realm—let it go.

Today's Nourishment:
I relieve stress by surrendering my stress over to a power greater than my own. I acknowledge that I am not alone; God is waiting for me to release my stress to Him. I am stress free and I feel at peace.

~191~
Gaze At The Stars

A warm summer night, a clear sky, relaxing in the hammock; the heavens above unfold in thousands of sparkling small bits of light and one large in complete circle. Star gazing, and planet watching, can be a very rewarding relaxing experience—especially if you allow yourself to be transcended in time and space.

Become a member of the sky-watching club. All you need are two eyes and an unobstructed spot to look up. Today, seek out a place away from the city lights and polluted air; look toward the heavens above you and watch the sky sparkle and shine with billions and billions of points of light from the Milky Way and beyond. Let your mind take you back to ancient times and truly see for the first times the awesome spectacle that greeted shepherds and sailors every night.

Today's Nourishment:
I spend time gazing at the stars tonight, allowing myself to be transcended in time and space, watching billions of sparkling bits of lights. I enjoy the summer and all other seasons by looking up, every chance I get. I feel relaxed and at peace—I deserve to gaze at the stars

~192~
Seek Spiritual Understanding

As you live spiritually in tuned with your world you open up to new ways of viewing life; taking your spiritual understanding to the next level. Now is the time to keep your mind open, let go of illusions, and eliminate closed mindedness. Seeking out spiritual understanding requires the use of all your senses; sight, sound, taste, smell, touch, as well as the inner sense of knowing. Pay attention to information that comes to you—in threes. These *signs* may appear in the form of a dream, a song, and everyday item, or delivered by human messenger.

Be reminded that your increased awareness may cause shifts in your life and career goals; simply follow your inner guidance and you will know that you are on the right path. Spiritual understanding will change your life—your thinking will expand in ways that defy normal logic. To quench your thirst for spiritual understanding, ask to be visited in your dreams. Travel with the angels while in a dream state to places where you learn spiritual truths and secrets. Ask that you be able to remember upon awaking these places you traveled, truths and secrets learned.

Today's Nourishment:
I am ready to take my spiritual understanding to the next level. I ask that for angelic visits to my dreams; travel to places to uncover spiritual truths and secrets. I am blessed with a sense of knowing and living spiritually in tuned with my world.

~193~
Open Your Heart To Trust

Open your heart and mind to trusting the goodness of life—learn to trust yourself, learn to trust life and to trust other people. Release negative, cynical, or destructive thinking in exchange for positive and believe that your highest good and greatest joy is being fulfilled. You have been given the essential love of spirit you need in order to trust and be truly life-affirming.

To be able to trust is an essential ingredient of happiness and ease; otherwise your energy is wasted on suspension, doubts, and fears. Trust gives you the courage to move forward with life and allows you to take risk. Opening your heart to trust is a vital component to your spiritual growth. Ask the angels of trust to open your heart to trust, helping you learn to value each experience and trust your perceptions. By listening to your inner Divine guidance will you develop the trust you need to progress through life and live more spiritually in tuned.

Today's Nourishment:
I trust in myself and in God, knowing that I am protected and safe from harm. My heart is open to trust and I trust in life and all it has to offer.

~194~
Give From Your Heart

Service to others is a way you can participate in your community and make a real and lasting contribution to the well-being of others. These acts of service may take the form of participating in government or civic work, warm gestures of caring from volunteer work, personal advisors or therapists. Simple acts of caring by offering personal favors or helping those who are in need; any form of assistance to another is an act of service. Giving from your heart and being of service to others help make this earth a more peaceful and fruitful place.

You are being urged to make a difference in others' live today. Ask for assistance in finding the inner and outer resources to give in the best way you are able. Help a young person find their way, spend time with the elderly, serve the homeless a meal, offer a listening ear or strong shoulder to a wounded heart. Those who willingly give from the heart and give their lives to the service of helping others, appreciate the spiritual function of service.

Today's Nourishment:
God blesses me with the energy, resources, and inspiration to be of service to others. Let me contribute to my community, give from my heart, and make this place a happier and easier place to live in.

~195~

Take Inventory of Life

To grow spiritually you must be willing to make necessary changes, eliminate what no longer serves your highest good, and to mend that which is unbalanced. In order to do that, you need to make periodical life reviews; today is such a day!

Today you are being guided to take inventory of your life. You have been blessed with the strength, courage, compassion, and sense of humor to take an honest look at your life. Spend some time taking stock of your life's travels, what lessons have been learned, and notice any patterns in your life that no longer serve your highest good. Work with your spiritual teammates to help you take inventory of your life, release such patterns, and be grateful for the blessings in your life.

Today's Nourishment:
I take time alone and work with my spiritual teammates to take an honest look at my life. I see that which I have traveled, lessons learned, and recognize those patterns I need to release for my highest good. I am grateful for the blessings in my life.

~196~
Heal The Unbalanced

The greatest art in spiritual life is finding balance in your daily life. Even with the responsibilities and duties to be performed as part of your daily life, you still have an obligation to your spiritual path. Add helping others and alone time into the melting pot of life and many times the bowl of life is unbalanced!

The demands of living and joys of living spiritually do not conflict unless you believe them to be so. The demands and joys can intersect and blend perfectly together, similar to a sunrise leads to sunset. The first step in healing the unbalanced is to have a positive attitude that the two can be blended; call upon God for help in healing the unbalanced and blending the daily demands with your spiritual life.

Today's Nourishment:
My spiritual life is blended with the demands of my daily life and is perfectly balanced. I have time for my responsibilities and duties and meet my obligations for my spiritual path. I enjoy all parts of my life—meeting responsibilities and devote time to myself for fun, rest, and exercise.

Guide Others

As you have already traveled down a certain spiritual path, you can teach others how to avoid the pitfalls and roadblocks. Since you have raised you own spiritual energy, you may feel a desire to retreat from the cares and responsibility of the world. You are being urged today, to guide others along their spiritual path.

The choice to enter into a relationship as a guide, mentor, teacher, or coach is a two-way street and rests in large part with you. Those that need guidance may not be far enough down their spiritual path to realize that they need an earth guide. But, you having already traveled the path know the path well and can help a great deal to speed the raising of their level of consciousness.

As a guide you are to enlighten, inform, share your experiences, and help remove that which stands in the way of spiritual knowledge. Guiding others is not about trying to convince or convert another to your new way of thinking. The best way to guide others is to be peaceful and happy, in that way, you are a walking advertisement for the benefits of living the right spiritual path. As others notice your peacefulness, they will soon ask you about the secret to your happiness.

Today's Nourishment:
I am peaceful, happy, and content with my life and my spiritual path; let those who are curious be place on my path. I am grateful for my past experiences, as they have led me down my path. I share my experiences with others, enlighten, and show others how to avoid pitfalls and roadblocks.

~198~
Seek Wisdom

Today's focus is on becoming receptive to the wisdom of God—finding wisdom in your life, and seeking wisdom in all your experiences. When you give yourself the chance to reflect, analyze, and filter your personal experiences you find wisdom. With this you can progress along your path, enrich your understanding, and deepen your spirituality.

Wisdom is an internal awareness which is projected on to the world around you so that you can live in peace. You need wisdom for your growth and spiritual development—without it you are at the effects of the physical world and can easily lose you integrity and personal identity. Seek the help of God to guide you to the wisdom within yourself. From this place within you can make healthy choices for your well-being and happiness.

Pray to be shown how to make sense of your experiences here on earth and how to find the meaning for yourself. Pray for wisdom for your healing and for the healing of this planet—through seeking wisdom you are able to find happiness and a sense of peace.

Today's Nourishment:
I receive the wisdom of God—seek out wisdom in my life and all my experiences here on earth. I ask God to guide me to the wisdom within myself and to make the right choices for myself.

~199~
Release Wanting

How much do you really trust that a miracle will happen after you have asked for something and have strong feelings about the outcome? After you have asked for the miracle, and believe that it will happen, how do you let it go? Your angels want you to know that you do not have to let go of the miracle you asked for, just the wanting of the outcome. You are to maintain passionate for your miracle, but as far as wanting an outcome—let it go!

Sound confusing? It's not really. Not when you look at wanting as a barrier to the results you requested. If you release the wanting, you are releasing the barrier that stands between the sender and the receiver. To want is to infer that something is missing—it creates fear. Your attention is focused on what you do not have instead on what you desire. You need to focus on the positive outcome you are seeking. When you say you want something you are pointing out that you do not have it! It's like seeing the illness and not the cure.

Find time today to sit quietly, think gently of your worries, fears, and the wanting. Find that place within that contains your fear—the pit of your stomach, your neck, or your heart. Feel the tension in your body as you think about your fears, worries, and wanting. Take a deep breath; slowly exhale relaxing the tension in your body that hold your fears, worries, and wanting. Do this several times until you feel the tension, fear, and wanting depart your body. You will feel lighter, calmer, and find that you have released the wanting along with the fear and worries.

Today's Nourishment:
I release the outcome of every act and event. I do not always know what is best, but I trust that God does and I start this day turning everything over to Him. God.

Volunteer

Volunteering gives you an opportunity to change people's lives, including your own. If you're feeling frustrated or overwhelmed by the news of a disaster, volunteering to help can be a great way to cope. If you'd like to support a cause but can't afford to donate money, you can donate your time instead. Helping others in need is such an important part of your spiritual path in life; helping others is a way of giving back and showing your gratitude for all your blessings.

You can choose what really interests you and who or what organization is most deserving of your time. If you like animals, help out at a local animal shelter. Most shelters depend on volunteers to keep the cats and dogs happy and well exercised. And when you're walking rescued dogs, it's not just the pooches that get a workout — you benefit too! If you like children, there are a multitude of volunteering opportunities from being a Big Brother or Big Sister to helping out in an after-school sports program.

You can serve food at a homeless shelter, donate to a food pantry, volunteer to spend time at a retirement community, help out at your church, or take part in a community cleanup day—the possibilities are endless!

Today's Nourishment:
I release the outcome of every act and event. I do not always know what is best, but I trust that God does and I start this day turning everything over to ~~Him~~. God .

~201~
Help A Child In Need

Each day, life sends many gifts and blessings to you. God loves you and has blessed you; and He wants you to help others. You can share these blessing with a child in need. You can help a child whom is orphaned, abandoned, ill, abused, neglected, or whose parents are not able to provide more than the bare necessities of life. Every child deserves to have their basic needs met, and live in a safe, secure, nurturing, and loving environment.

Helping a child in need is about giving something back and discovering the joy that comes from blessing someone else's life—especially the life of a child! Notice the many ways that you can make a difference in the life of a child in need. Helping provide children in need with a safe and nurturing environment can be accomplished through sponsorship, fostering, donations, volunteering, tutoring, or becoming a mentor to the child. Work with your spiritual team to find ways that you can make a difference in the life of a needy child. What you do today in the life of a child will make a difference in that child's future.

Today's Nourishment:
I am grateful for the gifts and blessing that life shares with me—I share my blessings with a child in need. I give of myself, my time, and resources to make a difference in the life of a child in need. The universe is very generous with me; I am very generous with others!

~202~
Open Your Heart

As you open your heart to be fully present in your life, for yourself and others, you call forth the miracles of healing, love, and tenderness. The benefits are immeasurable. You were made by a caring loving Creator; made out of miraculous love. By opening your heart to love, you encounter God.

If you have closed yourself off to protect yourself against emotional pain, ask for help in opening your heart in such a way that feels safe and secure. Ask your spiritual teammates to join you in removing the brick wall you have built around your heart; brick by brick. Replace the brick wall with a fence; a white picket fence will work. Within this fence include a gate that can be opened when you feel safe enough to let love in. Ask protection angels to stand guard at the gates, granting entry to only the most trustworthy relationships and situations. Work with these angels, letting them know how you are feeling and your desires. Keep in mind, angels are there to help you in all ways; but they can not act on your desires without your consent.

Today's Nourishment:
I open my heart to receive God's love. I replace the brick wall with a fence, allowing protection angels access to the gate, trusting that only the most worthy, trustworthy relationships and situations gain entry.

Resolve Conflicts With Love

Conflict can arise whenever people, close friends, family members, co-workers, or romantic partners disagree about their perceptions, desires, ideas, or values. These differences can range from the trivial, such as who last took out the garbage, to more significant disagreements which strike at the heart of our most fundamental beliefs and concerns. Regardless of the substance of the disagreement, though, conflict often arouses strong feelings.

Conflicts can lead to you and others feeling angry, hurt, or vulnerable. When you are in the midst of conflict and on the verge of losing control of your emotions, remember that love is always in your midst. Recall that you are always surrounded by love, from your Creator and his angels. Your emotions can be used as a tool for increasing conflict and fear or love depending on your decision.

It is not your role to change someone or justify yourself—resolve conflicts with love, compassion, and a sense of caring. Using love's approach to resolve conflict is to always remember the Divine nature of each person and relationship. Let go of any attempts to control how the situation will work out—focus instead on that everything has already been worked out for the highest good of all involved. This sense of knowing that all is as it should be, will allow you to enjoy your day regardless of the circumstances.

Today's Nourishment:
Regardless of the circumstances or situation, I remember that love is always in my midst. It is not my role to change another or to justify myself. I resolve conflicts with love, compassion, and a sense of caring.

~204~
Say, I Love You

Think about to the last time you said the words, "I love you", to a loved one. Was it last night, this morning, or perhaps last week? Often, we can remember to say "I love you" and show it during special occasions or crisis times. But more often when you become comfortable and feel close to someone; spouse, family member, sibling, or even close friend, those words aren't spoken as often as they should.

Everyone enjoys hearing that they are loved and appreciated. When you express how much you care or love someone, their soul shines with happiness, illuminating yourself as well! One of the simplest things you can do to show someone that you care is to say, "I love you", and say it often. Do not wait for a special occasion or for a crisis moment to arrive—start today, say it, sing it, write it down on a slip of paper; it really doesn't matter as long as you say it!

Today's Nourishment:
I tell my spouse, family, siblings, and friends, I love you. I give hugs, smiles, and behave in loving nurturing ways to express my love for others. Love is a powerful healing light that radiates from my heart to others.

~205~
Keep Open Mind

Walking a spiritual path requires learning, studying, and keeping an open mind. You are being guided now to keep your mind open and enjoy this time of spiritual growth. By keeping your mind open to new ideas, concepts, and spiritual gifts you will grow by leaps and bounds—spiritually, intellectually, and emotionally!

You are on the path of rediscovering the beauty of humility - that wonderful feeling of being just a speck in the universe, when you realize that there is infinitely more that you don't know compared to what you do know. You will learn how to embrace the inspiration of this chronic condition, and will drive you me forward on your new path. Keeping an open-minded attitude will bring enlightenment to your life and certainly make it extremely interesting!

Today's Nourishment:
I keep my mind open to the wonderful exciting information I am learning on my spiritual quest. I am open to new ideas, concepts, and spiritual gifts—rediscovering my life's purpose and seeking enlightenment.

~206~
Share Your Ideas

Do you have thoughts, ideas, or spiritual insights you wish to share with others? You are a spiritual teacher as well as an avid learner. Learning and teaching go hand-in-hand—as information comes to you, you in turn should share your ideas with others. Share thoughts and ideas that awaken your passion with others.

The more you share with others, the more lessons are reinforced within you. Be open to sharing new ideas; trust in your teaching abilities as you are more in tuned with the Divine. Know that it is safe for you to share your ideas and to teach others.

Today's Nourishment:
It is safe for me to share my ideas, thoughts, and spiritual lessons with others. The information and spiritual insights given to me awaken passions within—I share these ideas with others.

~207~
Embrace Victory

Your unwavering faith has resulted in your prayers being heard and answered. This is a time of celebration, rejoicing, and embracing victory! Focus on this moment and allow yourself the pleasure of savoring the flavor of victory—your reward for keeping the faith.

You are deserving of this time of victory! God wants you to live in victory. He wants you to live a passionate spiritual life every day—not in defeat or just going through the motions. As a spiritual being, you choose whether to walk in victory or in despair. Living a passionate spiritual life isn't automatic. You must open you heart and arms to receive all His blessings and then embrace the victory of answered prayers!

Today's Nourishment:
This is a time of celebration! Today I embrace victory knowing that my prayers have been heard and answered. God wants me to live in victory—He wants me to live a passionate spiritual life!

~208~
Hello From Heaven

Have you thought about Heaven lately? Wonder what it's like? Worried about your loved ones that passed? Your loved ones in Heaven are doing just fine—let go of any worries and anxieties. Keep in mind that your loved ones are in a place that has no tears, no pain, no sorrow—they now reside in a place of ultimate joy!

Your loved ones aren't far away; in fact, they are quite near. Heaven is another place for our souls to visit. Heaven is a beautiful place—a vast wonderland of activities. In your quiet moments, envision the most beautiful upscale vacation spot with all that nature has to offer, with fascinating possibilities, new sights, sounds, and new sensations. That is Heaven—where your loved ones now reside. Human beings were meant to be explorers, regardless of the age—in heaven, your loved ones get that chance. There is so much to see and investigate, so much to do and an endless amount of time to do it in. Your loved ones are busy going on sightseeing excursions to an incredible variety of cities, planets, galaxies, and beyond!.

Know that your loved ones are happy, free of all suffering, and want you to know that they are having a great time. They may visit you from time to time, simply to reassure you that they are, *okay*. You may notice dream visits from deceased loved ones simply to let you know that they are alright and help you to be peaceful.

> Today's Nourishment:
> *I let go of worries and anxieties over my deceased loved ones—they are doing fine in their new home. My loved ones are in the most beautiful upscale vacation spot I can imagine and having the most wonderful adventures. I ask the angels to bring me reassurance and messages from my loved ones in Heaven.*

Clear Your Space

Clearing your space is a powerful way to remove unwanted energy from your space and to fill your space with vibrant, positive, uplifting energy. The idea of purifying and blessing an area through a ritual clearing of the space is as old as time. In recent years, many have become more aware of the connection between their own energy and that of their space—just look at how popularity of Feng Shui has spread!

Space clearing is different from just cleaning up your house. This process involves focused awareness and clear intention—you are honoring your space, life, and family. Ask for spiritual guidance and assistance to be with you throughout this process. Keep in mind that simple and heartfelt clearings are more effective than elaborate rituals from which you feel detached. Joy and celebration are highly positive emotional vibrations that bring vitality to your space; so have fun while you are clearing your space.

There are many different ways to do clear your space. There are many books available on this subject or you may prefer to make up a ceremony of your own. Ideally, your home should be clean and tidy before you begin. Fresh flowers and/or incense bring positive energy into your space. Often a space clearing will begin with the lighting of incense and placing fresh flowers into a vase. Sound vibrations help to loosen stale, stuck energy. Harmonious sounds bring a lively, uplifting energy to your space after the old, negative energy has been cleared out. Put on a CD of beautiful instrumental music, or play a flute, guitar, or other instrument as you walk through your entire house. End your space clearing ceremony with a blessing—it can be as simple as a heartfelt prayer of gratitude on behalf of your home and family.

Today's Nourishment:
I plan my space clearing ceremony for my home—removing unwanted energies from my space and filling it with positive, upbeat, and clean energy. I honor my home, office, life, and family by blessing and purifying my space.

~210~
Use Feng Shui

The term Feng Shui means literally, *wind and water,* the forces that shape the landscape. It refers to a set of rules in Chinese philosophy that govern spatial arrangement and orientation in relation to patterns related to the Universal Laws, as expressed in the natural world. Feng Shui draws from this knowledge in order to produce environments that promote wealth, health, love, and happiness.

Feng Shui proposes arranging the space in order to reproduce the signs of nature that we recognize as life-nurturing and safe. How you react emotionally to a place is as important as proper architectural or interior design. It is essential that you feel comfortable and safe in your home or workplace in order to create environments where you can be happier, healthier, more prosperous and free.

Today, hold the intention of practicing Feng Shui and arrange your space according to the rules; making your life more harmonious, happier, and more prosperous.

Today's Nourishment:
I create a home and work environment where I feel safe, in greater harmony with my surroundings and in greater control of my space. I feel more relaxed. I have better relationships. I am more productive!

~211~
Reconcile With Your Past

Today, you awake to the new dawn of awareness, starting your day fresh, living magically in the present moment. It is now time to release painful traumas that distort your view of life. You are being guided to clear out the old and useless baggage of your past. Reconcile with your past and release the sorrows, hurts, and resentments which congest your energy and weigh you down. You need your energy and vitality to live in the present—in the here and now!

You can ask the angels to assist you in the process of letting go of the past and redeem your spirit. By releasing the past you are releasing the energy you have invested in the emotions spent on past people and events. By holding onto sorrow, bereavement, grievances, or resentments you are destroying the energy and enjoyment of the now. Pray for guidance to help you accept the past as it was and release the negative ideas of how it should have been. Ask that the lessons from the past help you develop into a more healthy-minded adult.

Reconciliation with your past is not about changing something which cannot be changed. It is about transforming your view of how the past was and how you can empower yourself now by making positive choices.

Today's Nourishment:
I release the painful trauma, old and useless baggage, of my past. I am no longer a prisoner of my past—I have reconciled with my past and release the sorrows, hurts, and resentments. My energy is cleared and I am empowered to making positive choices for today!

~212~
Use Your God-given Power

Are you ready to transform your life? Are you ready to acknowledge your magnificence instead of focusing on your limitations? Remember you were created in the image and likeness of your Creator; therefore, you have all of the power of your Creator within you! The power of Divine love, wisdom, knowledge, and spiritual powers are readily available to you.

You are entering a time when human consciousness is shifting; the veil that has kept you from remembering who you really are and from accessing your God-given powers is lifting. You have the spiritual power to see, hear, and feel Divine guidance. You have the emotional power to feel compassionate and a sense of caring for others. You have the mental power to tap into the universal wisdom of knowledge and information. This is the time to use your God-given powers and seek out spiritual knowledge—undercover spiritual truths and to shine with the radiant Divine love.

Let go of any fears, doubts, or worries connected with being a powerful spiritual person—you have an unlimited source of spiritual beings willing to relieve you of these fears. These spiritual beings are quiet, behind-the-scenes, and beautiful aspect of your power. Allow yourself to express this power—it is safe for you to use your God-given power.

Today's Nourishment:
Created in the image and likeness of the Creator, I have all the powers of God Him within me. I have the power of Divine love, wisdom, knowledge, and spiritual powers available to me. It is safe for me to explore and use these powers—I use my God-given powers with love.

~213~
Have Spiritual Courage

Living a more spiritual life goes beyond simply practicing *spirituality*. Spirituality is feeling one with the Divine and listening to what is revealed. To live spiritually in tuned with your world involves enhancing your human capacity for empathy and love, striving for justice, feeding your hunger for beauty, and fulfilling your yearning to create. Simply stated, living spiritually is putting love into action. This requires spiritual courage. Now is the time to trust your impulse to reach out to others, to help others, to challenge injustice—not out of hate, but out of love.

Recall others who have had this type of courage, those who helped Jews hide, even though it meant risking their lives and the lives of their families. Often when they were asked afterwards why they did it, they simply answered that they had to. This is true spirituality, listening to that inner voice to be caring rather than cruel. All God's children here on earth are born with that voice, that it is part of the essence of what makes us human. Babies, newborns, cry when they hear another baby's cry. They are born with empathy, with the capacity to feel with another.

You are being encouraged to have spiritual courage and act upon your impulses, stand up for your beliefs, challenge injustices, and become a warrior of light. Be a role model for others the most important form of spiritual teaching. Do not be afraid, be courageous, you are protected by your angels—ask and they will give you confidence and spiritual courage.

Today's Nourishment:
I am a lioness of God—infused with bravery, courage, focus, and action! I trust my impulses and reach out to others; putting love into action, helping others, and challenge injustices out of love. It is safe for me to practice spiritual courage as I am a child of God—protected and guided with Divine power.

~214~
Stand Up For Your Beliefs

Today, everywhere you look people think that it is the new hip thing to be called Agnostic and to deny a power greater than themselves. However, since almost everyone is doing it, why not fight that rebellion and stand up for your faith? Why not go to the top of a mountain and look all around at all the beautiful things God has created and scream it out? Yell that you believe in a power greater than yourself; your Creator, angels, guides, or the power of the universe!

Show everybody that you are a spiriutal being with a purpose here on earth! Standing up for your beliefs requires acting upon your convictions even if other disagree with your view. This does not mean to force your beliefs upon others or attempt to convert others to your way of thinking. Practice your beliefs openly, honestly, and without fear. For example, if you truly believe in the power of God and His angelic beings, do not be afraid to speak of your relationship with your God and the angels. Embrace your new spiritual path with your whole heart—being a role model to others!

This is a time for a multitude of spriutal awakenings everywhere; be that gentle voice that stirs the sleeping. You are being encourage tolive today within your spiritual truths—stand up for your beliefs and honor that which you know to be true.

Today's Nourishment:
I believe in a power greater than myself—I am a child of God, a spiritual being living here on Earth. I stand up for my beliefs in God and His angels; embracing my spirituality and being a role model.

Trust Divine Guidance

Does it seem that your prayers go unanswered? You ask for spiritual help or guidance, but nothing seems to happen? Have you been praying to meet your soul mate and he/she has yet to appear? Or perhaps praying to be reunited with that special one? Improve your finances? Regardless of what you pray for, most often when a prayer goes unanswered it is because divine guidance hasn't been noticed or is being ignored.

Human beings often expect one specific answer to their prayers and may not notice that which differs from expectations. For example, you pray to meet your soul mate, and received divine guidance to attend a spiritual retreat. However, you do not go to the spiritual retreat because you would rather attend friend's cookout where singles may be attending. By choosing to attend the cookout perhaps you missed out on meeting your soul mate. Now you assume that your prayers were not answered—you didn't listen to what was being revealed.

Some people don't trust the guidance being given. For instance, you pray for your finances to improve or become debt-free, you get a strong urge to start your own business or change careers. However, going from the known to the unknown is too intimidating orscary—so the strong urge is ignored.

The message for today is to listen todivine guidance; that inner voice, inner knowledge, or sense of knowing. You have thoseinnate abilities; sense of knowing, inner voice, gut feelings, even flashes of mental images! Be open to receiving and listening to divineguidance and you will see that your prayers have been answered!

> Today's Nourishment:
> *I listen to divine guidance received in all forms; inner voice, knowledge, or sense of knowing. I can always count on the support of the angels and my Creator. My prayers have been heard and answered—now I listen for instructions!*

~216~
Keep Yourself Grounded

You have been blessed with angels that work with you to give you guidance in all aspects of *grounding* yourself in material reality. Your senses have been blessed so that you may experience the world around you in and through your physical body. By using the earth element to ground your spirituality in the world of form, you have the ability to manifest your wishes, dreams, and desires. Shifting from creative thought to physical form requires the use of all your senses—grounding your energy gives structure, stability, and security.

Ask your angels to bless your senses and help you realize your dreams. The angels can bless your body so that you are freed from stress, tension, and worries—when you are well in your body you release good energy. Good energy heals yourself and those around you. This is how you make earth a better place to live; by actually being happy!

You are being encouraged to listen to your body and treat yourself respectfully—look after yourself by feeding, clothing, resting, and exercising your body. Ask for help with releasing abusive habits which weaken your body and release negative energies. Energize your senses by eating healthy foods; get sufficient rest, plenty of exercise, and courage to be yourself. Keep yourself grounded on the earth plane by expressing and sharing yourself.

Today's Nourishment:
I am inspired to look after my planet and the needs of my physical body with care and awareness. I ask for angelic help to feel well in my body, awaken my senses, and earth my energy so that I am able to manifest my gifts.

~217~
Know You Are Safe

As you are never alone; you are surrounded by angelic beings sent here by God, know that you are safe. Know that your future is filled with many fulfilling, happy, and meaningful moments. You will be given several paths from which to choose, experiences that invoke lessons and growth. You have the ability to guide yourself to the happiest and most fulfilling path—stay in communication with the Divine and those angelic beings seated by your side. Grant permission to be assisted and guided along your path. Know that you are safe—you have an infinite number of spiritual beings watching your back!

Breathe easy, relax, and release your worries and concerns—know you are safe.

Today's Nourishment:
I breathe deeply, relaxing my entire body and release all my worries— knowing I am safe. I am completely protected by the Divine and angelic beings at this moment and for all the days that follow today. Everything is as it should be and will turn out perfectly. I am watched over and protected—I am safe!

~218~
Bond With A Child

Do you know a child who is lonely or unloved? Know a child that needs extra nourishment, gentleness, and care? Perhaps a new mother is feeling overwhelmed and needs an extra pair of hands to assist with her newborn. There are angels that have been assigned the task of watching over all new beginnings, including new life. These angels watch over all new souls incarnated to earth; helping mothers and babies at births. Angelic beings protect and guide all those who help manage young babies and children. Every new baby and young person is protective, blessed, and cherished by angelic beings.

You are being guided today to assist these angelic beings—help nurture and sustain what is young so that it can grow strong, and resilient. Ask for guidance and protection for the young and tender in your life; blessing for families, friends, co-workers, and those we come in contact with daily. Touch the life of a child that is lonely, unloved, or needs special attention. Create a bond with a child—help heal deep wounds where there has been no love or even abuse. Work with a child to help them release pain, sorrow, and upsetting memories and help the heart to heal. Become an earth angel and give extra nourishment, gentleness, and care to a child. By helping a child to heal, you find healing for your own spirit.

Today's Nourishment:
I am a protective earth angel and watch over a child. I stand guard and protect all that is new and young in life—bonding with a child. I provide nurturing, healing, caring, love and caring to a child. By helping a child to heal my spirit heals and soars!

Express Your Feelings

Your feelings are a strong and elemental force which can unleash great waves of emotion. Repressed feelings can ferment, fester, and create a pull on your unconscious, demanding to be released and resolved. When you are open to expressing your feelings, emotions flow like water in a riverbed. You are being urged today to seek a balance in which you are aware of your feelings and no longer afraid to express them.

Your angels want you to feel what is true for you rather than suppress your feelings. Repressed anger, sadness, or anxiety will eventually draw you into a situation that, like a magnet, will pull your feelings to the surface. Ask your angels to help and guide you to experience the richness of your feelings and to find legitimate and creative outlets for them. You will be blessed each time you allow your feelings honest acknowledgement. You will be blessed with the ability to transform negative feelings into creative outlets—paint, sing, or dance out your feelings so that they do not stay bottled up inside festering into a gaping wound! Allow yourself to express your feelings and connect with the depths of your spirit!

Today's Nourishment:
I accept that I have feelings, open my heart, and express my feelings. I feel safe in expressing myself and my innermost feelings. I ask for angelic assistance and support I need to experience my feelings and balance my emotions.

Spread Your Wings

This is not a time to fear, don't hold back right now—the timing is perfect and you are ready to soar! Going from the known to the unknown is scary, but it is now time to transform that fear into excitement. Instead of being prodded and pushed past your comfort zone ask to be infused with eagerness—put on your Nike's, go to the starting line, and wait for the sound of the starting pistol! Be the first one to leap from the starting line! Sprint past your comfort zone and into the unknown—you are ready to fly high!

Release any fears you have to your angels. You are being called to welcome new opportunities, turn challenges into victories, and know that it is safe to listen to your heart and follow your dreams. Stay focused on love, for self and others, service, and spirit. Avoid skeptics or nay-sayers today. Surround yourself with positive, uplifting energies, and energizing persons. Inspire others today with your tales of victories and blessings; large and small!

Today's Nourishment:
Today I spread my wings, take flight, and soar to unknown territories! I am not afraid as I am surrounded by spiritual warriors who protect and guide me. They will not let me crash and burn; they are my navigators, co-pilots, and air traffic controllers—they are my angels!

~221~
Nurture A Child

One of the duties of assisting angelic beings with children is to help nurture and care for a child. This can be your child, a child in need, or your own inner child. All that is young and new requires nourishment and nurturing so that it can grow and become strong enough to survive. One of the most important qualities of embracing your spirituality is by service to others. Specifically for this day, you are to be of service in the form of nurturing a child.

Nurturing means showing a child they are loved and accepted so that they can grow and develop. Unconditional love is the key to nurturing a child, with help from your Creator, you can nurture a child, help them heal, and provide spiritual nourishment through love. There are many ways you can nurture a child and help them to heal, feel loved and be happy. Children have a way of connecting with other children in a way that many adults don't understand or know about. Sometimes just a glance or eye contact lets you know things that might take a thousand words to communicate.

One reason it's important for you to nurture a child is because you are also helping your own inner child in the process. You are teaching what you need to learn, so pay attention to the messages you deliver to children—those messages are meant for you as well.

Find time today to spend nurturing a child; your own child, other children, or even your own inner child. Spend time engaging in children's activities; play and laugh, be silly and carefree. Create a rapport with a child, listen to a child, give unconditional love to a child; letting them know they are safe, valued, and loved.

Today's Nourishment:
I give my attention and time to a child—offering nourishment, love, and caring. I allow my own inner child to come out and visit with me, taking time to acknowledge its needs. As an earth angel I accept the task of nurturing children, allowing them to heal, learn, and grow in love.

~222~
Surmount Challenges

Let today's message serve as a reminder of all the challenges and difficulties you have over come. Know this, the worst is behind you, you have surmounted previous challenges. While difficult, the challenges you have faced in the past were to make you stronger and teach you lessons. Take a moment to think back to a difficult period in your life. Are you a stronger, wiser, and more in tuned person from that experience?

Instead of wallowing in self-pity, bitterness, and being a victim, you have opened your heart with compassion toward others in similar situations. Being spiritually in tuned has allowed you to let go of any blame or negative feelings. By staying positive you are attracting new situations, loving solutions to challenges, and have a higher level of spiritual understanding. You are surmounting challenges at this very moment—by being spiritually aware.

Today's Nourishment:
I am a spiritual warrior with the ability to surmount any challenge or obstacle put in my path. I look for the lesson in each experience, release bitterness and anger, and open my heart with love to others.

~223~
Project For Prosperity

You have been blessed with the ability to project your own life of abundance; financially, spiritually, emotionally, and materialistically. At a child of the Divine who has traveled thus far on your spiritual path, acknowledged spiritual things, your material needs are provided for. Know that as you follow your intuition you can manifest your dreams into reality.

By projecting your dreams and desires out into the universe, infusing them with faith and positive energy, you simply need to open your arms to receive. An abundance of prosperity is being poured upon you and your life at this very moment. Some of the gifts will be in the form of brilliant ideas and some will come in the form of opportunities. Listen to the divine guidance you receive and follow these instructions. Work with the angelic realm to realize your highest goals and release any worries, doubts, or fears over to God. God wants to see you prosper and live a life of abundance, as God knows you will share these blessings with others. Project for prosperity—open your arms to prepare to receive all the blessings God has for you!

Today's Nourishment:
I have been blessed with a life of abundance and all my material needs have been met. I raise my arms and hands in praise and thanks, as more abundance is poured upon me and my life. I am grateful to my Creator for giving me so many blessings that I graciously share with others.

~224~
Pay Attention To Ideas

Know that God doesn't give you anything you can not handle, even if He calls you past your comfort zone from time to time. Divine guidance comes in many forms and often comes in the form of thoughts and ideas. This is the time to pay attention to ideas that come to you seemingly out of nowhere as these ideas are answered prayers!

Ask for, then open your arms to receive, all the love, support, and caring you need to bring your idea into physical form. This support will arrive in the form of spiritual assistance as well as help and support on the earthy plane. Your Creator uses others here on earth to help you manifest your ideas, so pay attention to those people who bring you opportunities, offer assistance, or want to help you in manifesting your idea into reality.

Yes, you are being divinely guided in this moment—take action to make your idea a reality!

> Today's Nourishment:
> *I pay attention to my ideas and thoughts as this is a form of Divine guidance. My prayers have been heard and answered. I listen to the guidance given and accept the help and support offered to make my idea a reality.*

~225~
Remember Who You Are

You are a much loved child of God. You are a powerful spiritual being filled with love, compassion, empathy, and creativity. You are made in the image and likeness of God—therefore you are perfect as you are! No need to alter your appearance, worry about flaws or perceived imperfections—you are perfect! Having been created by God, you embody Godlike aspects; your inner self is pure and bright in truth, and no mistakes can change God's handiwork for true perfection.

Do not be afraid of your magnificence, power, or spiritual wisdom. Take notice of your interactions today. Do you project yourself as a much loved child of God, filled with power and self-confidence? Do others pick up on the loving healing energy within and radiant toward you? Are you a walking bill board for being spiritually in tuned with your world? Ask for angelic guidance and assistance throughout the day—let the angels infuse your memory so you remember who you are!

Today's Nourishment:
I am a powerful spiritual being created in the image and likeness of God. I am loving, playful, powerful, compassionate, and have a creative soul. I do not fear my magnificence, power, or spiritual wisdom. I project myself for whom I am—a much loved child of God—I remember who I am!

~226~
Exhale Slowly

Too much stress simply results in irritability and can cause or worsen health problems. Learning to relax is the key to reducing stress. Becoming familiar with your own breathing patterns and changing them may help you relax. Your breathing pattern is often disrupted by changes in emotion. Sometimes, when you are anxious you tend to hold your breath and speak in high-pitched voice as you exhale. Other times, you tend to sigh and speak in a low-pitched voice as you exhale.

Today, focus on the manner in which you breathe when you are under stress. Do you hold your breath when tense? Do you let out a long sigh and subconsciously exhale? You are being reminded today, of the importance of invigorating yourself with deep cleansing steady breathes and to exhale slowly—releasing tensions, worries, fears, and other negative feelings. Throughout the day, especially when you are under stress or tension, take several deep breaths to awaken your energies and exhale slowly to release all negative feelings and emotions.

Today's Nourishment:
After each deep cleansing breath I release negative thoughts and sadness by exhaling slowly and steadily. With each breath I awaken my energies and exhale slowly to release all negative feelings. I practice this suggestion throughout the day—everyday!

~227~
Soften Your Heart

The spiritual practice of compassion is often likened to softening the heart. Compassion is a feeling deep within that softens the heart. When you soften your heart you experience a quivering of the heart by the suffering of others and moving on their behalf. The practice of softening your heart increases your capacity to care for others; reinforces charity, empathy, and sympathy. Softening your heart is good exercise for your heart muscle.

Today you are being guided to soften your heart in regards to all situations and those involved, including yourself. Allow yourself to feel the suffering of others within your inner circle, in the world, including your own. Don't turn away from pain; move toward it with caring. Go into situations where people are hurting. Identify with your neighbors in their distress. Then expand the circle of your compassion to include other creatures, nature, and the inanimate world.

Today's Nourishment:
I soften my heart in regards to all situations and those involved, including myself. I approach situations with a loving heart, increasing my capacity to care for others. I practice charity, empathy, and sympathy—softening my heart is good exercise for my heart muscle.

~228~
Be Observant

Stop. Be still. Open your mind and heart. Listen to what is being said. Observe what is being shown. Let go of your fears and doubts, as your prayers have been heard and answered. It may not feel this way, in the moment, because sometimes the answers come in unexpected ways. Perhaps you receive a *feeling* or opportunities are presented; passing a billboard with a message or you hear a song on the car stereo. Your prayers are often answered by receiving ideas or information through everyday ways.

Be extra observant today; notice everything you see, hear, say, think, and feel. For instance, if you hear the same song several times during the day,the song most likely contains a message you are meant to receive. Another sign of an answered prayer is finding a feather in an unusual place or appears seemingly out of nowhere. Angel's often leave a feather to show they are near because you associate feathers with angels. Be especially aware of help that comes to you—be sure to accept that help. You deserve this help and often times everyday people act as God's assistances, earth angels, to provide you with answers to your prayers.

Today's Nourishment:
I observe all that is around me—everything I see, feel, say, think, and hear. My prayers have been heard and answered. I am open to messages sent to me through everyday ways. I will accept help that is offered and give thanks.

~229~
Trust Yourself

You are being guided to trust yourself and have faith that you are loved by God and the angels—they are always with you. It is past time to lose fears that block you from enjoying full faith and trust. Your past disappointments may have distorted your faith in yourself, others, and even God. You are reminded that it is important to hold on to your faith—ask for spiritual help to lose fears and restore trust.

Everyone has made mistakes in the past, but mistakes have not destroyed your true nature—the essence of who you are, where you came from, and where you are going. You have omnipresent God within, and God is perfect. Trust in God and, in turn, He will help you to trust yourself.

Today's Nourishment:
I am loved by god and the angels; they are always with me. I relinquish my fears and doubts and have faith and trust in myself. Mistakes from the past have no hold on my present self—I have forgiven, been forgiven, and move forward along my path. I am truly blessed!

~230~
Take Time to Read

Drop that remote! Turn off the TV, video games and iPods, and curl up with a book! You are being guided to drop everything and read—find at least 30 minutes today for reading. This is an important time for you to read, learn new ideas or skills, listen, and grow.

Why read? The great minds and the great storytellers of the past speak to us in books and the mediocre minds too, if we allow them. Reading can provide insights and perspectives that watching a movie never does. Even though you are reading at this moment, take it a step further and get lost in a good fiction today.

When is there time to read you ask? Before you go to sleep at night, during the night if you can't sleep, early morning when you wake up, during trips, instead of TV, instead of movies—whenever. You can even read in the bathroom. Reading is your cure for boredom, your ticket for a cruise around the world of ideas—and it is fun. Follow today's suggestion and take time to read!

Today's Nourishment:
I take time to read, listen, and grow. I spend time reading a book each day. My mind is open for learning new ideas, exploring new places, and gaining knowledge through reading.

~231~
Dance With Serenity

Become a partner with serenity and disengage from struggle and conflicts. Make this a day for an attitude change and reframe your views. Learning to live spiritually in tune with your world requires you surrender your struggles, release your negativity and ego—accept yourself and become one with the Divine One. Dancing with serenity allows you to release emotional pain and live a life filled with ease and grace.

Start today by eliminating obstacles that clutter your life. Accept that you are safe, secure, and loved by an omnipresent being. Embrace your freedom of dance and engage in a dance with serenity—through crisis, change, and loss. Open your arms to the blessing that enables you to feel safe, comfortable, and fruitful in your life!

Today's Nourishment:

No longer a prisoner of struggles, conflicts, negativity, and ego—my attitude is one of peaceful acceptance. I am safe, secure, and loved by an almighty powerful God who blesses me with a wonderful life of abundance. Today I dance with serenity!

Freely Express Yourself

Are you feeling trapped in a negative cycle of events? Are you worried that this *bad luck cycle* may never end and afraid to embark on anything new for fear it too will fail? Perhaps you are feeling stuck or strapped and want to make changes in your life. You are being asked today to realize that you are the only one holding you back, keeping yourself in a self-made prison. Realize that whenever you have the power to be free, freedom happens.

God gave everyone the freedom of choice—everything you do is by choice and you are free to choose again. It is up to you to freely express yourself; your true thoughts, ideas, and desires.

Even those who are incarcerated behind prison walls have the freedom to choose their thoughts so that they may find some peace under their circumstances and surroundings.

Whenever you feel that you have no other option or alterative, ask God and God's angels for assistance. You will either be guided to do something different that you will enjoy or you will suddenly have a change of attitude, making the situation or task more acceptable.

Today's Nourishment:
I have the power to be free; to make different choices. I freely express myself, my true thoughts, ideas, and desires. I ask God for help with my life conditions—offering gratitude for his blessings.

~233~
Survive Disappointment

Disappointment is inevitable—your earth life can never consistently live up to your expectations.There are times when the one you love doesn't love you back; times when a seemingly loving spouse chooses another and leaves the marriage. Let's face it, life doesn't always turn out the way you imagined it will. It's up to you to decide how to get through those dark times.

Some of your greatestdisappointments occurred when others disappointed or hurt you. Sometimes they knew exactly what they were doing and didn't care. Whileother times, they were only doing the best they knew how to do with the tools that they had. Your ultimate success, happiness, and joy in your life should not depend on others—it depends on where you are at on your spiritual path and your relationship with God.

Naturally, you depend on people for certain things, and it is painful when they let you down. If you are in a good placespiritually, emotionally, andcomfortable with yourself, you are more equipped with surviving disappointments.Of course, you will still feel the pain butyour recovery time is lessened. Keep in mind that sometimes God allows disappointments to happen in order to bless you in some way.

Today's Nourishment:
I ask God and the angels to help me survive disappointment. I let go of illusions of pain and suffering. I am forever God's child and I allow God to heal my disappointments and hurts. My heart and mind are at peace.

~234~
Enjoy Simple Things In Life

Now that your longed-for aspirations have been delivered to you, it is time for you to enjoy the simple things in life. Perhaps they arrived in a different fashion than you expected, but your true desires were delivered—peace, tranquility, and happiness—manifested as you requested.

Now it is time to celebrate the endless opportunities for goodness and joy in your life. Be thankful for the beauty and simplicity of your life. Some of the simple things in life to be celebrated are the rising sun, a rainbow, and children singing and dancing. These are the basic joys of life, which remind you to celebrate these simple joys of life. Acknowledge all the goodness around you; give thanks for all that you have.

The angels are reminding you that your life can be one long celebration if you so choose. Let the joy of gratitude nourish your soul and give you the deepest feeling of grace. Stop for a moment today and give thanks for all the good things that are happening to you.

Today's Nourishment:
I thank God for all the good things that are happening in my life now. I enjoy the simple things in life, such as, a child's laughter, the feel of the sunlight on my face, the beauty surrounding me, and the joy of being in tune with my spirituality.

~235~
Take A Time Out

You are too busy. You have to do this and have to do that. Someone is always waiting for something that needs to be done. Rush, rush, and rush some more. Then there is the boss who wants you to work overtime. Push, shove, rush, and hurry; only to get home where more people want your attention. You need to take a time out!

How many times during a sporting event does the coach call for a time out? Every time the team needs to recharge, regroup, or plan the next move they take a time out. You need to do the same thing. You need to take a few minutes by yourself each day to regenerate for the next day.

Before you go to sleep from exhaustion, put your mind in open space. Calm your mind and put yourself out somewhere where it is peaceful for you. Tell yourself about the positive things that are going to happen tomorrow, that you are feeling great, and that life is awesome.

Let your mind see yourself being successful and full of energy the next day. Use your conscious mind to direct your subconscious mind to make you feel good in the morning and to enjoy a good sleep tonight. Relax all the muscles in your body; tell your muscles to relax tonight—from your tip toes to the top of your head. You do have a few minutes to direct yourself, even if it is the last few minutes left of the day!

Today's Nourishment:
I take a time out each day to regenerate for the next day. I release any feelings of guilt to my angels; I am deserving of this time out. My mind is calm and peaceful; I think of positive things yet to come to me and refresh my mind and body for the next day.

Believe In Angels

Dear Sweet Child,

Let us introduce ourselves to you. We are your Angels and we want you to know that we are with you today as we are everyday and have been since you were born. We know that you have lost faith in us and are leery of those who claim to know us.

Let us restore your faith by telling you how to find us again in your life. Look around little one and see us as we are everywhere. The gentle breeze you feel upon your face when none stirs the trees or grass that is us caressing you with love. The smile that plays at the corner of your lips that appears suddenly for no reason; that is us smiling upon you with love. The joy that fills you heart when you know that you have no reason to be joyful; that is us touching your heart with our love. The playfulness within you at times when it appears to others that you should be serious is us playfully touching the lost child within you. The laughter that escapes your lips when all else is quiet; that is us tickling you with our love. The whispers you hear that tell you what the right path to take are us guiding you with love.

Do not lose faith little one for we are here with you; loving you, guiding you, protecting you. Talk to us often little one for we miss hearing your voice call out to us. Ask us for what you need and want as we will answer your calls. We can not interfere will a human's free will unless ask. Ask for we will answer; trust your heart, accept our messages, believe once again little one for we do exist.

Your Angels

Today's Nourishment:
My angels are always with me, loving me, guiding me, protecting me. I talk to my angels often, ask for their help, and accept their messages. I am loved by my angels.

~237~
Keep A Dream Journal

You are receiving important messages during your sleep time, through your dreams. Think back to times you have awaken with the feeling that you have traveled or was told something vital during your sleep—but you can not remember. You can learn to remember your dreams, remember them in more detail or even lucid dream as long as you are dedicated and take the time to establish a habit of keeping a dream journal.

Once a habit of intention to remember your dreams is established over time, the importance is implanted on your subconscious mind and your subconscious mind will nudge you with memories of your intention to remember your dreams repeatedly—until finally you do.

Keep a spiral notepad, pen, and small flashlight right by your bed. Write tonight's date on a blank page, to imprint on your subconscious mind that you intend to remember your dreams. If you awaken during the night with a dream memory, you can use the flashlight to write it so you don't become completely awake. Even writing a couple key words can help jog your memory in the morning.

Today's Nourishment:
I pay attention to my dreams and keep a dream journal. I review my dream journal often and recognize patterns, repetitiveness, and themes. I am open to the messages that are being sent.

~238~
Embrace New Beginnings

You have completed one cycle and ready to begin another. It is important to focus on your future; do not worry about what has been left behind. This is a positive time in your life and you are experiencing a growth spurt, causing you to feel overwhelmed as so many lessons have been laid out before you; do not fear as things are working out for you highest good.

You are to embrace the new beginnings in you life. Put on your captain's hat, stand ready at the wheel, and steer the bow into uncharted waters. You are in the captain's seat for the first time and it's natural to feel some apprehension or nervousness; but trust that you are not alone. You have a host of spiritual shipmates ready on deck, one positioned on each side of you, several in the crow's nest and they will not let you fail. It is safe for you to move forward, keep checking with your spiritual shipmates who are in direct communication with the Divine.

Brush off any nervous tension as you gaze out across these uncharted waters—instead allow your soul to absorb the excitement and wonderment of the wonderful possibilities and opportunities that lie before you! You are on the threshold of a spectacular new adventure—embrace these new beginnings!

Today's Nourishment:
With a fresh outlook and heartfelt gratitude for the lessons of my past, I gaze outward to the uncharted waters that lie before me. I look forward to this day and to a bright exciting future with promises of God's blessings!

~239~
Express Your Power

Your personal power comes from a divine love within you. Your creator instilled within, a strong healthy sense of self. You have a personal power that includes several components: your self-esteem, your independence, and your initiative. It consists of knowing what your individual talents and resources are and having the confidence to act on them.

You have spiritual power—you can hear, feel, and follow divine guidance. You have emotional power and are empathic and compassionate with others. You have mental power that gives you the ability to tap into the universal wisdom of your Creator. You have a quiet and beautiful aspect of a true power, stemming from the divine love within you.

Release any fears you may have of this power—allow yourself to shine with divine healing love!

Today's Nourishment:
I allow myself to express my power. It is safe for me to be powerful. I express my power with divine love.

State Your Intention

Your experiences are created by your intentions. To create what you intend to happen you must clearly state your intention—be sure that it is clear in your own mind. You are being asked today to review your expectations. What would you like to happen today, tomorrow, or in the future? You are the director of you life; you create your experiences by revealing your intentions. Stating an intention is declaring a goal and your intention of achieving that goal.

When you declare or state your intention, use positive terms and be specific—state details, time, and place. Infuse your intentions with love, seeing yourself as successful, happy, and at peace. Understand that if you do not get your intention, it is because it is either not in your best interests or the universe's, and there is something to be learned from that.

Today's Nourishment:
I create my experiences by stating my intentions. I take inventory of my expectations and state my intention in a positive term. I am happy, successful, and at peace.

Clear Your Mind

Do you sometimes feel like you've lost yourself, or that you're not really yourself at all? Or do you simply want to grow or become who you should be? Or perhaps you are pushing yourself too hard and in need of rest. You are being reminded today that rest is a natural part of everyday life—it is alright for you to take some time to clear your mind. Seek out a place with no noise at all and sit down. If you can't find a completely quiet place, go where at least it is comforting sounds, and sit down.

Clear your mind from all thoughts. After clearing your mind, allow your mind to think freely or if you have a specific topic in mind, focus on that. Avoid dead end, angering, and solution-less subjects. Focus on subjects where you are certain you can find new ground and progress. Another option is to look into your life, or your inner self, and think about what's going on right now. Anything that will help you focus and see helpful pictures or thoughts. If you want, journal or draw. Pay attention to any ideas, thoughts, feelings, or sense of knowing that comes to you. Listen to this inner guidance—you will know that which is divine guidance and not just your imagination or wishful thinking.

Today's Nourishment:
I spend time alone in quiet thought; clearing my mind, and focus on my truth and priorities. I pay attention to ideas, thoughts, feelings, or sense of knowing that comes to me in my mediative state as this is Divine guidance.

~242~
Retreat To Quiet Place

In today's busy world, you may find yourself stressed by the crush of demanding jobs, numerous activities and other obligations that draw you away from doing the things in life that could ultimately bring you joy and well being. As hectic schedules and fast paced life-styles tax your body and mind, your spiritual energy is also depleted. You become disconnected from the very spiritual source within you that can restore your life to balance and wholeness.

Even when you want to seek services or counsel to better yourself, your situations, or your relationships, you are often squeezing those appointments in on top of an already too full schedule. You frequently push yourself until you are in crisis, and then franticly seek help to fix the problem. Retreating to a quiet place can lift you out of crisis mode and into a place of self-care and well-being for yourself and those around you. You are being guided today to seek out a quiet place to retreat to re-group, recharge, and rejuvenate yourself.

Today's Nourishment:
I find time to retreat to a quiet place and recharge myself. I do this without guilt or anxiety as I am worthy of taking time for myself. By retreating to a quiet place I allow myself the opportunity to be lifted out of a crisis mode and reconnect with my energy source.

~243~
Create Harmony In Your Surroundings

Think back when you were a child sitting in the branch of a large tree, thinking and dreaming—feeling in harmony with your surroundings. Perhaps you used to ice skate outdoors and felt a sense of freedom and happiness as you glided silently across the frozen water; feeling light as the air and as smooth as the frozen lake—feeling in harmony with your surroundings. As an adult now, looking back, do you now realize that sense of inner peace and connectedness was a divine experience, a powerful spiritual connection with all life?

Bring this same spiritual energy and transformation into your current life. Fill your surroundings with radiant harmony! Create harmony in your relationships—see yourself and others through the eyes of divine love. By shifting your viewpoint to the angelic perspective, you have the ability to create harmony in your surroundings regardless of the environment or situation. Shift current energies to create harmonious energy to support your personal growth and create positive change in your life.

As you become aware of the direct connection between the condition and quality of your environment and the quality of your life, you will see the positive effects of living harmoniously—you can improve the quality of your health, wealth and happiness.

Today's Nourishment:
I deserve peace, happiness, and harmony in my life—I accept it graciously. I create harmony in my surroundings by clearing my space of clutter, see myself and others through the eyes of love, and am aware of the direct connection with my environment and living harmoniously.

~244~
Know That You Deserve Abundance

Hear ye, hear ye—you have an inflow of abundance coming into your life! This abundance is arriving special delivery just for you; return address is God. At some level you have always known that your creator would take care of your needs. Your faith, even though it may have wavered occasionally, has been rewarded with the life of abundance that is on its way. Know that you deserve this gift from God—you are worthy of a life of abundance.

Today, rejoice in your abundance; materially, psychologically, emotionally, spiritually, and mentally. The more faith you have, the more you ensure a steady flow of abundance; release any fears and doubts so that you can enjoy this deserved abundance.

Today's Nourishment:
I relax in the knowledge that I deserve abundance in my life. I accept abundance graciously into my life. I release my fears and doubts and rejoice in the knowledge that all my needs are met today and in the future.

~245~
Meditate Daily

A quiet mind hears divine guidance (thoughts and ideas, inner voice, gut feeling, and visions) more easily. Mediation is very important to practice as a way to quiet your mind so that you can receive spiritual guidance in a clear concise manner. Start your day with at least fifteen minutes of quiet time; with your eyes closed take deep cleansing breaths, slowly exhaling, breathe deeply, slowly exhaling and feel yourself slip into a serene state of mind.

While in this serene state, you can ask for guidance from the Divine on any number of things, situations, relationships, or issues—prepare to listen for a response. It is not necessary to strain to hear—the answer will come at the precise moment and in the perfect manner. Do not worry if you do not receive an immediate answer. Continue to take deep cleansing breaths and allow yourself to relax. Remind yourself that receive divine guidance is a natural thing and that mediation is an everyday occurrence for you. The more you practice meditation, the easier it is to hear the guidance you seek.

Today's Nourishment:
Meditation is very important to me and my spirituality—it allows for constant communication with my creator. I practice meditation often so that I can receive much desired spiritual guidance from my creator.

~246~
Cultivate New Friendships

As you grow in your spirituality and become more spiritually in tuned a transformation is in progress. Not only are you are changing within with new thoughts, ideas, and perceptions, you are changing on the outside as well! Especially in regards to your relationships and the way you interact with others. You may find that you no longer have common interest with your current or former friends. Or wonder if you will meet like minded persons to cultivate new friendships with which you will share a close bond.

Know that changes are natural and necessary for growth and transformation, including changes in friendships. Now is the time to seek out new friendships with people who mirror your interests and goals. In order to meet new people who might become your friends, you have to go to places where others are gathered. The hardest thing about going out and doing anything in the community is doing it for the first time. It's hard for everyone. Ask God to give you the strength and courage to go to new places and cultivate new friendships. You will be glad you did.

Don't limit yourself to one idea or strategy for meeting people. Explore such ideas as attending a support group, attending community activities, or volunteering. Support groups are a great way to make new friends. It could be a group for people who have similar interests or a group for people of the same age or sex. Community activities like sporting events, theatrical productions, concerts, art shows, poetry readings, book signings, civic groups, special interest groups, and political meetings are great places to cultivate new friendships. Take a course or join a church. Let yourself be seen and known in the community. Becoming a volunteer is another great way to make new friends. Strong connections often are formed when people work together on projects of mutual concern. As a volunteer you are already with a group of people with a common interest and helping others at the same time! Whichever methods works for you is the right one—the main goal is to cultivate new friendships.

Today's Nourishment:
I am lovingly honest with myself and my friends—changes are occurring in my friendships. The time is right for me to cultivate new friendships. I ask for guidance in meeting and developing new friendships. I am guided to the places and activities where like-minded persons are gathered and I make new friends.

~247~
Mend Broken Relationships

Pay attention to recurring thoughts or flashes of mental images. Has someone from the past been on your mind lately? When recurring thoughts from an old relationship resurface, you should pay attention to what is being shared with you. These recurring thoughts and images may be a sign that you have unfinished business with this person. Ask for clarification and guidance as to why thoughts of a former relationship are resurfacing at this time.

Notice any feelings that occur when you think about this person or relationship. Are you tense, nervous, relaxed, upbeat or upset? Think back to the last time you interacted with this person—do you harbor any regrets or resentments? If so, take a deep cleansing breath and slowly exhale releasing any negative feelings—let the healing energy undo effects of any mistakes that either party made. The breathing exercise alone can be the healing that you need.

However, if thoughts continue to plague your mind, you may want to reach out to this person. The matter you reach out doesn't matter—you can write a heart felt letter that you never send. Sometimes writing down your thoughts and feelings has more therapeutic value that physically contacting the person. Upon completion you can destroy what you have written as a form of letting go and moving forward.

You may feel strongly guided to contact this person again directly. In this case, ask for spiritual guidance and for the interaction to be surrounded with the powerful healing loving light to make sure that the interaction is harmonious.

Today's Nourishment:
By practicing forgiveness and letting go of resentments and regrets, I mend a broken relationship from my past. I am willing to look past any mistakes made on either side—see only love within the situation.

~248~

Visit a Friend

You have just received some really good news. You are engaged to be married! You got the position for which you interviewed! You are going to be a grandparent! You are *ablaze* with desire to tell a friend the good news. Who would that friend be? Think about your friend. What is the history of your friendship—does it include a spiritual connection? What qualities in that relationship make the friendship special?

Now ask yourself, when was the last time you visited this friend? Maintaining and nurturing friendships is vital to your spiritual growth. Friends add a wonderful dimension to your life. God understand the importance of having at least one person here on earth you can talk to about your feelings and things that are going on in your life—someone you can relax and be yourself with. Taking the time to nurture relationships and cultivating a supportive network of people you can rely on, is just as important as your relationship with God.

You are being urged today to visit with a friend—someone to help you celebrate the good times as well as see you through the tough times. Find some time today to connect with a friend. If your schedules conflict, be willing to rearrange your schedule to find a time to get together—hang out, have fun, talk, and visit!

Today's Nourishment:
I realize the importance of my friendships and make time to visit with a friend. My friendships are a vital part of my spirituality—I nurture each friendship knowing they are as important as my relationship with God.

~249~
Navigate The Murky Waters Of Relationships

Relationships can be difficult to navigate due to one major variable—*the other person!*You can be trudging along, doing the bestyou know how to do, thinking that everything is going fine and suddenly you are in the middle of a relationship crisis. Some of life's darkest moments are due to the troubled times with others.

Any type of relationship can bring pain and disappointment—parents siblings, children, neighbor, co-workers, and so forth. Any of these relationships can cause a knot inyour stomach, lump inyour throat, or loss of sleep. Let's face it, relationships are important to everyone. No one can live without some type of relationship or personal interaction.

Much of what God wants for you to learn will come about as you grow in your relationships with the people put in your life. Just as every relationship is a learning experience, every relationship requires some sacrifice; every sacrifice has a reward. If you knew the rewards you wouldn't hesitate to make the sacrifices. Everyone needs to be loved, cared for, valued, and respected, but those needs aren't met when we *demand* them. Those needs met when you *give* them! Sometimes you must lay down your pride and your needs for the other person. Humbling yourself and putting the other person's needs first can resurrect a relationship that has suffered mortal wounds.

Focusing on your own spiritual path and asking for assistance can help you navigate through the dark waters of any relationship. When you are walking step-by-step on your own spiritual path God will help you through each crisis,you will see miracles. Being on the right path spiritually, emotionally, and mentally brings about transformation, restoration, and healing of any relationship crisis.

Today's Nourishment:
I am the co-pilot of my life, as God is the pilot—I focus on my own spiritual path. I ask for assistance to help me navigate through the dark waters of my relationships; knowing that being on the right spiritual path can transform and heal any relationship crisis.

~250~
Open Your Heart To New Love

Your heart yearns for love in abundance but you have bound your heart in a cold silence with emotions about the past. Your true nature is love and you must trust in its power to make the barriers disappear. You need to tear down the wall you have built so that new love can come in. Untangle your heart from the memories of the past—open yourself up to angelic healing powers. Release all the painful feelings from the past; just let them go. You will always have the memories, lessons, and love from past relationships. Today, you are releasing hurtful memories that created the wall around your heart.

Open your heart now, feel all those hurtful memories leave your heart clearing a path for a new love. Release old anger, resentments, tensions, worry, guilt, shame, sadness, grief, and regrets—everything that feels painful is now gone. The past no longer holds your heart as a prisoner; you are free to love again.

The angels have heard the cries of your heart and felt its yearning for a great love. Since you are on the spiritual path, you will be connected with a partner with similar philosophy and common interests. You are now ready to enjoy a great passion and spiritual companionship with a new love. You will be guided to your new love—if you are currently in a relationship, release this partnership over to the angels. They will elevate your current relationship into the great love your heart desires—open your heart to this new love!

Today's Nourishment:
I open my heart and release all hurtful memories; clearing the path for a new love. Free of all painful emotions, my heart is no longer a prisoner of my past—I am free to embrace new love. My heart is now open to new love!

~251~
Go With The Flow

Have you noticed a certain sense of unreality these days? Have you seen with a different perception? Do things look a little unreal to you? Good. Then everything is just as it should be. You are beginning to see things as the projections that they are. You are in the process of becoming totally aligned with your Creator—becoming spiritually in tuned with your world. That is why everything is as it should be—you are in the midst of a transformation, becoming total oneness with God. During the process of this transformation, all that is not in alignment with God will be purged.

You are being prepared to go to the next level of your transformation, where your veils will be dropped and you will experience yourself in your true nature; as a spiritual being, a conscious extension of God, as joyous participant in the dance of creation, and totally aligned with God and of the light. You are being asked to trust this process, go with the flow; unlike the salmon that swim upstream and struggle with the current—trust that all is as it should be and go with the flow.

Trust this transformation process and do not take it as something that must be corrected or controlled. You are evolving, changing, becoming more in tuned with your spiritual side; so you will have to let go and surrender more and more as things proceed. Think of yourself as a cork floating in an ocean, bathed in love and light and grace-filled. Let yourself go and feel the peace and the bliss that accompanies the letting go. Let yourself be lifted and carried and let yourself melt and be like a clear stream of the purest water. Ask not where your journey takes you, but just become the flow and it will all unfold perfectly, for you and for all. Go with the flow!

> Today's Nourishment:
> *I trust in this process of transformation and know that all is as it should be. I am totaling aligned with my creator and evolving into a more spiritually aware person. I am a conscious extension of God and totally aligned with God and of the light. I am relaxed and go with the flow—I am protected in all ways.*

~252~
Maintain Balance

Living in balance is fundamental to maintaining a good working relationship with God. As a spiritual adult, take notice of signs indicating that you are not seeing reality clearly and take responsibility to do whatever it takes to return to your inner state of balance. As a spiritual being live in loving appreciation of all life, including your own. Maintain balance in your life; stay on top of what is most important to you, reduce stress and anxiety, enjoy people, your community, and celebrate life. Maintaining balance in your life is essential to your emotional, spiritual, and physical health and well-being.

God can help you notice the signs from life and your body that you are out of balance before real problems manifest. God can pin point the cause of an imbalance to its source and to clear it there. Take time to communicate with God, asking for assistance and inspiration. Go to deeper levels in thinking, feeling, and sensing breaking through the blocks that hold you back. Maintain balance and under your inspiration and passions for your heart's desires.

Today's Nourishment:
I receive divinely inspired instructions on maintaining balance in my life. I stay on top of what is important to me; communicate with my Creator and am stress and anxiety free. My life is balanced between work and play, family and work responsibilities, and spiritual goals.

~253~
Best-Case Scenario

So often you allow your imagination to wander and dwell on the worst-case scenario, creating fear, dread, and uncertainty in your life. With this attitude, it's no wonder you are afraid to move forward from the known to the unknown. By creating this fear you have locked yourself in a prison—a prison of your own making mind you. But wait...if *you* made the prison, then *you* must hold the proverbial key to release set yourself free. Now how awesome is that?

Today adopt another perspective—instead of dwelling on the worst-case scenario, shift your energy and focus and ask yourself, "What's the best-case scenario?"

Give your imagination free-rein as you explore all the wonderful possibilities. Only think of positive outcomes, and allow yourself to become giddy with excitement as you consider all the options. You will be amazed at the shift in your energy and how powerful that energy can become as you nourish it. Throughout the day, keep your mind focused on the best-case scenarios; be optimistic and positive, and let your faith attract wonderful new possibilities. You are truly blessed!

Today's Nourishment:
My imagination gallops freely as I explore all the wonderful positive possibilities that can occur in my life. I am giddy with anticipation and excitement thinking of my future and what is in store for me.

~254~
Recapture The Magic

Think back to when you were a child and how the world appeared so fresh, new, exciting, and magical. As a child you naturally saw the world through the eyes of innocence and sense of enchantment. Children find delight and wonderment in the simplest things; the sky, colors, lightening, a lady bug, or a summer rain. Notice the expression on a child's face during moments as these, the expression of pure wonder—a sense of magical existence.

Somewhere along the way, you lost your sense of wonderment, that sense of magical existence. This sense of wonder and magic doesn't have to fade with time. You can recapture the magic and enchantment you experienced as a child. You are being gently nudged to recapture the magic and rediscover that sense of wonder and awe you experienced as a child. Remember that you are surrounded by a miraculous power—a magical and enchanting divine power.

As an adult boredom sets in because you find things dull when life seems static and routine, however, changes are occurring around you daily. It is impossible for anything to stay the same on Earth; it is your sensitivity to these changes that have become dull. By training your senses to notice and seek out these alterations and differences around you, you can recapture the magic that you felt as a child. Today, pay special attention to the variations and difference in each experience you encounter. Notice the colors, lighting, smells, sounds, and energy shifts and other nuances around you.

Today's Nourishment:
I open my eyes to the beauty surrounding me and am filled with a sense of wonderment and magic. I take notice of colors, lighting, smells, sounds, and the beauty of life. My heart opens and absorbs the magical and enchanting divine power that surrounds me.

~255~
Talk About Your Feelings

Sometimes the toughest thing about feelings is sharing them with others. You are a wonderful person in so many ways; it is now time to trust enough to reveal your true self to others. No longer do you need to hide your feelings from others or even from yourself. Expressing your authentic self is vital to your spiritual growth.

You are being guided today to honor your feelings by expressing and talking about them to yourself and those who care about you. Harboring your feelings and not talking about them with others can lead to misunderstandings with friends and loved ones. Trust that you would never be guided to say or do anything to hurt others feelings—you will be able to talk about your feelings and be given a new level of inner peace.

Today's Nourishment:
I am a radiant, successful, powerful, and a wonderful person! It is time to let others see my true self—it is time to talk about my feelings with my friends and loved ones. No longer afraid to be my true self—I shine with radiant loving light and others see!

~256~
Immerse Yourself In Music

Music elevates your thoughts, lifts your spirits above earthbound worries, and is a fuse to creativity. Have you felt guided lately to listen to a particular type of music, compose a song, join a choir, or play an instrument? These inner urging may be divine guidance that you may benefit from the healing properties of music. You are being guided to immerse yourself in beautiful music and add more music to your life.

Choose music that uplifts your spirit, which you care about, or want to learn about. Immerse yourself in music by listening to it, play soft background music while you dress, in the car, while at work, and even at play. Allow yourself to sing, whistle, or hum along with the music—feeling it rejuvenate your soul and uplift your spirits. Let your earthy worries and concerns be washed away by the gift of song and melody. Immerse yourself in music and let the healing begin!

> Today's Nourishment:
> *I add more music to my life. I play background music while at home, work, driving, or at play—I immerse myself in the healing properties of music. I sing, whistle, and hum, letting the music wash away my worries and cares of the day!*

~257~
Practice Self-Acceptance

Self acceptance is being happy and feeling loving with who you are at this moment. Some call it self-esteem, others self-love, but whatever you call it, you'll know when your accepting yourself because it feels great. You are a child of the Creator, made in His image and likeness—to practice self-acceptance is giving praise for your Creator's handiwork.

Today make an agreement with yourself to appreciate, validate, accept and support who you are at this very moment, regardless of the illusion presented by any problems. You are a magnificent creation of God—focus on giving yourself praise today as a way of praising and paying tribute to your creator.

Today's Nourishment:
I am a magnificent creation of God; made in His image and likeness!
I give praise to myself and pay tribute to my creator by practicing self-acceptance and being happy with whom I am in this moment.

~258~
Count Your Blessings

Do you have moments when you feel as if you have been abandoned? Do you feel that life's problems and challenges are too much for you to handle? Perhaps recent events in your life have caused you to be blind to everyday blessings. When life is the most challenging, know those are the times when God and God's angels bestow extra blessings upon you. Those are the moments when God assigns additional angels to watch over you and give you a double dose of love and strength.

Sometimes you may feel as if you are alone, but this is never the case—you are reminded that you are never alone. God and the angels are with you all ways; they cannot leave you ever. While challenges and life experiences may blind you to blessings, you are being asked today to look around and see how God has blessed your life. Today, view every event, relationship, situation, and interaction as an opportunity to grow, learn, and heal—see each as a blessing. Look around your everyday world and count your blessings; your loved ones, family, food, shelter, truth, justice, forgiveness, and a stranger's smile. Count your blessings of life, liberty, freedom, happiness, integrity, and friendships—and so much more. Look around your world and count your blessings!

> Today's Nourishment:
> *I find blessings within my everyday life. Instead of focusing on life challenges, I seek out the blessing in each situation, person, event, and interaction. My life has been blessed in so many ways; loving family, friends, my home, my job, forgiveness, compassionate, happiness—the list is endless!*

Welcome Spiritual Growth

Spiritual awareness is ongoing, and requires the willingness to open your mind to new possibilities. Empower yourself to become greater than you are now. Spiritual growth brings holistic healing into your life which touches all aspects of your physical life. Becoming more spiritually in tuned with your world opens doors you would never have imagined through your spirituality and awareness.

You are an aspect of the source that created you, and you have all its attributes, characteristics, and access to power that goes along with awareness. Free yourself to fly, move out of the box, and create your own truth. Open your mind and ask for all those things you desire are brought into your life. Embrace this time of spiritual growth and enjoy the process.

Although you love this reconnection with the creator, you may feel a mixture of emotions; confusion, excitement, fear, and a sense of wonderment. Release any fears, doubts, or concerns—trust that you are where you are suppose to be at this moment and all is as it should be. Open your mind, heart, and arms and welcome spiritual growth—read, study, learn, and meditate as often as you are able.

Today's Nourishment:
I welcome spiritual growth, allowing my thoughts, mind, and heart to be open to learning. I am an aspect of the creator with all its characteristics; I am a powerful spiritual being. I am free to fly, move out of the box, and create my own spiritual truths. I embrace and welcome this time of spiritual growth and enjoy the process.

Practice Spiritual Healing

Spiritual healing involves any technique that uses subtle energies for healing. Such energies are only now starting to be recognized by western medicine. Most eastern medical systems have acknowledged and used such forces for hundreds to thousands of years. "Chi" and "prana" are two of the better known names for these energies. They are related to, and can be directed by, a person's consciousness. Because of this, one can receive such healing forces either in the presence of, or at a distance from, the healer being worked with.

Typically spiritual healing is used to shift subtle energy patterns that may be obstructing the healthy functioning of life in the ordinary world of mind, heart and body. Healing is usually directed to an individual but it can also be helpfully sent to practically any collection of beings or situations. In general the more specific the target for healing is, the more energy that is available to promote recovery and well-being.

As you are eternally connected to the creator, you have the same healing abilities that others have. One of the reasons that it appears others are more effective healers than you is that they trust in the divine powers flowing through them. Methods that are commonly used for spiritual healing work include; prayer, visualization, understanding, caring, healing, protecting, using spiritual energy such as chi, prana, reiki, and personal spiritual realization. Instead of worrying if you are qualified or ready to practice spiritual healing, accept the fact that you have healing power and focus on embracing these divine powers. Enjoy the therapeutic gifts you have been blessed with; put them to use today without delay!

Today's Nourishment:
I embrace and enjoy the therapeutic gifts given to me by the creator—I am eternally connected to God and His divine love and energy. I am a gifted and qualified healer; I practice spiritual healing through prayer, visualization, caring, compassion, and spiritual energies.

~261~
Watch For Signs

You are being given messages. You have asked for guidance and help with a decision; guidance has been given. Pay attention to the signs given to you; these are messages from God. God is attempting to get your attention with signs. Signs can be anything that you see or hear three or more times or in an uncommon way.

These signs may be in the music that you hear, the red-tail hawk that flies above, or an object that is thrust in your path. For instance, if you hear the same song three times during one day, the song most likely contains a message you are meant to receive. Signs can be given in the form of a feeling, thought, or idea that you have. Trust what is being shown; pay attention, and watch for signs.

Today's Nourishment:
I am open for receiving messages of guidance and pat attention to my thoughts, inner voice, and anything uncommon. I ask for assistance in interpreting the signs given. I follow what is said, knowing that I am receiving divine guidance.

~262~
Talk With Your Guardian Angel

The presence of angels is such a wonderful magic to know and experience. Angels have an active place in your life because they work with you helping you with all your relationships; including your relationship with God. They give you protection and guidance and help fulfill your creative potential by making your life here on earth smoother and easier.

It is the deep hope of your guardian angel that you receive its unconditional love, which whispers divine melodies of encouragement. Please listen and be still, and sense the incredible loving presence of your precious guardian angels. Be still and learn to receive the unconditional love God sends you through this heavenly representative, your guardian angel.

You are being reminded, that no matter what you do in life, your guardian angels will never leave you—they are your protectors and guides, making sure you stay safe, happy, healthy and fulfill your mission in life. In order to fulfill this intention, you must work with your Guardian angels. Talk with your guardian angels everyday, asking for help and guidance, and then find quiet time to listen to what they have to say. You don't need a special place or situation to talk with them. Talk with your guardian angels while standing in line at the supermarket, driving in the car, taking a shower, or while enjoying your nightly stroll—it doesn't matter, just talk to them!

> Today's Nourishment:
> *I call upon my guardian angels to open my heart, my eyes, and my ears—to communicate with them. I talk with my protectors, guides, and heavenly beings throughout the day. While standing in line, waiting at a traffic light, walking, showering—anywhere is fine, as my angels are always there!*

~263~
Interact With Animals

Animals, like God, love unconditionally. They're always happy to see people, they offer their caregiver encouragement during those low points, and their devotion is touching and reassuring. Petting and talking to animals lowers stress in people and the animals they are interacting with. It can also be a great way to lift people out of isolation and loneliness. Pets are wonderful listeners and provide unconditional love.

You are being encouraged today to spend time with animals. If you do not have a pet of your own, visit a friend who has one, a pet store, or your local animal shelter. If possible adopt a pet from the animal shelter; the benefits to interacting with a pet on a daily basis are endless!

Today's Nourishment:
I make time for myself today by interacting with animals. As I interact with my pet, I am reminded of the unconditional love of God. My stress is relieved by petting and talking to a pet. I give myself the gift of interacting with animals.

Unconditional Love (Pee Wee Wallis, age 12 weeks)

~264~
Add Fun To Your Life

You have a lot of responsibilities and a need a steady flow of earned income to meet your responsibilities, needs, and perhaps an occasional something extra. However, you do need to take time out to have some fun as well. A regular dose of fun balances out your life and helps achieve your goals. Make some time today to have fun, laugh, and relax. It's a perfect time to kick back and add a little fun to your life.

It doesn't matter what you do nor do you have to leave home to have fun. For example, build a fort with pillows from the couch, water balloon fight, blow bubbles on a child's belly, finger paint, have a party, or color with crayons. The choices are as unlimited as your imagination!

Today's Nourishment:
I make time for fun today. I use my imagination and look for creative ways to add fun to my life. I feel happy knowing that I am balancing my life and making time for fun.

~265~
Notice Open Doors

Sometimes in order to move toward the future that the universe intends for us, you must leave something behind. Instead of standing looking longingly at the closed door, turn around; see the doors of opportunity ahead. You have every door open to you at this moment—there is nothing standing in your way, which door do you choose to walk through is your entirely up to you.

There is nothing holding you back but your own fears and indecisions. It is normal to feel overwhelmed with the choices available or insecure with your abilities for a particular door; rest easy beloved child of God. Your angels excel in removing fears, doubts, and offer clarity for every situation. All you have to do is ask for their help.

Today's Nourishment:
I can do, be, or have anything that I choose—my angels give me clarity, courage, and the strength to move forward on my path in positive ways. I embrace all life transitions with unwavering faith. I no long look longingly at closed doors, but notice open doors of opportunity knowing the choice is mine!

~266
Acknowledge Love Is Eternal

You are being reminded today that love is forever and to release the fear that love is limited. Let the fact that love cannot be lost and is eternal be the ultimate source of comfort and solace for those who grieve lost love. Love is permanent and remains a part of you through eternity. With each experience of love it becomes grafted on to your soul causing your soul to expand and develop. Love is a powerful divine source that enhances and enlarges perspectives of self, reinforcing that the universe is a safe and sweet place intended to provide you with peace and joy.

Love does not die with the physical body; it is eternal and can be recalled when you have need for it. Think back to a loved one that has since left this earthly plane—the love that was shared does not diminish. It stays with you, becomes apart of you and furthers your spiritual growth and awareness. When you bereave for a loved one ask your angels to comfort you with the knowledge that love can connect people through lifetimes. Some love can endure through ages of separation. You can consciously choose to remember the love of friends, family, teachers, or anyone with whom you shared love. Those memories stay with you and help defined who you are—acknowledge love is eternal.

Today's Nourishment:
Love is forever, is permanent, cannot be lost and remains a part of me throughout eternity. I embrace this eternal love; choosing to remember the love of friends, family, and those whom I shared love.

~267~
Notice Prosperity in Your Life

Today's guidance is simple and direct: notice all the prosperity in your life. Begin by counting your everyday blessings; love, beauty, happiness, health, energy, and so forth. Notice as you acknowledge your blessings with gratitude more are bestowed upon you. You were promised a life of abundance by the creator and that promise has been fulfilled.

Today's Nourishment:

God has been very generous with me for I am very prosperous. I see and experience a life of abundance and accept this prosperous life with gratitude. As I am blessed, I share with others and offer thanks to God.

~268~
Embrace Your Health

The more you focus on your well-being within yourself and others, the more you experience being well. Today, you are being urged to look past any physical earthly appearance of illness, injury, or disease and see the wellness inside yourself and others—especially within yourself.

Ask your angels for help with making positive decisions about the way you manage your life. They can help lead you to a healthy and wholesome life-style which supports your well-being and happiness. Ask for vitality to do all the things you love and to have abundant energy to handle all the tasks demanded of you. True health and well-being comes from being balanced in mind, body, and spirit—let yourself be guided toward finding this level of wholeness.

Embrace that you are already healthy, and so are those around you—affirm this often throughout the day and feel it in your body. You are blessed with good health and having divine healing available for any physical, emotional, or spiritual pains you may suffer.

Today's Nourishment:
I am perfectly healthy and whole, because God created me this way. I see only well being within myself and others. My angels help me live a healthy and wholesome life style to support my well being and happiness.

~269~
Know That Your Prayers Have Been Answered

Even though it may not seem like it at this moment, know that your prayers have been answered. They answers may come in unexpected ways; an intuitive feeling or new opportunity appear. Very often prayers are answered by giving you ideas or information in everyday ways. You are being reminded that things are being worked behind the scene on your behalf to manifest all that you desire. All that is required of you is to keep the faith and follow any inner guidance; the rest is up to God.

As with all fathers, your heavenly father is very happy to do things for you and support you in the name of love. Know that you do deserve all that you are given, and many times God enlists people here on earth to act on his behalf that bring answers to your prayers.

> Today's Nourishment:
> *I trust and have faith that all my prayers have been answered. Any worries or fears that I once had have been released—I trust Spirit to take care of all the details. I am happy to watch my prayers manifest in my life—I deserve and graciously accept all that God gives me.*

~270~
Accept Your Sensitivity

Sensitivity is a beautiful and powerful gift that allows you to receive divine guidance, feel your own and others emotions, have compassion, and respect nature. Know that there is no such thing as too sensitive. It is this sensitivity that allows you to know the truth about people, situations, circumstances and it's important for you to follow your gut feelings or hunches.

It is safe for you to be sensitive—it is a blessing. Today focus on accepting your sensitivity and avoid hard energies today. An *extra-sensitive* is like a sponge to the energies surrounding them, absorbing all energies positive and negative. Steer clear from harsh situations and relationships; be mindful of your eating and drinking choices so that you nurture your sensitivity.

Spend some time alone today in nature to further develop your sensitivity. Acknowledge that it is safe for you to feel deep emotions, as they are a part of your sensitivity.

Today's Nourishment:
It is safe for me to feel deep emotions; my sensitivity is a beautiful powerful gift. I accept my sensitivity and spend time alone with nature to develop this gift.

Love Is The Substance Of Life

Love lives at the centre of every living cell in your body, and in the heart of all living things. It is the key to all that you do and all that you desire. Open your heart to the love within, and know that love is the basic and fundamental substance of life. Ask for assistance in opening your heart and being aware of your soul, mind, and body. Pray to be able to connect with that oneness and remember the eternal and unconditional nature of love.

As you stand on the brink of a new day, take this gift of love with you and share with others throughout your day. Let the love flow through your body, removing old pain, anger, or hurt—let love grow and flourish within.

Today's Nourishment:
Dear God, help me love today; teach me how to love fearlessly, with gratitude and acceptance. Assist me in removing old pain, anger, or hurt; let love grow and flourish within—allow me to enter this new day with a clean and open heart.

~272~
Walk Barefoot

When you habitually wear shoes your feet become soft and tender. It is like wearing blinders and you are not able to experience nature fully. The shoes prevent your foot muscles from working the way God intended, and your feet become unaccustomed to various textures. . By walking barefoot for half an hour, three to four times per week, you can recondition and sensitize your feet to the point that walking barefoot is preferable to wearing shoes.

God intended for you to walk barefoot. Your feet have as many nerve endings as your hand. You are depriving a sensory organ when you wear shoes. Walking barefoot allows you to experience nature fully with all your senses and teaches a respect for nature. It's completely natural to walk barefoot. In fact, it is quite healthy and good for your feet to do so.

Feel your feet free of confining, hot, sweaty shoes today. Kick off your shoes and give your feet a chance to breathe the air, feel the sunshine—wiggle your toes, feel the various textures and temperatures of surfaces as you walk. Feel the grass, mud, dirt, and sand between your toes—it's wonderful! Avoid shoes as much as possible and you will soon discover that walking barefoot is one life's most simple pleasures.

Today's Nourishment:
I kick off my shoes and walk barefoot; feeling all the earth's textures— grass, dirt, sand, and mud. I wiggle my toes, flex my feet, and absorb the energy of the sun on my bare feet. God intends me to walk barefoot—I obey God.

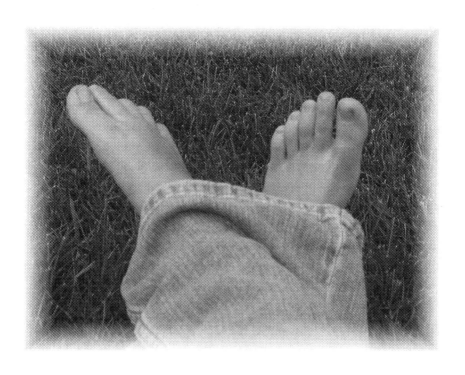

Barefootin' (photo by Nicole McGowan)

Love Is The Key That Unlocks

How can you expect different results when you continue doing the same things? Are you willing to unlock the chains that have you bound? There's only one way to do so; you must be willing to change. The key to change is a changed mind; a changed mind changes its actions; the key to change is God's extraordinary love. Love is the key that unlocks the chains that hold you back. Love is the key that unlocks the spiritually within for growth and progress in spiritual knowledge.

God's love is the glue of the universe. When you see all that surrounds you in the light of this extraordinary love, you acknowledge that love is the key that unlocks all things. Naturally, the love of romance and joining of two human beings is a wonderful place for a relationship of commitment and love. But the ultimate love of God's promises to us as spiritual beings is so much deeper. This love stems from the heart, to be sure, but it is also found in the spirit of doing right for the sake of right. It is found on the vibration of seeing into the soul of others and finding their love and light. The spirit lights up with our lessons of love with one another and acknowledgement that love is the key that unlocks. Today, ask for assistance in opening your heart—be mindful of your soul, mind, and body and be receptive to this extraordinary love. See love within those you meet today, in all your relationships and interactions, within all situations—begin this day with a clean and open heart. Love like an angel!

Today's Nourishment:
Dear God, I come to you today and ask for help in opening my heart to your extraordinary love. Take my hand and guide me away from old pains, anger, and hurts—let my heart be healed by your divine love. Assist me in loving without fear, see love within everyone, every situation and circumstances. Help me love like an angel. Thank you!

Release The Past

In order to live life successfully today and move toward the future that the universe intends, you must release the past. If you don't your past will color and taint everything you see and affect all that you do. If rejection and pain has been a part of your past and you haven't released those emotions and completed the healing process, you will experience every situation, event, circumstance, or person through the eyes of rejection.

Recall a time in your life that brought about *absolute endings* for you; people removed from your life, circumstances changed unexpected and swiftly, and you were able to sense a *clearing of the decks* for new opportunities, adventures, and growth. As difficult and scary as change may be—going from the known to the unknown is a daunting task—releasing the past is a necessary part of personal growth.

One of the biggest problems with moving out of the past is the unwillingness to forgive the people and events of the past. But by not forgiving the past, you remain attached and a prisoner of the past. As you begin your day, do so with a sense of wonderment and awe, and anxious to see what lies ahead!

Today's Nourishment:
I step out of the past and walk eagerly toward my future—I embrace the opportunities and adventures before me. No longer attached to the past, I experience a true sense of freedom!

~275~
Trust In Your Decisions

Decisions, decisions, and more decisions—your life is filled with decisions each day. Deciding what to wear to more complex decisions such as which career path is the right choice; you wrestle with yourself regarding the pros and cons of each side. Even when you know which direction you are leaning toward, you fear any possible negative consequence of your choice.

Today, let go of the stress and strain of decision making. Make the decision to not think about your options that you have been wrestling with—put the entire matter up on the shelve in the closet and shut the door for now. Relax your mind and be open to the divine guidance you are about to receive. God is waiting to help you be at peace with your choices—trust in your decisions. At this point you already know which the best choice is for you; it is so obvious that want to shout it from the rooftops!

Today's Nourishment:
I am at peace with my decisions—I have made the right choice for myself and my loved ones. I have clarity of thought, peace of mind, and an attitude of gratitude!

~276~
Affirm New Beginnings

Today is the start of a beautiful day! Know that what is happening in your life at this moment is part of something wonderful. If you have been experiencing havoc or chaos, realize that it is actually the beginning of a new way of life which was destined to happen at this time. If events had not happened this way, you would still be where you were and miss the wonderful opportunities destiny has in store!

Embrace the new in your life; new opportunities, people, situations, and projects. Naturally, changes can be frightening or overwhelming, but you are surrounded by a choir of angelic beings—call upon them if you feel afraid or nervous. They stand ready to give you a shot of confidence, infuse you with courage, and surround you with loving energy so that you can enjoy your new beginnings.

Today's Nourishment:
I am blessed to have new beginnings before me! I am thankful for the way events have unfolded in my life to this point. I send blessings to those who have crossed my path--even those who are no longer a part of my inner circle. Blessed be it is a glorious day!

~277~
Have Confidence In Your Feelings

Have you experienced a gut feeling in regards to a person, situation, or event? Or perhaps you have experienced warmth in your chest, tightening of muscles, goose bumps, or intuition? Do you dismiss such occurrences as *just a feeling?* You shouldn't dismiss or ignore such feelings, for God speaks to you through your physical and emotional senses.

Think back to the times you have ignored or dismissed your own gut instincts, only to realize later on how correct they were. You certainly experienced regrets when you didn't listen to your gut feeling or intuition. You are being guided today, to have confidence in your feelings—do not be afraid of the intensity of what you feel or confuse your own emotions with those of others. God is speaking to you through your emotions and wants you to listen to your intuition. For those occasions when you need clarity or have doubts about trusting your feelings, check in with God—*God* will give you clarity and ease any doubts or fears you have.

Today's Nourishment:
I have confidence in my feelings for this is how God speaks to me— through my feelings. I am thankful for this gift of feeling and can easily understand what God is revealing to me. It is safe for me to listen to my feelings and intuition.

~278~
Feed Your Passions

When you engage in activities that you really enjoy, time seems to fly. Even if it is just a moment—that moment is meaningful; you feel fully alive. Taking the time to engage in activities you're good at, share what interests you, or participate in things that bring you joy and adds meaning to your life. Today you are being nudged to feed your passions and engage in an activity that brings you pleasure or get you fired up!

As with any other living thing, whatever that passion may be, it must be fed on a regular basis. Keep a book related to one of your passions handy for those times you can't engage in the activity. This way you are still feeding your passion a snack even if you can't actually go fishing, paint, ride your bike, or write. Limited time for reading is no longer a problem with music and audio books readily available. You can listen to your favorite opera, music artist, or even learn about your favorite history era via your Walkman or IPod.

Even discussing you passion with other enthusiasts can uplift and revive your spirit. Reach out to another fisherman, motorcyclists, discuss flowers with a gardener, or visit a literacy chat room online for a few minutes—the choices are as unlimited as your imagination. Feed your soul with desire, even for a few minutes, and feel your spirit soar as you feed your passions!

Today's Nourishment:
I focus on feeding my passions by spending time thinking about activities that inspire or bring me pleasure. Each week, I devote regular time to these activities—nurturing and providing nourishment to my passions. I sign up for classes or groups, read books, discuss my passions with other enthusiasts.

Devote Time To Priorities

How many times have you said "yes" to a request, and then, the moment the words came out of your mouth, you cringed inside? As a spiritual being you are naturally driven to please or be of service. You aim to please others even when the commitment doesn't serve your needs, interferes with your priorities, or makes you unhappy.

An important part of your life's purpose involves making decisions about how to spend your time. When you are faced with so many choices; services to others, please others, work, family, spiritually you may wonder how much time to devote to each area. You have an obligation for self-care, to your soul, and to your spiritual path. For if these areas are neglected, all other areas in your life are affected.

A good way to start devoting time to your priorities is to ensure that every request is thoughtfully considered before you respond. Your personal mantra should be, "I choose how I spend my time, and how it reflects me, my physical, emotional, and spiritual needs." By having the time and space to think through the commitment and the resulting consequences, you can confidently devote time to your priorities—not the priorities of others.

Today's Nourishment:
I have plenty of time to devote to my priorities—self-care, of my soul, and devote time to my spiritual path. All other responsibilities fall into place; work, family, fun, rest, and exercise.

286

~280~
Remain Positive

Everyone faces hardship or challenges within their live, the most productive thing you can do when facing turbulent times is remain positive. A true testament to faith is to *believe* during the most difficult times, that things will work out for the betterment of all involved. There is a blessing within each circumstance, even if you can not see it at the moment. By continuing to hold onto the belief that all is well you uplift the spirit and energy of those around you and the situation itself.

Remaining positive in the face of adversity helps your body relax, clears your mind, eases worries, and allows for creative inspiration. Your bright outlook creates a positive energy force around you and those within your circle—avoiding the pitfalls of negativity and dark energy.

Vow to remain positive today, regardless of the situations, circumstances, or interactions with others. Of course, you must always be honest with your feelings—call upon your spiritual teammates to help you remain positive and have the best perspective on each situation.

Today's Nourishment:
It is my intention to remain positive about myself today—viewing all situations, circumstances, and interaction in the most positive light. It is safe for me to be happy, carefree, and upbeat in my attitude.

~281~
Stay Charged Up!

Today is devoted to staying charged up—invest time and energy in your priorities. This is the day you take action toward any projects and activities that you daydream about. Even a few minutes of energy devoted toward even one goal will make you feel happier and more energized.

Take a deep cleansing breath, you can keep your eyes open during this exercise, exhale slowly—take note of your first thoughts or feelings about priorities. What was the first thing that came to mind? Then what are you waiting for? Get ready, get set, and go—devote ten minutes to this one particular priority. If you need to, write it on a slip of paper and carry with you today so that you do not forget that you will devote ten minutes to yourself.

Today's Nourishment:
I start today with an attitude of accomplishment—I am charged up about taking action toward my priority. I am rewarded for listening to my inner guidance and devoting some time to my priority.

~282~
Resolve Disagreements

Conflicts tend to be a part of life here on earth and for the most part, they're often inevitable. Dealing with conflicts and disagreements effectively with love is a part of your life purpose. When conflicts and disagreements are handled inappropriately, the outcome can be destructive and are rarely in the best interest of either party.

Ask for God's help to resolve any disagreements you encounter with others and watch the arguments and conflicts immediately be resolved. When you ask for God's help, the hearts of everyone involved are opened and a sense of peace will surround the relationship. When working toward resolving disagreements, visualize everyone involved being open-minded and cooperative—this includes yourself. Trust the divine guidance you receive and know that all relationships contain blessings, growth, lessons, and love.

Today's Nourishment:
Arguments and conflicts are being resolved at this moment. The hearts of those involved have been opened and healed—all relationships are surrounded with a sense of peace and loving energy. I open my heart to receiving all blessings, lessons, growth, and love from all my relationships.

~283~

Find Your Center

Physical, emotional, mental, spiritual centering is one of the very basic corepracticesfor staying spiritually in tune or for your personal development. This practice promotes increased personal happiness and spiritual health. There is a way to self awareness and owning yourself and your energy. Start by focusing your attention at your spiritual and personal center—call in your energies and release any energy that is not yours. This is a starting point for a spiritual self-exploration and feeling your own integrity and wholeness.

To find your center, focus your attention and energy on yourself; balance within yourself—a spiritual version of pull *yourself together* so to speak. Bring your attention into the center of your head or you can focus your center in your heart. The location you choose is the place you feel most balanced and contained—where you are firm in self-awareness.

Visualize all your energy firmly connected to your chosen center and working optimally—see yourself filled with light, balanced, and harmonized.

Today's Nourishment:
I practice spiritual centering as a means to stay spiritually in tuned, promoting personal happiness, and spiritual health. I am self aware and own myself and my energy. I am centered, filled with light, balanced, and harmonized.

~284~
Release Hostility

Words contain charge and when combined with fiery emotions threaten the foundation of your relationships. You can upset someone not only with what you say, but with subtle facial expressions or physical gestures. Your life purpose is one of love; increasing love, approaching all situations with love, removing barriers with love, and sharing love. Your role is to minimize fear, face others with honesty, and acknowledge the divinity within every person and relationship. It is not your place to change others or justify yourself.

Use love's approach to release any feelings of hostility in your interactions—let go of any preconceived notion how the situation will proceed. Put your entire energy force on knowing that everything has already been settled for the highest good of all involved. Relax your defenses and enjoy your day regardless of the situation or circumstance.

Realizing that it is natural and healthy to feel your emotions about the relationship—your angels would never suggest deny them. Rather release any hostility attached to the situation or person and view the relationship through angel's eyes—through the eyes of love.

Today's Nourishment:
My life purpose is one of love and I am always connected to love. I worked through fiery emotions and release hostility in healthy caring ways. Everything has been settled for the highest good of all involved and I enjoy my day.

Purify Your Home

Just as your body and mind can pick up and store negative energy, so can your environment. Any fear-based sources that is in your home; newspapers, arguments within the home, television, or even using the Internet can bring dark negative fear-based energy into your home. In order to protect yourself from absorbing these negative energies or fear based sources, you will need to clear your surroundings on a regular basis.

To live spiritually in tuned with your world, your energy needs to be of the light and of the highest level possible. Today your are being guided to look around your environment, be it home, work, office space—any area where you spend part of your day. You will want to clear away the negative energies and allow light to circulate freely and lift the energy level of your surroundings. Some ways to clear the energies and purify your home include painting the walls, shampooing carpets, burning sage or incense, or putting crystals in various rooms of your home.

Of course, as you know by now, you can always call upon your angels to band together and circulate through your home, sprinkling the entire square footage with their divine healing loving energy and removing dark energy!

Today's Nourishment:
I take control of my energies and clear away negative energies from my home. I allow light to circulate freely and call upon my angels to lift the energy level to the highest level possible.

~286~
Appreciate Your Life

On your quest for living spiritually in tuned, happiness should be one of your top priorities. Learning to appreciate life is a very big aspect of that. You can be a happy person but until you take the time to appreciate the life you have, you will never reach your highest potential of happiness.

There may be a time in your life in which you feel worthless, that your life is horrible, and nothing will ever go your way. Whether you are suffering from a financial setback, feeling unhealthy, lost a job, or questioning your spirituality things can always get better. No matter where you life is at this moment—there are always ways to make it seem better. Today you are being urged to look through the fog, stop going through the motions of life, and realize how wonderful your life really is—today, find ways to appreciate your life.

Some of the best healing therapies available are pets and babies. Having a pet can get you through some very rough times because no matter what, they're always there for you. You can not help but feel happy looking at a baby—especially one that's laughing or smiling. No pets or babies in your life? Then look at the stars; stargazing is relaxing, fun, and gives a deeper understanding of life. If stargazing isn't your cup of tea—watch a bug! If all else fails, just watch a bug for a few minutes. Sound silly? Go outside and watch a bug for a minute—would you like to be the tiny little bug you're staring at? They don't experience the joy you can; they can't experience love, well-being, or the ability to directly enhance their lives. Even if that doesn't show you how great of a life you have, you'll probably start laughing when you realize that you're staring at a bug in the ground!

Today's Nourishment:
I spend a few minutes out of my day to realize how great my life really is. I am a much happier person and appreciate my life in so ways. I have been blessed with the perfect life for me!

~287~
Savor Each Day

Although it is exciting to look toward the future and wonder what is in store, true joy and happiness can be found by living in the present. Like a child in the backseat of the car on a long journey focusing on the final destination, worrying about "Are we there yet?" causes you to miss out on some of the most fascinating parts of the journey. Each day of your life's journey is filled with the joys of love, blessings, interactions, messages, humor, and captured moments.

Today, focus on savoring the day, all day long, cherishing every moment that you experience. Pay attention to the little things, as it is the littlest things that bring you the greatest joy and happiness. Be conscious of all your human interactions and the emotions you feel within each situation and event throughout the day. Be aware of details; sights, sounds, smells, and feelings—savor your day!

Today's Nourishment:
I notice the details of my day. I am consciously aware of all interactions, situations, and circumstance. I pay special attention to what I hear, see, feel, and think. I find humor in everyday situations and human interactions—I savor my day!

~288~
Seek Out The Blessing
Within Everything

Today you are to assume the role of lead detective and find the blessings within everything—Begin your investigation by asking yourself; *what's the blessing within this situation?* By putting this question to every event, interaction, situation you encounter you grant yourself the opportunity to grow, learn, heal, and promote love.

You experience growth by taking actions or reacting in ways that make you feel good about yourself. You learn by recognizing patterns of thoughts, behaviors, and emotions within each experience. For example, you may learn how to be more compassionate, understanding, or empathic during these instances. You experience healing when you are able to forgive others or situations and release hostilities toward others. Lastly, you promote love by behaving lovingly and speaking loving words.

Today's Nourishment:
I find the blessing within each human interaction, situation, and circumstance. I view everyone with the eyes of compassion, understanding, and love. I accept the lesson within each situation.

~289~
Nurture Your Mind

As a creation of the Creator, you are linked with the infinite wisdom of the Creator—all your mental gifts stem from Him. You are an intelligent and wise individual with the ability to focus and concentrate on any task given to you. Your mind is always at work, even when it appears to drift off or wander away from you or your physical surroundings—these little mental vacations increase your ability for clear thinking.

Nurturing your mind is as important as nurturing your body. Promote clear thinking by exercising your mind throughout the day. Find opportunities to allow your mind to wander; day dreaming is good for you. Stimulate your senses—change your scenery by taking a walk outside. Exercise your creativity and imagination by keeping a pad with you at all times—you never know when inspiration might hit you!

Today's Nourishment:
I nurture my mind; promoting clear thinking, keeping my mind sharp and alert, and generate creativity. I am intelligent and wise; forever linked to the most powerful computer server—God's mind!

~290~
Put A Bounce In Your Step

As a messenger of love and light you have a happy heart—physically and emotionally. There is no such thing as being *too happy* since God puts no limits on the amount of happiness he bestows on His children. There are times that you mistrust feelings of well-being and happiness; therefore today we focus on your ability to have a happy heart!

Know this, child of God; you were born to be happy; you have the inherent qualities of love, life, freedom, joy, peace and happiness. When you are joyful and happy, you are truly being yourself—you have a bounce in your step and a twinkle in your eye. Throughout the day, hold the thought of being happy and let that happiness to radiant into your core. Let this happiness feed and nourish your heart. Emit it wherever you go, through the bounce in your step, the twinkle in your eyes, and words that you speak to others so everyone will know that you are happy!

Today's Nourishment:
I am a happy person; I emit happiness wherever I go, by the bounce in my step, the twinkle in my eye, and the words I speak. My heart is happy and healthy for I am a messenger of love and light.

Remove Negativity

How often have you told yourself that you were not going to get that job? Or perhaps told yourself that even though walking and exercise helps others to lose weight, it won't work for you—nothing works? Been overdrawn on your checking account and told yourself that you had no way of getting any money to put back in there?

All of these things you say you can't do or won't happen for you will not happen with that attitude. Thinking negatively will keep you from getting the things you want or being where you want to be in life. The only person who can remove all that negativity out of your life is you. The most important thing you can do to remove negativity from your life is to have a positive train of thought about every situation.

You can't accomplish anything without having positive thoughts. Anything you want from a new job, losing weight or gaining financial stability requires you to think positive thoughts to succeed. There are always some blessings within all circumstances even if you can't see it—holding onto faith generates positive energy for yourself and others. Removing negativity from your life and maintaining a positive mind-set keeps you relaxed; your mind cleared, and helps you find creative solutions intense situations.

Make a pact with yourself today to remain upbeat and positive no matter what. Always be honest with others, check in with your higher self or angels throughout the today for guidance. Work through and difficult issues or situations swiftly, releasing any negative emotions, so that you can continue your day with a positive outlook.

> Today's Nourishment:
> *I see the blessing within all circumstances and hold fast to my belief that all is as it should be. I am upbeat and positive throughout the day no matter what. I work through any disagreements swiftly with love, release any negativity, and maintain a positive upbeat attitude.*

Practice Music Therapy

Music has always been a greater healer. Listening to music alleviates stress and is a significant mood-changer. When you were a baby in your mother's womb, you were influenced by the heart beat of your mother. You respond to the soothing music, perhaps associating it with the safe, relaxing, protective environment provided by your mother. Today you are being urged to practice music therapy and let the rhythm of the music or the beat calm and sooth your body and soul. Take a few minutes to read some suggestions on practicing music therapy:

- Take a twenty minute *sound bath*. Put some relaxing music on your stereo, lie in a comfortable position on a couch or on the floor near the speakers. Choose music with a slow rhythm—slower than the natural heart beat—music that has repetitive or cyclical pattern is found to be effective.
- As the music plays, allow it to wash over you, rinsing off the stress from the day. Focus on your breathing, letting it deepen, slow and become regular. If you need stimulation after a day of work, go for a faster music rather than slow calming music.
- When the going gets tough, go for a music you are familiar with—such as a childhood favorite or favorite oldies. Familiarity often breeds calmness.
- Take walks with your favorite music playing on the IPod. Inhale and exhale in tune with the music. This is a great stress reliever by combining exercise, imagery and music.

Listen to the music that you feel comfortable. Sitting down and forcing yourself to listen to relaxation music that you don't like may create stress, not alleviate it.

Today's Nourishment:
I practice music therapy and let the rhythmic sound of the music sooth me—I surround myself with music, choosing music with a slow rhythm and calming effect. I listen to music I feel comfortable with—alleviating stress. I am calm, serene, and stress free.

~293~
Know You're A Child Of God's

Forever a child of God's, you were created in love—you are forever wanted, loved, and cherish by Him. For those times you feel unworthy, unloved, or unwanted know that as a child of God you are the essence of love and caring. In this moment, stop and feel the depth of God's love for you. Breathe deeply, slowly, drawing in God's love—infusing yourself with divine love.

Today, see yourself as God sees you—with divine perfection and a gift created out of love. Feel how much you are loved and cared for. Release any feelings of rejection, abandonment, loneliness, and judgment toward yourself. Know that you are God's child—you are perfect, now and always.

Today's Nourishment:
I see myself as a child of God's—perfect in everyway. I am forever wanted, loved, and cherished by my Creator; I feel His love flowing through my body and wrapping me in its warmth.

~294~
Brighten Someone's Day

In the hustle and bustle of the everyday world, it is all too often that people and things are taken for granted. Let the people around you know how much you truly appreciate their presence in your life. Whether it is a co-worker, a superior, friend, or loved one, saying something a simple as "Thank you, I appreciate you" will generate a sense of pride and value. Giving compliments is an art in itself. It is about making a person feel good about themselves and even more important, feel special.

It is never too late to start showing a little appreciation to those around you. Today, brighten someone's day by letting them know they are important to you. Whether you send colorful flowers that say, 'I'm thinking of you', a card or note to wish everyday filled with happiness, color, and joy, or pick up the phone to reach out to someone—you will be amazed with the response.

Today's Nourishment:
I remember to reach out and let those around me know how much I appreciate them. Whether they are co-workers, family, friends, or casual acquaintances, I generate one gesture toward brightening their day.

Expect A Call

You have a great purpose during your time here on earth; there is a call from God on your life. Will you be ready to listen to find out what that purpose is? Are you in the dark about your purpose in life? Perhaps you have not received the call and are living as if you have, or you have received the call and living your life as if you have not!

Too often life can become too busy, too overwhelming with other *stuff*, or temptation pulls you in pursuit of riches and fame and you miss the call—and erased God's voice message by mistake. The direct line to heaven is ringing; don't turn up the volume on your life so that you can't hear God calling. Do not feel as if you are not special enough to believe that God has chosen you and that the call must be for someone else.

You have a destiny, a purpose, a life mission here on earth. You are worthy of doing great things. Of course, your entire life's purpose isn't revealed for you in one just call, it may take several calls before all is revealed. The first step is to ask God what to do with your life—then expect a call.

Today's Nourishment:
I step out of the noisy fast lane of life and find a quiet place where I can hear heaven's ring. I ask God what to do with my life and listen for His call.

~296~
Be Introspective

For spiritual growth to take place it is important to become introspective. This means that in addition to remembering the things that happened in the recent past, you must reflect on thoughts, feelings, beliefs, and the things you have experience to this point in your life. In order to gain useful insight, you must examine your experiences, your relationships, and your decisions. This insight allows you to enhance your positive traits and help you release the negative traits and allows you to become more spiritually in tune with your world and nourishes your spiritual growth. Moreover, it gives you clues on how to act, react, and conduct yourself in the midst of any situation.

Today, quiet your mind and be introspective about your experiences that lead you to this point in your life. Allow yourself to reflect on all the thoughts, feelings, beliefs, and circumstances that you have experienced. Ask for the courage and willingness to seek the truths that lie within—be objective, be forgiving of yourself, and focus on your areas for improvement.

Today's Nourishment:
I quiet my mind and am introspective on my life experiences. It is safe for me to reflect upon thoughts, feelings, and situations that have brought me this far on my path. I have the courage and willingness to seek the truths that lie within—I am forgiving of myself and focus on improvements.

God Is Like 7-Eleven

That's right, this is not a misprint—God is like a 7-Eleven store! How can one compare God to the *home of the Big Gulp?* Just like a 7-Eleven store, God can be found everywhere for your convenience. He never closes, and has everyday solutions to your problems. Need to satisfy a sweet tooth or an energy boost? Perhaps you are looking for an eleventh hour pick-me-up gift? If you are like most people you are constantly on the go with little time to spare.

This is how God becomes like a 7-Eleven store; He can satisfy any sweet tooth by nourishing your soul with His sweetness and provide you with a quick energy boost throughout the day or night. His gift of love and healing is your eleventh hour pick-me-up—and if you are on the right spiritual path, He is with you constantly while you are on the go with no time to spare! Ideally, you should find time to attend a place of worship, but for those times you can't, know that God understands. You can talk to God wherever you are—outside, in the shower, driving to work, in your home, in the office, or standing in line at the 7-Eleven—God is there!

> Today's Nourishment:
> God is my own personal 7-Eleven store. He is everywhere for my convenience, He never closes, and He is my solution for my everyday problems. He satisfies my sweet tooth with His sweetness and gives me jolts of energy with His divine love throughout my day. God is my 7-Eleven store!

~298~
Allow God To Help

God takes great interest in His [god's] children. As one of God's children He [god] takes great interest in you—your care, your happiness, and your emotional well-being. When you are upset or troubled, like a good father, God stands ready to help and enfold you in His [god's] loving arms. Even during those times you feel misunderstood or abandoned, God is with you, loving and protecting you.

He [god] is your biggest fan, ready to take on whatever you throw at Him [God]. When you allow God to help and work with Him [god], there are no limitations—wonderful things happen when you coordinate your efforts with God. Of course, this means you must keep the lines of communication open, especially during those troubled times. Resist the temptation to shut God out or close off your heart and mind to him during difficult times; allow God to help you.

When you allow God to help you with all things, you will see how much He [god] loves you and the depth of that love. His [god] love exceeds the capacity of words to explain it—yet, if you allow God to help, you will feel it!

Today's Nourishment:
I am loved, cared for, and cherished. God accepts and loves me just as I am—I allow Him [god] to help me. I ask God to help me throughout my day. He [god] is my biggest fan.

~299~
Infect Others With Smiles

You already know that smiles are contagious in the best sense of the word; you smile at someone and they smile back. Today, your task is to go out into the world and infect as many people as you can with smiles!

See how many people you can give your smile to—spread joy and gladness through a simple facial expression. Watch the facial expressions of those you greet with a smile—see their eyes light up. Infect others with smiles today; you'll brighten the day for many, including yourself, as you give your smile to others!

Today's Nourishment:
I go out into the world and infect others with my expression of happiness. It brings me joy and gladness to know that my smile infects others with cheer—I enjoy being the fuse that begins the chain reaction!

~300~
Have Integrity

As you travel down your spiritual path it is important to maintain integrity in all that you say and do. Integrity is doing the right thing because it is the right thing to do—it is keeping your word, doing what you say. You have integrity if you complete a job even when no one is looking. You have integrity if you keep your word even when no one checks up on you. A person with integrity accepts financial accountability and personal reliability. Integrity is not manipulative, prone to arrogance or self-praise. Integrity is honesty at all costs; having the guts to tell the truth, even if it may hurt to do so.

Today, pay attention to your thoughts, actions, and the words you speak. Do your actions and words reveal that you are a person of integrity? Do you say what you mean and mean what you say? Do you do your best to follow through and do what you say? Do you do the right thing simply because it is the right thing to do? Notice your thoughts and feelings as you go throughout your day—have integrity in all that you say and do.

Today's Nourishment:
I do the right thing simply because it is the right thing to do. I keep my promises, complete a job, and accept financial accountability, even when no one is checking up on me. I am honest in my words and actions—I have integrity.

~301~
Be Sincere

The virtue of speaking truly about one's feelings, thoughts, desires is vital to your spiritual growth. It goes hand-in-hand with being honest, doing the right thing, treating others as you want to be treated, and seeing others through the eyes of love. Being sincere carries risks, as it leaves you vulerable to the outside world. At the same time, you expect your friends, your lovers, and others to be sincere.

Being sincere means, don't be kind and caring as a means to an end. If you just want to be kind and caring so that you can gain preferential treatment, it's quite the opposite—it's deceptive, shallow and cruel. Be nice because you want to look back on your life and know that you were a kind and caring person, no matter what.

Today's Nourishment:
I am a kind, caring, sincere person in my actions, words, and expressions. I am honest and do the right thing simply because it is the right thing to do—treat others as I would like to be treated. I look back on my life and know that I am living a sincere life.

~302~
Respect Others

Being respectful to another person's thoughts, feelings, and actions helps strengthen your own self respect and character. Respect is having gratitude and saying thank you—being appreciative to another person for their time, help, and being nice. Respect is listening to others opinions, without being judgmental and having empathy. Today pay attention to how you treat others; respect others by showing compassion and kindness.

Respecting others, simply stated, is treating others the way you wish to be treated. Bullies often try to force others to respect them but the emotional reaction they really get is fear. You should show by example that other people should not be bossed around when you want them to do something. And never communicate with insults, or sarcasm.

> Today's Nourishment:
> *I pay attention to my actions, words, and interactions with others. I practice being respectful in all my interactions, situations, and relationships. I treat others with respect as an example of what I want to be treated.*

~303~
Pour Your Heart Out To God

God is here for you twenty-four hours a day, seven days a week, and three hundred sixty five days out of the year—in other words, continuously. When you are upset, disappointed, lonely, sad, or feeling rejected, pour your heart out to God. Tell him everything that you are feeling, even the unpleasant feelings you are experience. Although, God knows everything, there are no secrets; it is good for you to talk to Him about these things. He supports you in everything and He loves you unconditionally.

Today's Nourishment:
God is my trusted confidant and I pour my heart out to Him. He is my best friend—in good times, in bad times, whenever I need a shoulder—I can count on Him.

~304~
Choose Inner Peace

By attaining inner peace you will attain everything else. All the satisfaction, all the fulfillment of worldly and heavenly desires, comes from God. The inner realization of your eternal harmony, or your eternal wisdom, and of your power comes from attaining inner peace. If you do not get these, you will never find satisfaction, no matter how much money or power, how high position you have.

Inner peace offers you the possibility of living in a way that is congruent with your natural rhythms and cycles; honoring your gifts and abilities. Once you have resolved the conflicts within, your life begins to take on a deeper sense of peace and order which allow you flourish as the unique person you are. It is only when you choose inner peace that you can truly become creative. Without inner peace you are limited to continually re-enacting the painful traumas of your life.

Today, ask to be guided toward healthy situations and to people who will allow you to attain inner peace. Focus on becoming internally stiller and less reactive to external conflict around you. Ask to be wrapped in a cloak of comfort to let you be at peace with yourself.

Today's Nourishment:
I reconcile opposite forces within myself and my life. I find solutions to conflicts and am guided toward healthy situations to foster inner peace. I ask for guidance to learn how to be a peace with myself and let go of the painful traumas of my life.

~305~
Call Parents

The topic of talking with God on a regular basis has been covered previously and you realize the importance of maintaining a personal relationship with your Heavenly Father. As important as this relationship is for your spiritual growth, the relationship you have with your parents here on earth is equally as important. Regardless of your previous relationship with your parents, it is vital to your spiritual growth to work toward a healthy attitude in all your relationships—especially the relationship with your parents.

In today's busy world, you sometimes forget to call your parents or perhaps view a phone call to your parents as yet another task on your *to do* list. Today, you are being reminded to call your parents. You can talk to your parents about anything—talk to them about everything! They love to hear from you. Try to set aside some time each week to pick up the phone just to talk to your parents. You will be amazed how good it will make you feel by sharing a portion of your day with your parents—and they will be thrilled to share part of their day with you!

For those readers whose parents have passed on, you can still talk to your parents right now. Simply close your eyes imagine the parent you would like to speak to in front of you and have a mental conversation with him or her. Just because they have passed on to the other side doesn't mean they no longer want to hear from you!

> Today's Nourishment:
> *I call my parents and share my life with them—big, small, personal, or just a quick hello. It makes me feel better knowing that I am working on maintaining a relationship with my parents—they are happy to hear from me!*

Feel God's Love

God is sending you love as you read these words. Become aware of your breathing and notice the tender emotions that you receive each time you inhale. You are drawing in His love within—feel its warmth and let it bring you balance and healing.

Today, God will be sending you this feeling all throughout the day. If you become lost in the day and forget to notice His presence, that's just fine with Him. Just know that He is here when you need a shot of love or reassurance. Every time you breathe know that you are inhaling His love—feel it!

Today's Nourishment:
I breathe in the warm loving feeling knowing that it is God's love. With each breath I inhale I sense God's caring presence—I think of Him often and allow myself to feel His love.

~307~
Practice Empathy

Empathy involves being aware of and sensitive to the feelings and situation of another person so that you have an experience of life as that person would know it. Although this is difficult to do with peoples of other ages, lands, and cultures, you need to develop the ability to empathize if you are to truly live spiritually in tuned with your world.

The phase most often used to describe empathy is *walking in another's shoes*. When you practice empathy with someone, the first challenge is to listen to them as openly as possible—without expectations or judgments. Keep in mind, this person is not you. No matter how similar they may seem, they came through a substantially different set of experiences. Race, class, gender, culture, region, family history, and personal history all have their influences.

Empathy is an intellectual, emotional, and, ultimately a spiritual discipline. Like all others, it requires consistent and patient practice. Practice helps you listen openly at the times when it isn't easy. Insight helps you distinguish your emotions from theirs. Be patient with yourself. Give yourself room and time to grow.

Today's Nourishment:
I am aware of and sensitive to the feelings and circumstances of others. I do not pass judgment on others as they are born of different situations, experiences, and personal upbringing. I listen openly and practice empathy.

~308~
Comfort A Grieving Friend

Don't know what to say to your friend? How do you act around them? What can you do to help? What does one say to a friend who's faced a death of someone in his or her life? You don't have to know what to say. No words can take away the pain of losing someone you love. It is more important to just be there, a shoulder to cry on, an ear to listen, or the warmth of a hand. Sometimes the steadiness of friendship is the best remedy for the grieving process.

There are many ways you can offer your assistance during such a difficult time. Ask your friend what you can do specifically for the friend and family. Maybe someone from out of state is having trouble making it to the funeral. Or maybe this loss will cause financial hardship. Keep in mind, sometimes practical gifts of time and energy comfort more than words—help with the housework, cook, have a meal sent over, or help with yard work. Be dependable. So often as time passes, people forget to ask how the bereaved are doing and the cards stop coming. Make sure your friend isn't forgotten. Send a card or note every month, especially during the holidays and the anniversary of the loss.

Remember different people deal with loss in different ways—be aware of what your friend needs. If they need to talk, be willing to listen. If they do not want to talk, don't force the issue. If they need to cry, cry along side them. If alone time is needed, respect that and don't take it personally—don't rush any one through the grieving process.

As you walk along your spiritual path, you will be called upon to comfort others often, but not in your own strength. Remember that you're not alone. God will help you and guide you in comforting a hurting friend.

Today's Nourishment:

I spend time and offer comfort to a hurting friend. I offer my assistance where it is needed most; cooking, cleaning, financial, or the leaning of an ear or shoulder. I send caring notes, cards, and check up on my friend long after the initial grieving process. I feel good about who I am and knowing that I am comforting my grieving friend.

~309~
Surround Yourself With Color

Think of your life as a canvas waiting to come alive with color. Colors are a vibrant and active part of our lives, from the enchanting reds and oranges of the most amazing sunsets, to the cool sparkling blues of the clearest oceans, they enrich and surround us with beauty. Make color an everyday part of your live. Look around you, you can find color every where, inside and out. It has long been thought that color carries with it a specific energy or meaning that has the ability to influence our own energy and how we feel.

Color is a powerful element in your life and can enhance your life and the lives of your loved ones. Colors affect you emotionally, physically, mentally and spiritually—your walls, clothes, fabrics, or flowers. Surround yourself, ground yourself, and support yourself with colors.

Today's Nourishment:
My life is a canvas waiting to come alive with colors—vibrant reds and oranges, cool soothing shades of blue and natures hues of green and browns. I surround myself with color—adding energy and excitement to my day!

~310~
Think Outside The Box

You have heard the term, *think outside the box*, but what does it actually mean? Thinking outside the box is a cliché or catchphrase used to refer to looking at a problem from a new perspective without preconceptions. In other words, you must think creatively or be original.

From where does this the inspirations come that inspires these unique outlooks and breakthrough ideas? It is all around you—it is within every spiritual being here on earth. Many perceive thinking outside the box as if it were an uncommon occurrence. It is not so uncommon at all. It may seem so uncommon to many, due to being stuck in the way reality is perceived. You could be one of the card carrying members of the thinking outside the box club, if you would just take the chance to being and living in the moment.

By eliminating the wall you built around your self and your thoughts just for an instant we permit the beauty and revolutionary breakthroughs you seek, to enter into our conscious experience. Thinking out of the box can only happen by being the experience and living in the moment. Today, pay attention to thinking outside the box and absorbing the experience of each moment every situation, event, interaction, and circumstance—opening the door to greater possibilities.

Today's Nourishment:
I spend time thinking outside the box and viewing my life with a new perspective. I absorb the experience of each moment—savoring the details of each interaction, situation and circumstance. I open door to greater possibilities and follow the path my heart and soul guide me to.

~311~
Know That You Belong

If you ever feel as though you don't belong or fit in with others, remember that God created you to be here. A sense of belonging comes with shared interests, habits, or hobbies—sometimes it may be necessary to participate in activities related to your interest as a means of expanding and developing new relationships.

You do belong here on earth and you have a life purpose that this world needs. You are unique, as all God's creations are, but you have a lot in common with others. Today your goal is to find similarities you share with others. This may require a filter on your thinking cap or thinking outside the box but you will soon begin to see commonalities.

Remember, you have a choir of angels that surround you—they are your loyal companions and friends. As your angels love you, so shall others here on earth—know that you do belong.

Today's Nourishment:
I belong here and fit in with others. I find similarities and reach out to others. I am happy, pleasant, and cheerful—people like me and want to spend time with me.

~312~
Delight In The Sunlight

Sunlight is something taken for granted, yet sunlight is an integral part of your life here on earth. Indeed without sunlight there would be no life; sunlight warms the Earth with life. Sunlight is indispensable to good health and peace of mind.

Many people fear the sun's ultra-violet rays and hide from the sun—do not deny the healing power of the sun. The human race evolved and thrived under the light and energy of the sun. The sun was once used as a general tonic to heal almost everything and man has run naked on this planet under the sun for centuries. The sun is the source of energy for all plants and animals. Delight in the sun's powerful rays for increased health, longevity, and spiritual well-being.

Today, spend fifteen or twenty minutes delighting in the sunlight—there are so many fun things you can do or simply do nothing but soak up the sun rays. Give into your spirit of adventure and tap into your playful side by spending some time outdoors today. Infuse your day with the benefits of the sunlight: spend time outdoors, sit near a window in your home and office, or invest in a skylight so that you can absorb the benefits of the sun. Make a point today to delight in the sunlight to support your health and happiness.

> Today's Nourishment:
> *I spend time outdoors today, delighting in the sun's powerful rays—increasing my health, longevity, and spiritual well-being. When I am stressed I inhale deeply, consciously inhale fresh air, feeling the sun's healing powers infuse my body—I feel invigorated, energetic, and refreshed!*

~313~
Know You Are Wrapped In God's Love

At this exact moment, know that you are wrapped in a loving embrace—you are wrapped in God's love. Give yourself a moment to soak in this love, feel it seep within your heart, drink it in and feel its refreshing nourishment within your soul. It is important for you to nourish and recharge yourself with God's love on a regular basis. Today, you are being blessed with waves of loving supportive energy from God. You need not be consciously aware of the details of this process, simply know and accept that you are wrapped in God's love and enjoy the benefits of this love.

Today's Nourishment:
I am surrounded by heaven's love and wrapped in God's love. This love seeps within my heart—I drink it in and feel its refreshing nourishment deep within my soul. I allow myself to soak up God's love—I am grateful to have such a loving God.

~314~
Give God Fifteen Minutes of Your Day

God is your Father. You do not need to call him "Master, Sir, Your Honor", or some other note worthy title but simply "Father". His love for you goes far beyond the love you have for your own children, and He wants you to be happy here on earth. But like a parent, He loves to spend time with His child—even a few minutes a day can bring a smile to His face.

Like most adult children, you sometimes get so caught up in living your life that you forget to stop by and visit with your Father. But like a parent, He understands that you are a busy person—He blesses your life even when your visits become infrequent. Like a parent, He doesn't mind when it appears He sees or hears from you during crisis moment. After all, children will be children. He shakes His head gently when the holidays come around and you finally make your way to a place of worship to give your yearly thanks—he knows what is in your heart, He's your Father.

He knows what is good for you and what will make you happy. It may not always what you want and what you think will bring you happiness— but Father knows best. You are being encouraged today to visit with your Father—give God fifteen minutes of your day. That isn't much time, but it would mean the world to your Father. Surly you can find fifteen minutes to pop in and say hello, chat for a few, let him know how you are doing and what's new with him. And then as you are ready to dash back out again, you can turn to Him and say, "Thanks Father!"

Today's Nourishment:
I give God fifteen minutes of my time today. He is my Father and He enjoys my visits; I will stop in, sit for a few, chat and tell him what's been going on in my life since my last visit—then I will express my gratitude for all that He does for me and the many blessings He bestows upon me.

Feed Your Curiosity

Curiosity may have killed the proverbial cat. However, curiosity is one of the most important aspects of life. It is through a desire to find out something that you are able to learn, grow, gather information, stay active and alive, and are able to progress along life's path. A lack of curiosity can lead to a lack of life, rather than the opposite.

Think back to when you were a child—being curious about the world around you was an important part of learning. As a child you showed an interest in wanting to find out about how things work and often asked why things happen. Life was very seldom boring back then—to many things to learn, explore, and investigate; you fed your curiosity on a daily basis. Just as feeding your curiosity was important to the learning process back then, it is just as important today as an adult. Enhance your life by feeding your innate sense of curiosity. Become the explorer, investigator, and an adventurer again—add luster to your life; feed your curiosity!

Today's Nourishment:
I feed my innate curiosity; I am an explorer, investigator, and an adventurer. I seek out mysteries, determined to figure out the 'why's' and 'how's' of thing within my world. I feed my curiosity and add luster to my life!

~316~
Live Within Truth

Do not discount any belief because each person is entitled to their own beliefs, their own truth. Respect the absolute individuality of each person, but live within your truth. Just as you are entitled to your belief and truth, each person is entitled to express their truth openly and honestly. It is now time to live within your truths and stand firm on your beliefs—listen to your intuition and inner voice. Let God be your strength and be the guiding hand that protects what is natural and pure within.

Ask for assistance to live within your truth faithfully while honoring your talents and gifts. God will grant you the courage to live from the deep knowledge within which respects your abilities and the strength to stand by your convictions. He can also help you succeed in developing your individual gifs and fully expressing yourself. By living within truth and holding to your beliefs, you are making a valuable contribution to the spiritual development of humanity simply by being who you are. In situations where there is conflict between what you know to be right and what is being represented as truth, ask that you be shown the absolute truth—live within that truth.

Today's Nourishment:
Dear God, nurture my strength and my conviction that I am making a valuable contribution to humanity. Help me to see what is real in every situation where my insight and intuition are called upon to direct and guide me. Light the way to the truth within my heart—give me the courage to live within that truth.

~317~
Watch A Red-tail Hawk Fly

Hawks are one of the most intriguing and mystical of the birds of prey. According to some Native Americans the red-tail hawks are the messengers, the protectors, and the visionaries of the air. The sky is the realm of the hawk. Through its flight it communicates with humans and with the great creator spirit. It awakens your vision and inspires you to a creative life purpose. The red of the red-tail reflects a greater intensity of energy at play within your life; physical, emotional, mental, and spiritual forces. It teaches the balance necessary to discover your true purpose in life.

Native Americans believe that by following the path of the hawk, you will be led on the right spiritual path. When you spot a red-tail hawk flying above, perched on a treetop, or utility post pay special attention to your inner voice, thoughts, or feelings at that moment. The red-tail hawk is a messenger that brings you information about yourself. He works with in tandem with your spiritual team to bring you guidance for your spiritual walk

You are encouraged to watch for the red-tail hawk today. Let this bird be a catalyst, stimulating hope, new ideas, and visions for the future. Know that when you watch this magnificent creature of the air, it brings messages that may help teach you and others to be open to the new. Let him lead you to use your creative energy in manifesting your soul purpose.

Today's Nourishment:
I look upward to the sky for the red-tail hawk paying attention to my inner voice, thoughts, and feelings. I am receptive to the messages brought to me by this splendid bird. I accept the lessons, messages, and energies brought by the red-tail hawk.

~318~

Admire Wildflowers

Plants and wildflowers provide a spiritual link between nature and human beings. Nothing soothes the soul quite like the sight and smell of these beautiful creations of nature. Not only are wildflowers beautiful, but useful, for without them life of every kind on earth would be in danger of extinction.

Your nature angels are waiting to be your tour guides on a wildflower walk. Take time today to admire the wildflowers around you. Visit your backyard or take a nature walk; stroll along at an unhurried pace and with a watchful eye. Take a long drive through the countryside; a field of brightly colored wild flower with the vivid blue sky as the backdrop is a beautiful sight. This presents an excellent opportunity to get some floral shots or kick off your shoes and walk barefoot across the field of wildflowers. If you live in an area where wildflowers are not accessible, visit a botanical garden or stop by a local florist shop and purchase a bundle of fresh cut flowers for yourself. Savor the bright colors, the sweet fragrance, and the warm feeling you feel within you.

Today's Nourishment:
I ask my nature angels to guide me on a wildflower walk; admiring the bright colors and sweet smell of these creations of nature. I feel the soothing affect this activity has on my soul. I take time out of my busy day to stop and admire the wildflowers growing in fields.

Disheveled Daisies (Photo by Nicole McGowan)

~319~
Take A Long Drive

It is in your blood! As the weekend approaches, the sky expands with sun and the weekend is open with possibilities. You find yourself opening a road map, tracing with your finger a route you never noticed before. You look toward the horizon longingly; thinking about some highway that leads to mountains or canyons—who knows all the wonders such a highway might lead you to? Not knowing is half, the fun, the excitement, the adventure!

Today, find a road map and look up routes that you have never traveled—take a long drive. Put your favorite CD in the car stereo, turn the volume up, roll the windows down or put the top down and just drive. Feel the sunlight on your face, wind in your hair, hear the music playing, and feel your stresses and worries be blown away as you travel down the long road!

Today's Nourishment:
My road map is open to the unknown. I gather up my collection of favorite tunes, pack a few necessities, service my car, and take to the road. Wind in my hair, sunlight on my face, and my favorite tunes—life is great!

~320~
Be The Director Of Your Day

What kind of day would you like to have? If you desire a positive, upbeat, and optimistic day, then allow yourself to visualize and feel only those energies. You are the director of your day—you decide the best possible outcome of any given situation by your attitude. Know that it is within you to have extraordinary experiences. Know that you deserve all the greatness that life has to offer. Make the decision to have a wonderful extraordinary day. If negative thoughts or emotions threaten to darken your day, simply ask for spiritual assistance in removing this negativity. Transform those negative energies into positive ones—make this day super wonderful!

Today's Nourishment:
I will focus on staying positive, upbeat, and optimistic. I deserve to have a wonderful day and experience only the best possible outcome in any situation or relationship. Blessed be, I am the director of MY day!

Experience True Freedom

Celebration of your freedom is more than what is written in the Declaration of Independence. It is up to you to decide what energies are acceptable in your life. The first step toward personal freedom is to make a declaration. This declaration you make for yourself can be established once you have taken some time to observe yourself in a very detailed way. This is a step towards personal freedom.

By observing yourself, your behaviors, thoughts, and attitudes you display, you can find ways to free yourself of negativity. This is not about judging one self. No, it is about watching yourself and how you react to daily events. Or, perhaps in watching yourself you may observe that you are not reacting. You may observe that you are often in situations that you allow others to *step all over your energy field* or you may find yourself barking at people too quickly! You may later wish you said or did this or that. Regardless of what you may observe about yourself, the key is to not judge yourself and just observe!

The key to true personal freedom is to find a happy balance. Being the individual you are, you may find this balance in a different ways. There are many paths to balance. You may find self-observation, meditation, plenty of sunshine and fresh air, regular exercise, lots of fruits and vegetables, good vitamins; laughter, plenty of rest as well as play and more laughter, all contribute to balance in your life. While you may be pulled off your target occasionally, you can just as easily be put back on track.

Today's Nourishment:
I focus on self-observation, observing my behaviors, thoughts, and attitudes and find ways to free myself of negativity. I set goals to maintain a happy balance and strive toward personal freedom.

~322~
Remember Heroes

There are men and women who are currently serving, have served their country, and gave their life for their country to allow you to have the freedoms you enjoy today. During peace times they served within the county and around the world, often away from their families for long periods of time. During times of conflict they served under dangerous conditions, often being wounded, changing their lives forever.

These servicemen and women are *spiritual warriors* in the sense they serve to protect, stand up for those who can not stand up for themselves, strive to correct injustices, and stand up for their beliefs. Think of all the freedoms that you enjoy; freedom of press, freedom of speech, freedom to demonstrate, freedom to worship, freedom to own property, freedom to travel, and the freedom to vote. Who guaranteed all these freedoms? Not the reporter, public speaker, campus organizer, minister, salesman, travel agent, nor a politician— but rather the *spiritual warriors* of yesterday, today, and tomorrow. It is the servicemen and women who protect and guaranteed all your freedoms—some who are buried beneath the very flag they died for.

You are being asked today to remember these heroes—these *spiritual warriors.* Give a moment of silence in their honor, turn on your headlights for a moment, visit a memorial, or simply say, '*thank you*'. Recognizing the legacy of those who died to protect the very freedom that enables you to read this book is something that can strengthen and unite everyone.

Today's Nourishment:
I remember the men and women assumed the role of spiritual warrior by protecting my freedoms. I admire their courage and their spirit; grateful for their service; respect their sacrifices; and salute them with pride!

USS Arizona Memorial Wall (photo taken by CPL Joseph L. Santel)

Get Involved With Your Community

Many people are so exhausted by the end of the workday that they opt to just collapse in front of the TV and relax in the evening. They never think that maybe, just maybe, getting involved in community activities is the path toward revitalization. Part of living a more spiritual life requires being involved with the world around you. Getting involved with your community is a part of that involvement.

Today's focus is on the getting involved with your community. Not only is it the right thing to do, getting involved in your community gives your life balance, expands your horizons, and connects you with others in the community. Additionally, getting involved gives you a better understanding of community issues and allows you to act on their beliefs about social change and social justice.

There are numerous ways to get involved with your community; you could help out at a soup kitchen, read to children in day care, visit people in nursing homes, deliver flowers in the hospital, or serve on a political or social action committee. Set aside some time today to find ways that you can get involved with the community that you live in.

> Today's Nourishment:
> *I seek out ways to be involved with my local community—I am revitalized, balanced, relaxed, and feel a sense of togetherness. I volunteer my time to help others within my community by visiting the elderly, helping the young, and assisting the sick.*

~324~
Learn To Be Calm

In today's world, life is so arranged that you seldom have a moment to collect your thoughts or personal contemplation. Between the demands of work, family, and social activities, there remains little time for just *being*. Even when free moments do arise, the time is often filled with television, or music, or magazines. Of course, there is nothing wrong with any of these activities, and they are encouraged, but in moderation as they can rob you of a great treasure—moments of quiet solitude.

As your life becomes more turbulent and busy, you need to take time to be calm, to be quiet, and to cultivate peace. Think about it, how can you ever hope to be spiritually in tune with your world, if you cannot even bring a few moments of peace into your life? Why not take 15 minutes a day to tap into your inner reservoir of peace. You don't have to be sitting in a quiet room or walking in the woods to do this. Just retreat into your soul. Open your heart to your creator; listen to your breathing; shut out the surrounding noise, for just a moment.

Have you ever been to a public swimming pool on one of the hottest days of the summer when it is crowed with boisterous children and adults? You are surrounded by the sounds of yelling and laughing. All the splashing and frolicking makes the water choppy. But, dive a few feet into the pool and, suddenly, all is quiet. The water is peaceful, calm. You have that same type of reservoir within your soul—no matter how busy or turbulent your life is at the moment, there is always a place to go that is calm and serene.

Today, find some time to escape within to that quiet place within of solitude—reflect, contemplate, and recharge yourself. Today, learn to be calm.

Today's Nourishment:
I stand barefoot and go deep inside myself. I close my eyes, breathe deep, and draw in a natural energy. I am completely with myself able to reflect, contemplate, and recharge.

~325~
Trust In God's Mercy

When you are faced with an unbearable situation remember God offers you *God's* love as a living reality and feel the shift of energy or change in circumstance. It may be in small and subtle ways that you experience mercy. It can be in the form of a friendly phone call when you are at a low point in your day or a gentle boost of confidence when you are feeling unsure of yourself. It could unfold in many situations in which you do not control. For instance, you could meet a person that changes your life or you could be accepted, or rejected, for a job or course of study. Some may consider these acts mere coincidence, however, trust and accept it as the gift of God's mercy, who is working to make your life fulfilled and easier.

With this awareness of *God's* mercy and intervention you gain an understanding that you do not have to strive and push yourself. Nor be harsh and punish yourself when things do not work out as you think they should—trusting in God's mercy as another gift of *God's* love.

Pray for understanding and acceptance of this guidance and intervention—release the constant need to control and accept that God's mercy is constantly being given. Trust in God's mercy and allow it to move you through the rough patches of your life.

Today's Nourishment:
I trust in God's love for mankind and am conscious that I am protected and guided. I am grateful for the blessings in my life and trust in God's mercy and allow God to navigate me through the rough patches in my life.

~326~
Capture Memories

History has always been about famous, important people but it is important to preserve your own life stories—today is about capturing memories. Find ways to preserve those fleeting moments—capture the emotions of each milestone, each moment of joy, every holiday shared, and each smile and laughter exchanged.

No, this isn't an advertisement for a photographer studio, scrap-booking business, or a digit make-over session. You may think to yourself that you have an ordinary life with nothing out of the ordinary to *capture*. No one has had an ordinary life. Everyone has had at least moments of extraordinary—that includes you!

Think back to a time when you lost a loved one and memories of time shared were all that you had to cling to. Capturing memories is an important part of living—especially after a loved one is gone. As time passes, memories can fade and dissolve in the mind, forever lost and distorted. Today, focus on ways to preserve ordinary everyday moments that are, in reality, extraordinary moments from an extraordinary life. Whether it is a collection of writings, images and documents, it is a window into the life to be shared across the oceans and beyond the boundaries of lifetimes.

Today's Nourishment:
Ordinary everyday events suddenly become extraordinary. I recall moments of time shared with a loved one that has passed and cling to the memories—reliving precious moments through captured memories. I preserve ordinary moments through writings, images, photos, memory books, and keepsakes—let these memories be a window into a life shared.

~327~
Share Your Heart

Is there any way you can become more loving that you are at this moment? Can you fill your heart with more loving kindness? Despite the fact that others are less than perfect, can you think loving thoughts about yourself and others? Sometimes progress in life is measured by income or clothing size, but what really matters is how much you love while you are here on Earth.

What matters most is your capacity to share your heart—to feel, receive, and be more loving. The most important thing to remember about your time here on Earth, is that your purpose is to love; it all its forms. In order to love openly and freely, you must be willing to share your heart. You have everything you need to allow your heart to open wide and permit more love and affection to enter and exit. Let go of any fears, doubts, or blocks—recall you handed those over to God.

Today, allow yourself to be more loving, caring, and affectionate. Look past flaws and imperfections and see only love…share your heart.

Today's Nourishment:
I am more loving. My heart is filled with loving kindness and I think only loving thoughts toward myself and others. No longer afraid or filled with doubts, I open my heart and share it with others.

Have An Adventure Day

In keeping with your spiritual existence while here on earth, you must feed your soul's craving for adventure. Venturing from the known to the unknown allows you the experience of learning and growing. Although you may resist the unknown out of fear or feelings of awkwardness, there is a certain amount of excitement that appeals to your soul!

Set aside some time, once or twice a month works, and have an adventure day. Take a day when you do something different. Schedule this day in advance. Choose an activity that you haven't done before; step out of your comfort zone. Get out of the house. Explore, and let your world teach you things. The activity is up to you. It can be something you think would be fun like riding a rollercoaster at the amusement park. It can be something that scares you a little; eating a new foreign food, or going to the symphony if you don't know classical music. Or it can be something cheesy or touristy that you'd be embarrassed to admit you did—gem mining, or a carriage ride through the city, or the carnival that shows up in the mall parking lot every summer.

Adventure Day can last a whole day, or an overnight, or just a few hours. But keep it simple and local so that you don't make it into such a big deal that you never even do it. The goal is just to do it!

Today's Nourishment:
I feel adventurous—dedicating at least one day a month to have an adventure. During my adventure day I do things that I haven't done before, are fun, and allow the world to teach me things. I realize that I have nothing to fear going from the known to the unknown—it is exciting and it feels my soul!

Write A Love Letter

In today's high tech society where the majority of people are now communicating by cell phone or email and unfortunately the art of the love letter writing seems to have been forgotten. But how do you write a love letter? Letter writing is a practice that has been neglected in an era of e-mail and text-messaging.

Letters are considered a much more personal form of written communication. It's something tangible—a personal touch. Paper, pen and ink can be felt and seen as well as read. It can be saved in a special place and rediscovered years later to be experienced again.

Now is the time to express your heart on paper—today you will write a love letter. Pick up a pen and start writing. It may sound intimidating, but love letter writing just has one simple rule--speak from the heart. Write a letter to your loved one as if you were together and talking.

Woo your beloved with words by remembering one very particular moment you have shared. Re-create that moment by recalling the small and intimate details that give it a special place in memory. Memory itself is rooted in the body, so use all your senses: touch, taste and smell are the most intimate. Spend five minutes with your eyes closed and think of the best time you've shared with your love. Take out a piece of paper and write to your love what you remember, from beginning to end. One moment you'll always remember. Include sights, sounds, tastes, smells, and images of that time.

Simple and heartfelt is best. 'I love you for your sense of humor.' 'I love you for your compassion.' 'I love you for your patience.' Love letters need no flowery language, or perfect rhyme. All that's required is giving the heart a chance to express itself.

Today's Nourishment:
I express my heart today through writing—I write a love letter to a loved one. I will speak from the heart. I use loving words, recall memories, and express my emotions using simple and heartfelt words.

~330~
You Are Love

God is pure, divine, and all encompassing love. This love is the only feeling that exists in heaven. As God is your creator your soul was conceived and created with Divine love. As a creation of God's your soul is eternally connected to God and in turn, connected to love.

The physical form you have is but a small aspect of who you are—your soul is the core of your being, the source of divine love. You are forever surrounded, much like a warm bubble bath, in this warm caring soothing feeling of love; you both give and receive.

Today, be aware of this eternal connection to this divine love and know that you are love. Express affection to yourself and others, paying extra attention to how his makes you feel comfortable and at home. You are love!

Today's Nourishment:
God and the angels are pure, divine, and all encompassing love, therefore so I am. Everything about me is love—I express this to myself and others, sharing this love with all that I am encounter here on Earth. It is who I am—yesterday, today, and tomorrow.

~331~
Age Gracefully

As you progress on your spiritual path, you are guided to make careful and wise decisions for your highest good and the highest good of others in your care. You have spiritual assistance available to help you mature into a wise being capable of handling responsibilities and making wise choice to enhance your life and well-being—how to age gracefully!

Regardless of your current age, you will continue to grow and mature and with maturity comes responsibilities—this is the nature circle of life. When the weight of your choices feel too much to bear, ask for assistance and support in finding the right answers. You can pray for blessings and guidance to help steer a course through life; you can pray to be led to love and joy; that your decisions come from love and not based on love of power.

Be mindful of the needs of younger or less responsible people entrusted to your care. Ask to be lead to find the peace and wisdom which comes with maturity—to be guided to what is truly right for you instead of what feels good for the moment. Have the courage to cultivate wisdom and the ability to handle power so that you are not abusive. Let those who are entrusted in your care feel safe with you. Ask that the angels bless you with self-respect and strength of character so that you age gracefully with wisdom and maturity.

Today's Nourishment:
I understand my growth process as move toward maturity and cope with the responsibilities of adulthood. I ask for assistance and support in making the right decisions—that they come from a place of love. I am blessed with self-respect and strength of character—I age gracefully.

~332~
Live Today As If It Were Your Last

Think of those folks you knew that have passed on to the other side. How many of those folks do you think knew that they were living their last day on earth? Sometimes due to an illness or a disease a person may understand that their last day may come sooner than they hoped, but no one knows which day will be their last.

The hour of death is unknown; many times it comes suddenly and without warning. Not to be morbid or cause unnecessary fear, but consider what if this were your last day to live. What would you do? Who would you spend time with? Who would hear the words, "I love you"? Who would you show your love to? Who would hear your final farewells?

What are you waiting for? This may very well be your last day on earth, there are no guarantees. When is the last time you hugged your kids; your parents, your spouse, or those special in your life? When is the last time you told your loved ones you loved them?

Live today as if this was the very last day of your life here on earth—seek out ways to express your emotions and love for others, do those things you have been putting off, savor each experience, each emotion, smell, sounds, and sights. As you begin your day, do so with the mind set that this could be your very last day and make the absolute most of it!

Today's Nourishment:
I begin this day with the knowledge that this could be my last day on earth—it is the theme for my day. I savor each moment of this day, reach out to my loved ones, show affection and love toward those in my life. I take steps to ensure my relationships are right with those that I love.

~333~
Step Out Of The Past

Today is the day that you step out of your past! It is now time to walk away from all those negative situations, events, and emotional scars. In order to live in the present and move toward the future to fulfill your destiny, you have to step out of the past. If you don't, it colors everything you see and affects all that you do. For example, if you have experience betrayal in your past and have not yet found healing, your future experiences will be viewed through the eyes tainted with residue of betrayal.

You are being asked to surrender your past and walk out of it step by step. See yourself as a child of God created in God's image and for God's purpose. Not forgiving the people and events of your past keeps you bound to it—becoming an emotional prisoner. Getting free from your past doesn't happen overnight. Ask for help with forgiveness, resentments, and those emotions that bind you to the past. Once you step out of your past, don't look back.

> Today's Nourishment:
> *I release my past to a higher power. Everything I have done and all that was done to me has been handed over as I walk away from my past. I am healed from all the emotional damage from my past—it no longer affects me today.*

Passion For The Present

Maintaining a passion for the present means embracing where you are at this moment and trusting that is where you are suppose to be—at this time. Trust that timing is perfect because when you follow your spiritual path, your creator controls timing—and God's timing is perfect!

When you come to accept that the timing is perfect you can be content no matter where you are, as you know that you will not be left in that spot forever. It is just a matter of time before things change. Furthermore, if you are in a good place right now, it won't last forever. You'll soon be moved into stretching beyond your comfort zone to move to an even better place. Get ready for the ride!

Focus on living your life in the present, content with where you are currently planted. If you are not in a place you want to be right now, refuse to let that frustrate or intimidate you. You will not stay there for long. There is no need to be stuck in your past or worried about your future for you will miss the richness of the present. Experience the wealth of each moment creating a passion for the present!

Today's Nourishment:
I am where I am supposed to be at this moment. I am content where I am at this moment—it is just a matter of time before things change. I am no longer stuck in my past. I experience a passion for the present.

~335~
Open Up To New Ways Of Viewing Life

Your spiritual quest has enticed you to dig a little deeper, going beyond mere belief, accepting that you and others here on earth are spiritual beings. Your spiritual understanding is rising to another level as you open up to new ways of viewing life.

Your mind is expanding, opening, and you are being invited to move to a higher level of understanding. Now is the time to let go of limited thinking, pay attention to signs, and open up to new ways of viewing life. Spiritual guidance is being sent in various forms—flashes of a mental image, feelings and emotions, a sense of knowing, and thought form.

Embrace this new way of viewing the world. Know that your increased awareness is another level of spiritual understanding; be not afraid, but rejoice in knowing that you are in the midst of a spiritual awakening and are being guided through these changes!

Today's Nourishment:
I let go of limited thinking and open my mind up to new ways of viewing life. It is safe for me to embrace this spiritual awakening and I welcome this new level of spiritual understanding.

~336~
Focus On Your Spiritual Growth

As a divine being you are connected to the universal consciousness, and are capable of, and possess the gifts of intuitive abilities. Some individuals display more developed extrasensory perceptions, while others have a sense of *knowing* without any actual proof of knowing why. The most beneficial methods for enhancing intuitive gifts are through ways that promote inner balance, meditation and disciplined spiritual practices.

While everyone is not intended to become professional intuitive or psychic, development of these inherent abilities allows a closer alignment with God and provides essential spiritual growth. You are being nudged to focus on your spiritual growth—read, study, learn, and meditate as you are guided. Listen to your own inner guidance for enhancement of your inherent gifts. During this time you may feel a mixture of confusion, fear, excitement, anxiety, and wonder—surrender any fears to God. Do not worry what impact your new spiritual pursuits have on your job, marriage, or friends—trust that you are supported, loved, and guided each step of your new spiritual path.

Today's Nourishment:
I make time to study, read, learn, and meditate as part of my spiritual learning. I listen to my inner guidance for instructions to enhance my spiritual gifts. I am supported, loved, and use my God given gifts to help myself and others.

~337~
Notice Fleeting Mental Images

You are not just a physical being, but also spiritual being living within an infinite universe filled with infinite possibilities. Your studies have expanded and opened your mind to your inherent extrasensory perceptions, allowing your spiritual sight to awaken fully. Known as clairvoyance, this spiritual sight may come in different forms; dreams, colorations, angelic beings, spirits, symbols, or other scenes not visible to the naked eye.

You have been blessed with a highly sensitive sense of inner sight that, up to this point, has been napping just below the surface. Pay attention to fleeting mental images and trust that you are being shown only that which you need to know. Trust that the same power that brought you to your spiritual path will show you only loving images. Enjoy you spiritual sight and trust the mental images!

Today's Nourishment:
I have spiritual sight. I open my mind to receive the universe's gifts, knowing I am blessed with a highly sensitive sense of inner sight. I notice fleeting mental images, embracing my connection God, His messages and guidance.

~338~
Pay Attention To Recurring Feelings

As it has been discussed, divine guidance is given in many forms. You can receive guidance in the form of recurring feelings—referred to as clairsentience. Clairsentience is an intuitive and involves what is commonly referred to as gut feeling, woman's intuition, or *that little voice within.*

Do not be afraid of these deep emotions or intense feelings, as they signify a form of divine guidance. As God speaks to you, a feeling or keen awareness is perceived and emotions and empathetic feelings can be relayed through the impressions. You can ask for help to distinguish between your own feelings and those of divine guidance. You are being guided toward people, situations, and places that hold clear and loving energies. Please pay attention to recurring feelings and follow these feelings as they are answers to your prayers.

Today's Nourishment:
I receive divine guidance in the form of clear feelings. I ask for help in sorting my feelings enabling me to notice, understand, and follow the guidance given.

~339~
Notice Thoughts And Ideas

Have you ever just known something without really knowing how or why? This sense of knowing is referred to as claircognizance; no one tells you, you didn't read it in a book, you just know it. That is exactly how you feel when a thought, idea, or instant knowledge comes to you—there are no words spoken and your entire body confirms that you simply know.

This sense of knowing comes from God, transferring the information to your mind in the form of thoughts and ideas. All great inventors, writers, scientists, and researchers stem from the same universal sense of knowing. Don't discount your thoughts, or dismiss them as dreams or common knowledge. As you evolve and become more spiritually in tuned, your thoughts and ideas are prone to a higher frequency and are trustworthy inspirations. Trust that you are tapped into divine wisdom and guidance at this time; it is important to notice your thoughts and ideas.

Today's Nourishment:
I pay attention to thoughts and ideas that come to me—these are answered prayers directly from God. I trust that the thoughts, ideas, and sense of knowing are of God and I am receptive to what is being revealed. I no longer discount this sense of knowing and ask for clarification when confusion threatens the messages I receive.

~340~
Listen To Loving Guidance You Hear

Did you ever stop to think about where some of your thoughts come from throughout the course of your day? Think back to a time when you were faced with a crisis or dangerous situation and a *little inner voice* sent you a warning. In the face of danger or crisis, you tend to listen, trust, and instantly respond to that inner voice though you may not be sure why. That voice within that you hear is true divine guidance. Normally this type of guidance is given to you in the form of repetitious messages—as most divine directives are repetitious, loving, and to the point.

Known as clairaudience, you can hear messages in thought form from the spiritual realm. You *hear* what is being said in thought form messages. You may actually receive guidance messages in the form of talking or singing in your head, yet there are no auditory sounds. Do not fear this form of communication with God as many receive loving guidance in this manner.

Listen to the loving guidance you hear in your head; when the information comes through, there may be pressure on top of your head, body sensations such as chills, tingles, hair standing on end, or other sensations. Do not worry that you are being mislead, as this is but yet another method to communicate with God and the angels.

Today's Nourishment:
I listen to the loving guidance to comes to my in thought form. I am not afraid as this is but yet another way to communicate with God—hearing ~~His~~ God's *loving guidance and follow* ~~His~~ God's *directions.*

~341~
Ask For A Purpose

If you are wondering about your life's purpose or want a greater sense of meaning, begin asking for it! That's right, you can ask for anything, why not ask for a divine assignment, greater meaning to your life, or for explanation of your life's purpose. When you ask for a specific assignment or greater understanding, completely release your request to the universe with a sense of knowing that your request will be heard and answered.

Be alert and watch for opportunities that are put in your path, strong urges, or repeated information given to you by others. For example, if others continue to comment on your musical talents and abilities explore the possibilities as they may be pointing the way to your mission.

By asking for a purpose or special assignment, you are displaying your willingness to be of service while here on earth. Ultimately, the greatest beneficiary of contributing to a sense of tranquility to the world is you— giving always yields the greatest rewards.

> Today's Nourishment:
> *Dear God, I ask that you reveal my life's purpose; give me a divine assignment that uses my talents and abilities for the highest good of others. I want to be of service and bring a sense of tranquility to my world while I am here on earth. Guide me where I am to go—I will follow. Thank you!*

~342~

When You Are Angry With God

God does not make bad things happen to people. For those times when all seems lost and that joy will never be in your heart again—know this, He *God* never gives ugliness or hurt. Agony is already within the human condition. No one escapes life's troubles or lessons.

When the worst is upon you, even the loss of a loved one, so is the best. When you are faced with the grief of such a loss, look around you, see the faces of those who mourn with you and know that no matter how lonely you feel in that moment, you are not alone.

If during these times you find yourself angry at God—this is alright. God understands.

When you feel betrayed by someone, it takes time to forgive and renew the friendship. When you are mad at God, really mad at Him *God*, it takes time to heal your relationship with Him *God*. When life has been hard, unkind, unfair, or painful, it was not God who hurt you. It was another's free will being used in a way that you can not yet understand. Every event of your life is part of a bigger plan no matter how awful, unfair, or painful it may seem. If you need to, yell at God. Tell Him *God* why you are so angry with Him *God*. Scream. Shout. Cry. Go ahead—let it out, all of it. God is all powerful, He *God* can handle it. Then ask for God's help. It has always been there. It will always be there. God brings strength, joy, and love.

> Today's Nourishment:
> *It's alright to be angry with God. I express my angry*, hurt, and sense *of betrayal to God. I scream, yell, cry, and tell God why I am so angry. I release all my anger and ask for His *God's* help to heal. My overwhelming emotions of sorrow and grief are replaced with feelings of unconditional love—God's arms are around me.*

~343~
Give Into Tears

Life is not easy but trust that you are being supported in every way. The lost of a loved one often leaves the survivors torn between wanting to continue living for others and wanting to die just to be with the one who has passed on. People who have been affected by a death or other loss are likely to experience feelings of grief. Grief is not an emotion anyone enjoys, but it an important part of healing. As people grieve they may experience a variety of emotions including shock, sadness, depression, anxiety, hostility, guilt, fear, and, with time, acceptance. They may also move back and forth between good memories and bad memories.

While the grieving process is difficult, there are things that can help people heal more quickly. Talking with trusted friends and family members about your memories, feelings, and thoughts will be helpful. Keeping a daily routine will help you create a sense of stability as you reorganize your life and your worldview.

And lastly, crying. That's right; allow plenty of time for crying. Giving into tears has a cleansing affect and helps release feelings. Let's face it, there are times when giving into tears is the most effective way of releasing emotions. Crying is a form of cleansing—a method to letting go and releasing emotions. When you are done crying, you feel lighter, and more at ease. Having a good cry usually makes you feels a little better about yourself, your world, and your prospects of having some control. It is not as if your loved one has returned or you have come to accept the lost. Life hasn't gotten any better, but your perspective of life and yourself has. You may still feel sad, hurt, and betrayed, but you are less likely to feel rotten and depressed.

So the next time you are overcome with the urge to cry, do not try to suppress the tears; give into them and allow yourself to have a good cry—just remember you are not alone—God has sent angels to weep with you.

> Today's Nourishment:
> *I give into my tears. My tears serve as a form of cleansing—releasing my pain, sorrow, anger, bitterness, and sense of betrayal. I cry as if my heart is broken—as it is. I feel lighter, relieved, and a sense of calm after my cry—as if I am not crying alone.*

~344~
Angels Weep With You

God's angels specialize in healing and they are with you all the time, especially during the difficult times. Angels are with you during painful times and bestow extra blessings and loving energy around you. Perhaps you have recently experienced a set-back, disappoint, or even a loss of a loved one and need extra help right now. Ask God to send angels to surround you in this moment with more divine love than ever. When you are crying in the darkness imagine your angels are beside you caressing you and loving you.

Sometimes it may feel as if you have been abandoned, but you are being reminded that you are never alone. As a matter of fact, additional angels have been summoned to surround you as you read this, giving you extra support, love, and light. You have not been abandoned, God and your angels are not gone and they cannot ever leave you. For those who have lost a loved one, be assured that there are angels of comfort who come to the bereaved soul who is still living and they do what is necessary to help you get through the difficult time. Angels weep along side you—trust in this.

Today, remember to ask for spiritual help in all situations, starting the moment you get out of bed. Request help throughout your day, with normal mundane things; driving, walking, exercising. Request help healing your grief-stricken heart, cry alone no more—let God send His angels to weep with you.
God

Today's Nourishment:
I remember that I am not alone. I know that God can direct a choir of angels to surround me and infuse me with their divine illuminating love. When I am mourning the loss of my loved one and crying out my grief these angels weep along side me.

~345~
Identify Highs And Lows

If you have difficulties relating to God you are slowing your spiritual progress. You have a clear sense of the need for balance in your body, mind, and spirit. It is now time to focus on you and find out what you want to be, to do, or to have in your life. Now is the time to identify those areas that need to be strengthened—these areas relate to actual behaviors not opinions. By identifying and focusing on these areas that are affecting your spiritual growth you can work to strengthen the needed areas.

Begin by looking at specific areas of your life and your performance in each area; personal, mental, work, health, family, spiritual, play, and social. As you review these areas rate your current performance on a scale of one to five. For example, if you feel you give yourself adequate time each day for reflection, privacy, and doing something that makes you happy rate yourself somewhere between three and five.

By identify highs and lows of areas of your life, you will identify the areas of importance and those areas you may want to improve. With this insight you can now ask for guidance. Here are a few questions to get you thinking:

- How can I raise the quality of my life?
- What can I read to challenge my mind?
- How can I find more time for fun and play?
- How can I reunite my family?
- How can I bring more friends in my life?

Work with God and your angels for those areas that need attention—become partners with the spiritual realm and work with them daily to find answers to all your problems. Strengthen all areas of your life so that you are living more balanced and spiritually in tune with your world.

Today's Nourishment:
I identify the areas of my life which are deficient and ask specifically for what I want to be, to do, and have. I ask God and my angels to remove all personal blocks that have been blocking my progress. I receive help from God and the angels willingly and graciously—my spiritual progress has quickened!

~346~
Increase Quality Of Life

Now that you have a sense of the need to find balance in body, mind, and spirit. It is now time to focus on *you* and find out what you want to be, to do, or to have in your life—increasing the quality of your life. The first step in this process is to recognize the areas in your life that needs to be strengthened. By focusing on these areas you will clearly see where you are inhibiting your spiritual growth and self-esteem. Once you identify the areas which stunt your spiritual growth, you can ask for help in working through them.

In spite of the personal blocks which have been hindering your progress, God has provided you with a spiritual team of angels, which have much to offer—simply ask specifically for what you want to do, to be, and to have. Ask how you can increase the quality of your life!

Today's Nourishment:
I ask the angels to heal the areas in my life that are hindering my spiritual growth. I recognize the areas in my life that are weak—and work through them. I increase the quality of my life by discovering what I want to be, to do, and to have in my life!

~347~
Find A Spiritual Buddy

What is meant by a spiritual buddy? A spiritual buddy is a companion or a friend with whom you have a mutual sharing of spiritual interests. Having a spiritual buddy includes getting together for fellowship, but there is more to having a spiritual buddy. There should be a spiritual and personal discussions, contact via letter, phone or visits. If you cannot see each other frequently, a telephone call is the next best form of communication. Letters are much less effective.

Having a spiritual buddy includes a conscious effort to get to know others and establish strong ties so that you can encourage them, have them encourage you, resulting in your growing together in your spiritual walk. This results in your being able to pray effectively for one another, and to establish strong bonds of lasting friendship.

God and the angels can help you with all your relationships, including assisting with finding the right spiritual buddy for you—simply ask. The angels can support you through any misunderstandings, miscommunications, and provide you with creative ways to overcome differences. As you grow spiritually, so should your friendships—ask for help in locating a spiritual buddy.

Today's Nourishment:
I have a wonderful spiritual buddy in my life for I am a good friend. I ask God to help me in my life and in every area of my relationships. I enjoy sharing and bonding with my spiritual buddy.

~348~
Surrender Your Dreams

Most everyone experiences a period of time where it appears that life is standing still and seems like every door is closed with no new ones in sight. Often this occurs when the mental image of what you want to happen isn't happening exactly as you believe it should be, and then you think *nothing* is happening. When this happens you end up in a stagnant wilderness of frustrations and confusion because you have made idols out of your dreams!

When God wants to make change in your life, and you are willing to let God, all that is unnecessary is removed. In the process, anything that hinders your future growth in removed from your life in order to prepare you for the wonderful things ahead. Your life may appear barren during this period, but in reality you are being freed from anything that does not bring forth life. Think of a rosebush that has been pruned back to nearly nothing—for months it looks like pathetic dead sticks that will never produce again. But come springtime, the barren rosebushes blossom and bloom profusely. First only little buds appear, then one-by-one they open and burst into beautiful shades of pink, red, rose, and white flowers!

That is what is in store for you when you surrender your dreams and ask what God wants you to do. This process of surrendering your dreams to do as God, your creator, intends is called pruning. Surrender your dreams to God and let God put dreams in your heart to give you vision and inspiration—to guide you to the right path. Make sure the dreams you have are not from your own earthy desires, but are from God—then your dreams will be realized.

Today's Nourishment:
I surrender my dreams to God and ask that they be replaced with God's desires for my life. That does not serve my highest good or God's future plans are removed to prepare me for the future that God has intended for me. I release frustrations and confusion—I graciously let God lead me to the right path.

~349~
Banish The Clock Watcher

Does the watch upon your wristown you or your life? Do you look at the numbers of the digital clock change and feel like you must hurry? Tick tock, tick tock...does it feel as if time is slipping away from you? Even now, you have most likely glanced at the clock at least once--wondering how much longer until you have to get the kids ready, leave for work,before lunchtime, or until your next meeting.

Whatever the case may be keep this in mind—you are meant to have breaths of delights in your life! Notbe a slave to aband of numbers upon your wrist orflashing neon numbers on your desk. For just one hour today, pay no attention to *tick tock*. Banish all thoughts of time from your mind and your lips. Watch your mind slow to a place of rest and tranquility—a place where new thoughts and ideas are born.

> Today's Nourishment:
> *I am banishing my timepiece, ignoring the flashing numbers, and will not watch the clock today. I tune out the ticking of the clock; banish all thoughts of time from my mind—allowing my mind slow to a place or rest and tranquility!*

~350~
Leave Hurt Behind

Have you felt a sense of betrayal? Felt you were compromised or unloved? Know this child of God, the person who hurt you has betrayed him or herself. This person has caused a ripple effect and caused you great pain instead of showing you divine love. Now you are burdened with the pain and hurt inflicted by this person—hurt no longer. By focusing on this hurt you will cause more harm to yourself.

Leave the hurt behind—leave this path of painful contemplation. You are doing yourself an injustice by holding on to the hurtful situation. You need to heal. Cleanse yourself of the hurt, leave it behind, and rid yourself of the deep wound left by those who disappoint you. Ask your angels to form a circle of love around you—let them warm you with their loving divine energy. Know that you have done nothing wrong, and you are God's precious child of love. Though you may have stumbled like a toddler taking the first steps, you needn't punish yourself or another person for the trips and falls—all God's children here on earth stumble when learning to walk.

Today focus on forgiveness and overlook others shortcomings—even as you follow your inner guidance that tells you when to keep away from another being on earth. As you heal through forgiveness you will attract those in your life who treat you with honor and respect.

Today's Nourishment:
I let go of hurt and allow myself to enjoy life. I ask my angels to circle me with their love and warm my heart. I delight in the fact I no longer have hurt and pain in my heart.

~351~
Tithe

Tithing is the ancient tradition of contribution 10 percent of your income to a cause of your choice, yet it means so much more than giving money. There is truth to the saying that the more you give the more you receive. By giving you are increasing the abundance that comes in your life. For example, if you long for more time, then volunteer your hours helping others. If you want more clothing, furniture, or other material items, then donate similar items to charities or others in need. If you desire more financial abundance, then make a monetary donation as you feel guided.

Giving jump starts the cycle of abundance that works through the universe. It begins the moment you give—not for the purpose of receiving, but for the pure joy of giving.

Today's Nourishment:
I tithe out of a desire to give, because it brings me joy and is part of my giving nature. I give effortlessly and receive for the pure joy of it.

~352~

Release Insecurities

For those times you feel insecure and worry that no one really cares for you, loves you, or even likes you, know that you are lovable. It's during these times that God and the loving angels surround you will divine healing love, shielding you from the painful emotions associated with insecurities. You have asked for help with healing and releasing negative emotions, therefore, you are protected from yourself during these bouts with insecurities.

It is during times such as this that you truly are, *your own worst enemy*, because you feel unloved, unwanted, abandoned, and unworthy. Because of such negative feelings you begin to attract circumstances and relationships that confirm such beliefs—self-fulfilling prophecy. Do not indulge in self-pitying thoughts and emotions, child of God, for it is destructive and self-defeating. Naturally, it is part of your humanness to feel doubts and insecurities from time to time. The moment you start to feel these negative emotions, call upon your angels for help release insecurities.

You are being reminded today, that your angels are standing by ready to send you loving rays of confidence and healing powers. It is your free will that dictates if you desire to wallow in self-destructive thoughts, even God can not help. God or the angels can not do anything unless you call upon them to help. Call upon God and the angels the moment you begin noticing such damaging hurtful thoughts—ask for help and release these feelings of insecurity.

Today's Nourishment:
I work with God to release my insecurities and replace them with new feelings of empowerment and love. I realize my worth as one of His children and know that I am cherished and loved.

~353~
Know That God Is Right Here

It may seem as if Heaven is some faraway place and God is unreachable. Heaven is a dimension that exists all around you and you can feel God's presence or see ~~Him~~ God within everything; ~~He~~ God is right here.

God moves where you move and stands next to you always—although ~~He~~ God will never interfere with your free will, ~~He~~ God is ready to help you every moment of every day; all you need to do is ask.

Today's Nourishment:
God is right here by my side. I am loved, supported, and surrounded by ~~His~~ God loving healing energy now and always. ~~He~~ God is poised ready to help me as soon as I ask

~354~
Spend Time With Relatives

When you pick up any magazine, it's easy to find an abundance of articles to help you organize your life. Most offer tips for cleaning out the closets, shuffling the papers on the desk, finding ways to balance work and play. What about organizing your time to find some precious, extra moments to spend with your relatives?

Although there doesn't seem to be enough hours in a day to manage work, home life, and family activities, let alone spending time with relatives. Today's focus is on finding time to spend with your extended family—your relatives! Think back to your childhood memories and visiting with relatives; playing games with your cousins, picnics, fishing, and talking with aunts, uncles, and grandparents.

As today's society becomes increasingly mobile and self-centered, family ties with relatives become less strong. Now days most families are lucky if they plan an annual family roundup—and then many relatives do not make time to attend. Perhaps the older relatives still attend, but as they get older and die, the younger generation will have little or no ties with the relatives at all.

It is up to you to make the time to spend with relatives. While it may require some creative planning on your part to get grandparents, aunts, uncles, and cousins in one place at the same time, the benefits are immeasurable. Do not let scheduling conflicts and logistics stand in your path—get creative. The angels excel at removing obstacles and thrive on creative ways to overcome challenges; ask for their help.

Today's Nourishment:
I reach out to my relatives and start planning a family gathering. Pulling our resources and creativity, we plan and execute a family get together—grandparents, aunts, uncles, and cousins all in one place. Scheduling conflicts and logistics are no longer a problem as I release those concerns to the angels—all will go smooth and I am delighted that I spend time with relatives.

~355~
Reach For God's Hand

Loss is a part of life that everyone must experience. It's the part that no one likes and wishes they never had to go through. But you will—everyone does. When a loss is severe and you feel like a light has gone out inside and nothing can turn it back on, know that the light of God's love can restore the light. God can soothe your pain, heal the wounds, and fill the empty place in your heart.

During the dark times of loss, whether it is the death of a loved one, disease or injury, divorce, a straying child, the end of a relationship, or loss of home and money, you grieve because someone or something is no longer a part of your life. Life as you knew it is forever altered—it will never be the way it was. The manner in which you envisioned your future—with that person, job, and capability—is severely shattered. These types of losses bring such pain that you wonder if you will survive and if you do will the pain ever go away. You wonder if you will hurt forever or if life will ever be normal again.

While every act of compassion, caring, sympathy, and love given by others is a great comfort and helps with the grieving process, only the healing power of God and the angels can restore you again. Mere humans can't say magical words to make the pain vanish—people don't always know what to say during times of loss. Beside, what words can make it better? However, when you suffered a deep loss, only God and the angels can sustain you and make you whole again.

If you suffer any kind of loss, let God put God's arms around you—reach for God's hand and let God guide you through the grieving and healing process. God knows of your pain and suffering and will give you the comfort of God's presence and healing power of God's love. God will send a heavenly host of angels to surround you with healing divine love. Even if the tears seem to never stop, continue to hold fast to God's hand and you will make it through the grief. Tears may come and go and return again when you least expect it—the constant will be God's love and healing.

Today's Nourishment:
Dear God, take my hand and fill this empty place that has been left in my heart. Be the one constant in my life that will never be lost to me. Even though there are times that I am overwhelmed by the pain and tears of my lost, I know you will be there to hold my hand and sooth me with your healing love. Help me to get past this grief and learn to move forward with my life.

~356~
Hit The Brakes

When is the last time you just sat and did nothing? Or watched the sunset from your quiet place? Or stopped and really listened to your favourite tune? Unfortunately, doing things like that is uncommon in a busy life. There are so many things you believe you need or have to do that you don't take time to recharge and just stop occasionally.

Today it's time to hit the brakes and realize there is more to life than rushing and doing things every second of the day. Being overly busy results in you being tired and less creative, it keeps you pumped up and without time to reduce the pressure. Work related issues fill your mind and you get overwhelmed and lose track of where you are going as you are so caught up in the tasks at hand.

Would you ever drive your car for years without changing tires, giving it a service or an oil change? What about an animal such as a horse–would you ride it all day without giving it a rest? If cars and horses deserve a break, don't you think you deserve a break from busyness? Of course you do—and today it is time to hit the brakes, take a break from everyday busyness, and enjoy doing nothing.

Today's Nourishment:
I take my time today, treating myself to periods of doing nothing—I am stress free, relaxed, and recharge myself.

~357~
Ride In Tandem With God

As you have developed a more personal relationship with God, you have come to the realizations that God is more than an observer, judge, or score keeper. God isn't sitting up in Heaven keeping track of wrongdoings to determine who merits heaven or hell. Having a close relationship with God is like riding a bike—a tandem bike; where sometimes you lead and other times you let God lead.

When you are in control, you know the way but it is a rather boring ride—predictable routes, routine, and traveling the shortest distance between two points. However, when you switch places and allow God to take control life suddenly becomes an adventure! Life becomes exciting, adventurous, thrilling, and sometimes scary—but you always end up in the right place at the right moment.

Being the wise God that God is, God sometimes sits back and lets you at the controls—like good parents do. For those times you have crashed and burned; end up in places you are *not* suppose to be, or end up completely lost and struggling to find your way home. It is those times when God gently moves you onto the back seat and pedals you out of the mess you were in!

And the wonderful thing about it is—God has never once said, "I told you so!" God simply smiles, shakes God's head in amusement, and gently takes your hand. How awesome is that?

> Today's Nourishment:
> *I switch places and allow God to take control of my life; God takes me to the most wonderful exciting places, we ride at breakneck speeds, over hills, through valleys, and rough terrain—I am not afraid, as God always knows where we are going and protects me.*

~358~
Be True To Yourself

Do not deny what you really want or who your really are. The issues about what is right and wrong for you personally are of great importance. Perhaps you've struggled to meet other's expectations for you, educationally or career-wise, because you simply wanted to do something else? Perhaps others want you to behave in a certain way and you don't like it?

There are many feelings, views, opinions and principles that you are having trouble expressing and living by, and suppressing them is causing internal conflict. If you are struggling to be true to yourself, seek the comfort and understanding of someone who you feel able to express your real thoughts and feelings to. It may be difficult to see the reality of your own situation from within it, so seek out the help and guidance of someone you trust to give you an alternative perspective.

It is important to be true to yourself and not simply conforming to what others expect of you. You have a choir of angels at your disposal; seek out their assistance, advice, guidance to help you find ways to be true to yourself.

Today's Nourishment:
I am who I am. I will be true to myself. I will no longer deny what I want or who I am. I will seek out assistance, guidance, and advice to overcome my internal conflicts.

~359~
Take Bubble Baths

Bubble baths aren't just for kids. A nice, hot bath is a great way to relax and unwind. Bathhouses have historically been used for their therapeutic, healing properties. Bathing in these natural, mineral-rich waters was said to relax the mind and benefit rheumatic, inflammatory and muscular ailments.

Sometimes totally immersing yourself in something you find totally relaxing and cleansing is the best thing you can do for yourself. It can also help you relax, particularly with some aromatherapy bath salts. Soaking in a warm bath is an indulgent way to soothe aching muscles and sore feet, relieve stress and some time for you.

Do this at least a few times a week. Unplug the phone, lock the bathroom door, fill the bath, select your favorite bubble bath, light the aromatherapy candles—lavender relieves stress and sandalwood relaxes, and indulge in the essence of the soft silence of the perfect bubble bath. You may want to put on a little background music to help you relax—this is your perfect bubble bath.

Today's Nourishment:
I take care of myself and my body by relaxing in a bubble bath. I appreciate how it helps me relieve stress, soothe aching muscles, and the therapeutic benefits.

~360~
Tap Into Your Potential

You have the power to achieve great things, if only you can tap into your natural-born, but often hidden reserves of talent, energy, imagination, focus and grace. That is the message of today, tap into your potential! Begin your day by focusing on your gifts, losing the fear of success, and start living at your highest potential. Take a moment right now to imagining what your life would be like if you tapped into your potential and went from where you are at this moment to where you want to be.

Today, ask your higher power for guidance on tapping into your gifts and lose the fear of success—start living your at your highest potential.

Today's Nourishment:
I tap into my natural-born talents, energy, imagination, and grace. I know that it is possible for me to tap into my potential, be successful in my professional and personal life, and have a life of abundance.

~361~
Learn To Believe

At God's direction, your angels will bring what you ask for, if it is for your highest good. Angels are incapable of bringing anything but the best gifts—as loving, healing, Divine spiritual messengers of God, you can not receive harmful gifts from your angels. When you ask your angels for something, be it material, spiritual, or emotional; believe that which has been asked is already yours. Know that you are worthy of receiving what you have asked for. Believe that God, through God's angels will bring it to you.

Once you have asked expectantly, as though the request was already filled, there are no barriers. You many have doubts that stem from you own self-limiting beliefs or your self-esteem. Low self-esteem often interferes with your ability to ask, but even more so, your belief that you will receive. Know that asking involves expectancy and believing involves trust; together they allow you to show trust in God's ability to bless you with gifts.

Today's Nourishment:
I asked expectantly, as if my request was already filled; as it is. My angels will bring what I ask for. I am worthy of receiving what I ask for—I trust in God's ability to bless me with gifts.

Know That God Works Overtime

When you are struggling with a decision, standing at a crossroad, or unsure which way to turn, know that God works overtime. Unlike traditional advisors, God does not have specific *open for business* hours nor does He have an office. God is everywhere; His door is always open and He works overtime. Feel free to ask God for guidance any time, day or night—He will provide answers.

If you awake at three in the morning with an idea, a feeling comes to you while driving home from work, or even while showering your inner voice speaks to you; know that is God speaking to you. You do not have to wait until you go to a house of worship to talk with God. He is everywhere, within everything, and fortunately for you—He works overtime!

Today's Nourishment:
I turn to God today; asking for guidance and direction. It doesn't matter when I talk to God, as He is always available, has an open-door policy, and works overtime. I am fortunate to have a loving understanding God that is readily available for me.

~363~
Stop Struggling

As long as you are searching for something, you are sending out the signal that you don't have it! You do not have to struggle or strain to find what you are looking for, simply hold to the belief that it is already yours. Keep the faith that is will come to you effortlessly and easily, and listen for guidance, follow guidance given, and it shall be yours.

Today, stop struggling to achieve your dreams—relax and let it happen. Determine what it is that you desire, thank God that it has already been given to you, and feel grateful for the fact that God has already answered your wishes, before that wish was spoken. Write a detail description of what you want today and sign it with a large 'thank you'. Smile to yourself, fill your heart with gratitude and enjoy knowing that you will receive a quick turnaround from God!

Today's Nourishment:
I no longer struggle and strain, I let things comes to me. I no longer search for an item—I send my desire upwards to Heaven, allowing God to send me my wants, desires, and needs. I feel gratitude before my desires are granted—I accept them graciously.

~364~
Ask For Directions

Do you feel lost at times, sweet child of God? Do you struggle to find you way at times? Do you waver between faith and doubt? Do you feel as if you are traveling in circles going nowhere? You have a God that is ready to guide you any time you call upon Him for directions. Let God be your compass and lead you out of darkness. God's compass is in perfect order at all times! .

Perhaps you do not take the time to check it often enough and only use it when you are far off the path God has for you. Use it often and it will guide you always—one foot in front of the other, showing you the correct path. Sit quietly in contemplation and feel God standing near. You will know He is near by feeling His presence—it is not your imagination, He will draw nearer to anyone who calls Him. Ask God for directions—ask Him to show you this compass that will lead you on the right path.

Today's Nourishment:
I focus on feeling God's presence within me, feeling His steady warmth and love within my heart and mind. I sit in quiet contemplation and ask for directions—God shows me his perfect compass and leads me on the right path.

~365~
Spiritual Gain For The New Year

As you embark on a new year, lay aside those diet books, weight-loss plans and every fat picture taped to the fridge. Instead, open your heart, soul, and mind to what God wants for you. Your weight loss starts with a spiritual gain plan based on following His guidance. When you think of your New Year's resolutions, do not focus on the bad habits that you want to quit, like drinking or eating too much. This year, focus on a good habit that you want to add, such as spiritual vitality, growth, and approaching each situation with love and compassion.

If you want to lose weight this upcoming year, start by making a list of people you need to forgive, including yourself. Make a list of all that you feely guilty about; all the resentments you still carry within. This process will reduce a ton of weight that you may be carrying around. Ask yourself, "Is it fat that I want to lose; or guilt, resentments, or anger and bitterness?" Next, make a list of all the people and things that you are grateful for. After you have forgiven yourself and others; released the guilt and resentments you will be at peace with yourself. When you focus on the spiritual, the will and power of God will dissolve the anger and resentment. You'll discover that the weight will naturally come off as a spiritual response to prayer and living your life more spiritually in tune with the world around you!

> Today's Nourishment:
> *I start this year by making a list of people I need to forgive; list of things I feel guilty about, and resentments hiding within. I ask God to help me forgive myself and others, release the guilt, resentment, anger, and bitterness. I pray to be shown my path and ways to remain spiritually in tune with my world—and know what God wants for me.*

Notes

Notes

Notes

Notes

Notes

Special Tribute

This past summer we, meaning myself, my daughter, and my son made a trip to Tennessee. This is not a pleasure trip that we traveled—this was one of those trips everyone must take at some point in their life, but dread the idea, and hope to put off as long as possible. Our final destination was a storage unit in a town, until a few months previously, we never heard mention before. It was within the walls of this storage unit, my children, their grandparents, and their younger sister began the daunting task of sorting through my former husband's personal belongings. In other words, they began "cataloging memories."

His home had been cleaned out and memories placed in a storage unit sparing his children from seeing the place where their father took his last breath. Their father was the proverbial pat rack and the family was faced with sorting through 45 years worth of memories crammed into a rented storage unit. Seriously he did not get rid of anything—he still had a record player and a vast 33 LP collection! My children and his family sorted through all the furniture, household items, clothes, tools, each box, crate, papers, pictures, films, etc. etc., and 'cataloged' the items. They decided among themselves what to keep for sentimental value, historical value; items to set aside for Good Will charities, and which personal items the kids wanted as keepsakes.

My children didn't want their father's things auctioned off or sold off bits and pieces at group sale. They decided to go through his things themselves-each taking various items for keepsakes and giving the rest to charity. The girls plan on using some of his old t-shirts to fashion into keepsake quilts. My daughter loved his watch, his old worn recliner-and broke down over a picture of the two of them dancing when she was ten. My son's treasure chest held home movies from the past 20+ years-memories on film. The youngest daughter was drawn to the Disney movies, swimming pool, and the books he read to her. His mother cried upon discovery of the unsigned birthday card he wasn't around to give her; loving touched his rosary choking back tears; let's face it a mother cries when a child is taken from her. His father, in spite of all his talks of 'down-sizing' lovingly and proudly carried his degrees, framed achievements, awards and college yearbooks to the truck. All that stuff; all those things and they just wanted something to cling to-a way to capture memories of their father, their son, their brother. Memories are all they want-all that is left of a man's life after 45 years.

As for myself, my moment came when my daughter slipped the golden ring I had placed on his hand so many years ago into my hand. As I gave into the flood of emotions, I was asked if there might be a keepsake I wanted even though it had been years since I was his wife. I looked around at my children and his family; thought about the man who was a part of my life for 20 plus years, a good father and a good man. As for a keepsake to recapture a memory; I choked back the tears as I realized I had all the memories I could possibly store-cataloged and stored within my heart.

In Loving Memory

Gregory Michael McGowan
November 12, 1961 - June 6, 2007

Gregory M. McGowan, Christmas 2005 with children (left to right), Nicole Marie, Anthony Ray, and Samantha Dawn sitting on his lap. As the father of my two children, he gave me the chance to enjoy the blessings of motherhood. Long ago he made me his wife and even though we traveled different roads, we continued to love and raise our children as one. Forever in our hearts, Greg will be deeply missed; he leaves the world his legacy...his children, his family, and those of us who knew and loved him.

Donations in Greg's Memory Appreciated:

American **Red Cross**
PO Box 4002018
Des Moines, IA 50340-2018
www.redcross.org

Meet Professional Coach and Advisor
Lil Mel

Melody "Lil Mel" McGowan, author, spiritual advisor, and founder of Let Your Heart Heal Life Coaching, is available for speaking engagements, public appearances, support groups, book signings, radio talk shows, seminars and workshops. By participating in one of Lil Mel's professional consultations, seminars, or workshops you will gain understanding, insight, guidance, and personal empowerment for making the right decisions for your life and spiritual path. Additional services offered include: fund raising opportunities, private phone sessions, and private and corporate events.

For more information or to inquiry about Lil Mel's availability visit:

Let Your Heart Heal Life Coaching

Website: *www.lilmel.com*
Email: *lilmel@lilmel.com*

About The Author

Melody R. McGowan, author of *Ramblings from the Heart*, is a life coach, counselor, and professional advisor who specializes' in relationship, family, and personal counseling. Affectionately known as, *Lil' Mel*, she is the founder of Let Your Heart Heal Life Coaching, an Internet based outreach program that offers professional coaching, counseling, consulting, and spiritual guidance. She provides clients with understanding, insight, guidance, and personal empowerment through personal consultations. Through her practice she has impacted the lives of thousands clients world-wide, by providing counseling, spiritual guidance, empowerment and motivation, and inspiration.

A practicing clairsentience, claircognizance, and spiritual advisor, Melody is an ordained minister and holds a Doctorate in Metaphysics, M.A. and B.S. university degrees in counseling, human resources, and education. Melody has been using her formal training combined with practical solid advice to help literally thousands of people see their way clearly to making the right decisions for their lives and guide them along their spiritual path.

Answering the call to help others, she expanded her practice to reach others through books, media outlets, speaking engagements, support groups, private and corporate events, and workshops. By offering fund raising opportunities she helps organizations raise funds through proceeds from book sales.

Additionally, Melody is a single-mother of two adult children, a military veteran, and currently resides in a small community in southern Illinois. For more information on Melody and her private consultations, speaking engagements, private and corporate events, book signings, and workshop availability, to subscribe to her free e-mail newsletters, or for information on fund raising opportunities, please visit her Let Your Heart Heal Life Coaching website at www.lilmel.com.

Postscript:
Letter From Author

In my first book, *Ramblings from the Heart,* written after the sudden death of my finance', I shared a collection of poems, anecdotes, and inspirational messages drawn from my own personal heartbreak and tragedy. It was my personal journey asI traveled through the grieving process and learnedto live again.

Now I offer the sequel, *Sweet Tea for the Soul: Daily Nourishment for Living Spiritually In Tune with Your World.* Traveling through the grieving process and learning to live again was a long winding road with many curves. Each day I was challenged to renew my faith, find strength to meet life's challenges, and find inspiration in the daily process of living. Plagued by an unquenchable thirst, I sought out spiritual nourishment in the hopes of becoming more spiritually in tune with my physical world.

Many of my clients come to me after experiencing major life altering event, crisis, or stressful transitional period in their lives. As it is my life's purpose to offer emotional and spiritual nourishment to others, as well as guide them along their spiritual path, my sessions include various ideas to help calm, heal, renew their energies, and restore balance and harmony. I do not take my profession lightly—I practice what I teach. In order to be more effective in helping others along their journey, it is imperative for me to maintain a life that is calm, balanced, and free of negativity and drama. Within these pages you will find daily guidance suggesting a specific action, thought, or theme that has allowed me to become more spiritually in tune with my world. Now I pass along these messages to you as I have to my family, friends, and clients. Although not a substitute for your personal religious beliefs, these messages are meant to enhance every facet of your life.

As you continue to enjoy *Sweet Tea for the Soul*, may these daily messages serve as welcome refreshment to you, quench your thirst, and provide spiritual and emotional nourishment. Let these messages serve as a reminder that God is watching over you day and night. Open your arms, heart, mind, and soul so that your life is illuminated by His loving healing divine light.

From my heart to yours,

"Lil Mel"

Melody, "Lil Mel", McGowan

CPSIA information can be obtained at www.ICGtesting.com
Printed in the USA
LVOW041631290712

292033LV00001B/306/A